REAL-LIFE STORIES
told by THE HIRED GUNS *who were*
THERE WHEN *the* SHOOTOUTS OCCURRED

CAMPAIGN ★ WAR ★ STORIES

Edited by **Ladonna Y. Lee**
and **Michael Payton**

TONY PAYTON

www.tonypayton.com

Allegiance Press

The Right Answers for America

Campaign War Stories
by Tony Payton

Edited by Ladonna Y. Lee and Michael Payton

Printed in the United States of America

ISBN 1-594672-38-5

Allegiance Press
10640 Main Street
Suite 204
Fairfax, VA 22030
www.allegiancepress.com

(703) 934-4411

Dedication

To the men and women who have the guts to put
their name on the ballot,

Their volunteers and staff who believe in them, and,

The citizens who show up on election day and choose our leaders.

Table of Contents

☆ ☆ ☆

Preface ix

Book One — The People in Politics..**1**
   Chapter 1 — Political Legends 4
   Chapter 2 — Stars in the Business.....................................21
   Chapter 3 — Legends in the Campaign Business.................31
   Chapter 4 — Men and Women Who Run for Public
                  Office 39
   Chapter 5 — Road Warrior Adventures 50

Book Two — Modern Political Campaigns **55**
   Chapter 6 — Tapping Public Opinion.....................................59
   Chapter 7 — Digging Up Dirt on the Opponent 64
   Chapter 8 — Raising Money to Pay the Bills 67
   Chapter 9 — Winning in the Streets 77
   Chapter 10 — Making the Classic TV Commercial 80
   Chapter 11 — Television and Radio Spots That Work 91
   Chapter 12 — Debates Don't Usually Matter.......................98

**Book Three — The Myths and Reality of Campaign
                Strategy** **101**
   Chapter 13 — Strategies That Seem to Work 105
   Chapter 14 — Dynamic Events That Re-deal the Cards.......110
   Chapter 15 — The Art of Counter-punching 114

Chapter 16 — When the Opponent Buys Ink by
　　　　　　the Barrel 120

Book Four — Winning the Big Enchilada 130
　Chapter 17 — The New Hampshire Primary and
　　　　　　　Iowa Caucus...133
　Chapter 18 — Political Party Conventions 144
　Chapter 19 — Presidential Debates Often Have
　　　　　　　Consequences 149
　Chapter 20 — Presidential Campaigns in the
　　　　　　　Homestretch..158

Book Five — When Campaigns Go South................................166
　Chapter 21 — The Art of the Dirty Trick 169
　Chapter 22 — Exposing Real Mischief................................176
　Chapter 23 — A Classic Case of Shooting Yourself
　　　　　　　in the Foot...180
　Chapter 24 — Just a Bad Day at the Office 187
　Chapter 25 — When TV Goes Bad.....................................193

Book Six — Good War Stories Well Told 203
　Chapter 26 — Good Stories Live on in Campaign Lore.......205
　Chapter 27 — Only in Louisiana 230
　Chapter 28 — More Good Stories, Told Shortly 249
　Chapter 29 — Comedians in the Political Business.............263

Bibliography 277
About the Author 287
Index 289

Preface

When George Washington first sought public office as a candidate for the Virginia House of Burgesses in 1758, he was busy on the frontier and unable to campaign in person. However, he instructed friends to campaign on his behalf among the 391 eligible voters in the Mount Vernon area of northern Virginia, and he provided a sufficient budget to do the job right. Like any good pols who wanted to assure victory for their mentor, the campaigning friends are said to have plied voters with liquid refreshment while asking for their support of Washington at the ballot box. The record reveals they provided a quart and a half of rum, wine, beer and hard cider for each of the 391 voters, and Washington won in a landslide.

Political people have been gathering around places where liquid refreshments are readily available and retelling old campaign war stories ever since. The beauty of many campaign war stories is that they can be told just as they happened and still be plenty entertaining. They don't require a quart and a half of booze and lots of elaboration to make them better, or more believable.

So what we have here is more than 150 stories from campaign professionals about their work in campaigns all over America. The author, thanks to the ruthless editors, left another 600 stories on the cutting-room floor. And there could have been 4,000 more. I collected stories from more than 100 men and women in the business; over 60 of them are included. I could have collected stories from a thousand people.

In the campaign business, it's the tradition and the practice that you only work one side of the street. If you're a Democrat, you work exclusively for Democratic candidates. If you're a Republican, you work only for candidates running under the GOP banner. A few people try to work both sides, but they're looked upon with suspicion from the professionals in both major parties.

The author admits it up front: I'm a Republican. I've been a Republican as long as I've been voting. I've never voted for a Democrat for any office. And I don't intend to change now. Oh, a few times way back when, I'll admit I skipped over a couple of down ticket races on the ballot, where I knew the Republican was a scumbag or a crook. But I never gave the Democrat opponent the satisfaction of getting my vote. My parents were Republicans and, they said, their parents were Republicans during the 1930s when Franklin Delano Roosevelt was president and being a Republican was not the most popular political point of view.

Collecting campaign war stories from my Republican colleagues was easy. I knew them all and have been friends with most of them for years. We've done business together, worked on campaigns together, been in the trenches together. I'd heard many of their best stories and was anxious to get many of them on tape.

But it's another matter with the Democrats in the business. Of course I knew many by name and reputation. I've been on the other side against half the Democrats I collected stories from. Some even told stories about the very campaigns where I'd been the consultant and strategist for the opponent. Interesting, very interesting.

But my newfound Democratic friends were as forthcoming – and many as good or better at telling war stories – as any of my Republican friends. And they had a whole bunch of new stories I'd never heard before. I guess we've been drinking in different bars.

But it turns out I like people in the campaign business, regardless of the side they're on. Whether we're Democrats, Republicans or independents, we're all in the business to win, we're all trying to advance a cause and we're all professionals. While we play hard every time, there are not many dirtballs in this business on either side of the street. A few "flash in the pan" people come into the campaign business, last one or two campaign cycles and then are gone. But if you've been around a while – 15 election cycles for the author – you're doing several things right. First, you're on the winning side more than the losing side. Second, you've built a reputation as a straight shooter who isn't ripping off his or her clients. And, third, if you've been in the business a while, you're doing a lot of repeat work. Old clients are hiring you over and over because they like your style, they like your work and you're getting the job done for them.

Lastly, this is a book of stories about democracy. We Americans are proud to say that our system of government is the world's longest-running experiment in freedom. Nowhere else on the planet have people been able, for so long, to go of their own free will and run for public office, whether it's for the school board or for president of the United States. And, of course, democracy means something very important – there will be winners and there will be losers. The stories in this book tell about successful campaigns for the U.S. House of Representatives, U.S. Senate, the presidency and state offices. Stories about victory are a lot more fun to tell, and probably more compelling. But for every winner, there was someone who didn't get elected. A lot of stories are about those campaigns too.

Democracy is strong because Americans actually show up and vote on Election Day in large enough numbers to be significant. Like they say in Chicago and New Orleans, vote as many times as they'll let you.

I want to personally thank my neighbor and best friend, Ladonna Lee, for her constant encouragement, her valuable criticism and her editing help. It's true that writing a book is a lonely business, and her continued support is immensely appreciated. I want to thank Betti Hill and Lynette Brown, two ladies in Helena, Montana, who have faithfully transcribed more than 100 tapes of interviews. This may sound easy until you recall there are interviews from New Orleans, Boston, New York City and Arkansas, among others –folks who could barely understand each other if they were in the same room chatting face to face.

I also want to thank the 100 political professionals – Republicans and Democrats – who put up with my hounding them for stories, then put up with my e-mails with editing questions. And they all did it for nothing, or maybe they did it because they, too, love the campaign business.

A special thanks goes to the candidates who have had the guts to put their names on the line and run for public office. Without them, there would be no book about campaign war stories. Every story is about a Democrat, Republican or independent candidate who, I believe, started down the trail of running for office with the very best of intentions, with deep concern for their community. Without good men and women willing to step up and run, we would have no democracy.

—*Tony Payton*

BOOK ONE

The People in Politics

People in the world's second oldest profession probably took some lessons from those in the oldest profession. Money, or the equivalent thereof, was changing hands. Favors were being done. Some were requesting laws be enacted on the matter. What better time for the political class to step forward proclaiming they would take the necessary action to make all sides believe they were being accommodated? The political class was, thereby, born of necessity. And political campaigns to decide which politicians would be in charge and which would sit on the sidelines were certainly not far behind.

Those who have found their niche in the netherworld of politics, for the most part, started at a very young age. Many, in fact, were born into the business. Countless is the number of youngsters hauled off to New England town meetings by their politically interested parents. Lots of kids were there at the precinct meetings in big-city and small-town America, while their parents participated in the first step toward nominating partisan choices for high public office. And for many young people, the dinner table conversation at home each evening often centered on the political issues of the day.

Still others got the bug to become active in politics when some great issue kindled their interest. Thousands of young Americans took to the streets during the late 1960s and early 1970s protesting the war in Southeast Asia, and many have maintained an ongoing interest in political issues, though the Vietnam War is a quarter of a century into history. Thousands of young women burned their bras as a symbol of protest during the early feminist movement. Many, though now wearing bras more frequently, are still active in politics.

Churches of a number of faiths have been incubators for political thought and campaign action, regardless of the Constitution's admonition to keep church and state separate. The pro-life protesters, who match the pro-choice opposition in numbers and enthusiasm, are often from the kneeling benches in the Catholic Church. Conservative Christians get their start in political activism from the altar calls in the conservative churches, most often in the Midwest and the South. The most conservative church doctrine is that of the Latter-Day Saints and, as a consequence, Mormons dominate conservative politics, not only in Utah, but also in several other nearby Western states. None of the conservative churches, however, are able to match the fervor that comes from the pulpit of black churches in support of Democratic candidates.

Politics, unlike industry and finance, is a people business. If anything, politics is most like sports, with heroes, everyday players, managers, fans, statistics and a playoff, like the World Series. Could anything in retail sales be the equivalent of the 1999-2000 presidential campaign between Texas Governor George W. Bush and Vice President Al Gore? Bill Mazeroski homered in the bottom of the ninth inning in the World Series of 1960, giving the Pittsburgh Pirates the world championship over the New York Yankees. It was the only time in baseball's storied history that a World Series ended with a home run in the last at bat of the last game. The United States Supreme Court did for Bush what Mazeroski did for the Pirates.

Most people get into politics because of their interest in philosophy or political ideology or a specific issue. Some feel passionately about the gun ownership issue. For others, the environment is a passionate cause. Those without often feel strongly that the government ought to be delivering more and better services – like shelter for the homeless. Those with deep pockets often feel strongly that the government takes too much from the rich and gives it to the poor. Robin Hood would have been in the former group.

But there are other reasons to become politically active. The do-gooders and the daily press would have you believe the only reason someone runs for public office is to gain "power." While this may be true in a few cases, very few people run for public office with the idea of becoming all-powerful, in political terms. More people go to political meetings to meet new and interesting people than to get into politics for the wrong reasons. It probably could be proven that more young lawyers run for county attorney in one of the 3,140 county jurisdictions in this country, with no hope of winning, but with the hope of building a better and bigger law practice, than those who run for power. More people see politics as fun, exciting and interesting than get into the business to make money the wrong way. It's probably true that you can find a hot date while stuffing envelopes at a campaign headquarters quicker than you can by hanging out in watering holes. Well, maybe not, but close.

Finally, there is a large group of people who get involved in politics to change the way things are being done by the incumbents. Stories abound, from practically all 50 states, of a young mother who decides the local schools are not teaching her kids what they ought to be learning. She takes matters into her own hands, files for the school board in the next election, wins, and proceeds to get the local superintendent fired and replaced with someone more to her liking. It happens every election somewhere in this great land of ours.

These are the stories from people who, for whatever reason, decided politics and political campaigns were their calling.

CHAPTER 1

Political Legends

☆ ☆ ☆

The pollsters say that 90 percent of the American public can tell us who the President of the United States is. A year after the 2000 presidential election, probably three-fourths of the country's voters could tell you that Bush won the election by defeating – depending on who's counting – Vice President Al Gore. Try asking the public who ran against President Bill Clinton in 1996 and less than a third could say the correct answer was Senator Bob Dole of Kansas. Fame is a fleeting thing.

Many famous people in politics got that way trying to be elected president. Think Harold Stassen, for openers. But some are well known and they didn't even try to become president. Ask people who the oldest man in the United States Senate was in 2001and not too many will mention Strom Thurmond of South Carolina, but mention Thurmond's name and half of the politically aware people in America will recognize who he is. Thurmond, by the way, was governor of South Carolina when he ran for president back in 1948 as the States' Rights candidate, but few people alive today voted for or against him.

Richard J. Daley was mayor of Chicago from 1955 until he died in 1976. Anyone with the nickname "The Boss" is a legend in politics. Former New York City Mayor Rudy Giuliani is a legend, but maybe legend status just comes with being a two-term mayor of the nation's most important city. Arizona Senator Barry Goldwater is a legend, not only because he ran for president in 1964, but also because he is credited with moving the conservative agenda into the forefront of American political thought. Conservative Republicans in every state will tell you they started in politics going door to door for Goldwater in that unsuccessful campaign against President Lyndon Johnson. John F. Kennedy is legendary for the same sorts of reasons. Not only was he elected president in 1960, but he energized an entire generation of young Democrats. So fame for some is not as fleeting as for others.

Here are some stories about a few legendary figures in American politics.

Meeting Ronald Reagan the First Time

I was 20 years old and the chairman of Young Americans for Freedom in Michigan when I first met Ronald Reagan in 1964. I had traveled to San Francisco for the Republican National Convention, and out in California I met my counterpart, Jack Cox, who was chairman of California Young Americans for Freedom. Cox said Reagan was wonderful and very helpful to young people.

I was nervous just at the prospect of talking to a movie star. Having grown up in the '50s, meeting anyone from Hollywood was exciting. Cox got Reagan on the phone and he introduced us: "Mr. Reagan, here is Emmy Lewis." I said, "Mr. Reagan, how do you do?" I told him I was very active in YAF in Michigan and that we'd had good luck raising money. I told him if he ever got to Michigan I would love it if he would give us a couple hours and we would arrange a meeting of some potential major donors and maybe he could give a little talk. This would be a great event to raise some money.

He told me he didn't fly. I don't know if he or Nancy had a dream about dying in a plane crash, but he took trains everywhere. The next thing he said was, "I don't get back East very often. I'm from the Midwest." I thought that was a bizarre expression. But I guess anybody out there thinks anything east of the Mississippi is back East. But he said if he ever did come to Michigan, he would be very happy to help.

Next Reagan asked, "Are you going home right after the convention, or are you staying in California for a while?" I said I was going to Los Angeles to visit my mother's sister. "Oh, well I live in Los Angeles," he responded. "I would like to meet with you." This is typical Midwesterner. I will never forget it.

Now, he didn't know me from Adam. I was a nobody. I was barely 20 years old. And here was Ronald Reagan saying, "Give me a call when you get down there. Mrs. Reagan and I would love to have you come over to the house."

I was just taken aback. I said, "Oh, Mr. Reagan, how nice of you. I would love to do that." Then I hung up.

Like a typical young person, I prepared myself to be disappointed. I thought, *When I get down there I will call and he will forget. He won't remember my name, or he will be busy or something.* But I called him anyway, and he answered the phone and said, "Oh, yes, Emmy. I am delighted to hear from you. I don't know what your schedule is, but can you come over today? How about this afternoon at two o'clock?" He gave me the address to the house they lived in before they moved to the White House.

I drove up and knocked on the door. A housekeeper answered the door, and Reagan came right up behind her to welcome me. As she opened the door wider, Reagan greeted me personally and invited me in. He had a nice sports shirt on, brown slacks, brown socks and red corduroy slippers. I thought, *Oh, man, this is Hollywood. Slippers at two o'clock in the afternoon!*

He invited me into this family room with a beautiful view overlooking the Pacific Ocean. Mrs. Reagan came in and we were introduced, and Mr. Reagan and I visited for two hours. One of the things we talked about was Michigan Governor George Romney and how he had refused to endorse Goldwater. I just trashed Romney, not rudely, but Reagan agreed. We talked a lot about foreign policy, and I didn't have a lot of expectations. I was blown away by his knowledge of history.

All these years later I am delighted in the memory of, year after year, writing these letters over Ronald Reagan's signature, knowing that he had, on his own initiative, invited me to his house—and here I am as God would have it.

—Emmy Lewis

Strom Thurmond's Longevity

Factoid: Strom Thurmond ran as a write-in candidate in the Democratic Party primary in 1954. He won with 63% over Democrat Edgar Brown with 37% and became the first person elected to the U.S. Senate on a write-in campaign.

On the morning of the George W. Bush Inaugural on January 20, 2001, I brought my 7-year-old daughter to the swearing-in ceremony at the Capitol, and we were supposed to go to the Minnesota Society Reception beforehand, but we received some bad information and ended up at the Trent Lott magnolia and mimosa reception.

Since we were not dressed for a formal reception, we were loitering around trying to figure out where to find the Minnesota people so that we wouldn't have to wait forever for the swearing-in ceremony.

My 7-year-old was quite excited about all this. So we were waiting by the elevator and she was over by the window watching the men put together a cannon outside that would be fired during the ceremony.

Senator Strom Thurmond walked up with his ever-present aide. We're standing by the elevator, and I turn and nod politely to the senator and say, "Good morning." And all of a sudden his aide got this panic-stricken look on his face and must have realized he forgot the senator's hat or something. So he took off back to their offices.

The senator was standing there by himself. He looked over at me and said, "Is that your daughter?" I said that she was. "She's beautiful. Bring her over here." I had heard a lot of things about the senator but thought it was interesting that he was addressing this comment to my daughter.

"I think I even have something here for her," he said. He fishes around in his pocket and comes out with a handful of candy. Libby was much appreciative and she said thank you. "Is this your first inauguration?" Thurmond asked her. She said that it was, so I asked the senator how many this was for him.

He looked at me, and thought and thought, then with a smile he said, "I've been to all of them." —*Bob Bissen*

Senator Thurmond Lives On

Factoid: South Carolina Senator Strom Thurmond, born in 1902, was first elected to the South Carolina State Senate in 1933.

Back in the late 1980s, I used to work out at a place called the Center Club in Arlington, Virginia. I would come home, eat dinner with my family and then go work out, finishing about 9:30 each night. Senator Strom Thurmond would come in frequently, and he was not young even then. He would swim laps – this guy was in tremendous shape.

He would often be one of the last ones in the steam room, as would I. We never said more than "How are you doing?" But one night I get there and Thurmond is lying down on his back with his arm over his forehead. I sit down in the room for three or four minutes, but it's unbearably hot for some reason. I think, "I can't take this, it's too hot," and I look at Senator Thurmond and wonder how he's doing it. But then I look at him again and notice that his chest is not moving at all.

I'm convinced I am going to be around when Strom Thurmond draws his last breath. So I said, "Senator? Senator?" a couple of times and got no response. First I thought, should I nudge him? Then I thought, if I'm touching some guy in the steam room, that's very inappropriate behavior.

So I said, "Senator" again and still got no response. Then I start thinking about the headlines. "Naked Senate administrative assistant discovered with Strom Thurmond in steam room." All these things went through my mind for about two minutes. I was absolutely intimidated.

Then suddenly he said, "What time is it?"

I said, "I'm sorry, I don't have my watch on."

And he said again, as senators will, "What time is it?" meaning go find out for me. I was so embarrassed and so relieved that I went out, put my clothes on without showering and went in search of a clock.

—Tom Mason

The Wit of Gene McCarthy

Factoid: Minnesota Senator Eugene McCarthy captured 41% of the vote in the 1968 New Hampshire presidential primary. President Lyndon Johnson got just under 50%. Twenty-six delegates were awarded to Johnson and 12 to McCarthy.

W hen I worked in the McCarthy movement in the 1960s, I got the chance to see Senator Gene McCarthy up close and personally. He had a great Irish wit. It is often said that Irish witticism comes in only two flavors, welcoming or sarcastic. Gene had the gift of cutting witticism.

He was on *Meet the Press* in the late 1970s, right after Vice President Walter Mondale had announced he was going to run for president. One of the commentators said, "Now, Senator McCarthy, you served with Walter Mondale. You come from the state Walter Mondale comes from. What kind of man is Walter Mondale?"

McCarthy looked into the television and replied in a slow, drawn-out manner, "Oh, yes, Fritz Mondale. He has the very soul of a vice president."

One day I got on an airplane going to Washington in 1975. Gene McCarthy was sitting there. I was glad to see him because I had heard he had just suffered a stroke and I was somewhat concerned about his health. I sat down next to him and told him that story.

I said, "You know, my favorite quote of yours was about Fritz Mondale, when you said he had the very soul of a vice president."

He said, "Well, it's worse than that. You know, in 1976, Carter required that all the vice presidential candidates, because of the Eagleton fiasco of the election before, which he wanted to guard against, must submit an affidavit detailing their complete medical history. There were five people under consideration. They all submitted complete, infinitely detailed affidavits, with every conceivable medical malady that had ever befallen them.

"Fritz, of course, got his in first," he continued. "He detailed the drugs he was taking for the hypertension he was subject to. The very last person to submit the affidavit was Frank Church. Senator Church revealed in his affidavit that as a result of a wartime injury, he only had one testicle."

McCarthy said, "As soon as Fritz Mondale found out that Frank Church had disclosed this in his affidavit, he saw fit to submit another affidavit. We all thought he was going to say he had no balls at all."

The entire first-class section in the airplane just died! We had just taken off from the Minneapolis airport, and it must have been ten minutes before people could stop laughing.   —*Vance Opperman*

Bush Goes One for One for Denver Bears

Factoid: In the 1984 presidential race, the Reagan-Bush team got 63% of the vote in Colorado to easily capture all eight of the state's electoral votes.

During the 1984 campaign, Vice President George Bush on a Friday afternoon flies into Denver to give a speech to the Colorado state party that night. We arrived at our hotel and did a press conference. I went to the lobby and ran into Whitey Ford, Juan Marichal and Warren Spahn, three Hall of Fame baseball heroes.

I said to them, "What are you guys doing here?"

They said, "We're doing an Old Timers game tonight."

I brought them to the vice president's holding room.

Of course, Bush just loves these guys because he's a baseball player at heart. We walk into the holding room and Marichal says, "Do you want to come to the game with us, Mr. Vice President?"

Bush said he couldn't because of security.

They left, and we had a long talk with the Secret Service. If no one knows we're going to do something, you can do it because there is little security risk. The vice president said, "I really want to go to that game."

We called Marichal back and said Bush was going to come, but that they couldn't tell anybody.

Marichal asked if the vice president would like to play or hit.

All I could think of was Gerald Ford falling down the stairs. I said, "Gee, I don't think that's a great idea."

He said, "Would you ask him?"

I agreed to ask him and, of course, the vice president immediately said, "Oh! I'd love to play!"

No one knew we were coming. It was for the Colorado Bears, which is a Triple A league team. We were in the locker room, changing into the Bears uniform, and I'm pitching him whiffle balls, getting a couple strikes.

This was right after Mondale announced in 1984 that Gary Hart was not going to be on the ticket, so I'm afraid Bush might get booed. We went from the locker room to the dugout in this closed van. In the van are Warren Spahn, the vice president, the Secret Service agents and myself. We get to the dugout and still no one other than the players know that Bush is there.

They announced Bush as a pinch hitter, a former NCAA All American and team captain at Yale, George Bush. He got a tepid response, but that's all you care about. He got a single, so I am pumped. I grab the bat, and I'm just psyched. This is great!

We stayed a little bit longer, and then Bush asked if they thought he could play first base.

The next thing we knew, here was the new first baseman, Vice President George Bush. Now he got a standing ovation. The first guy up hit a single to right field, and Bush went to the proper cut-off spot. The fans don't notice it as much as the players. They yell, "Hey! You did good! Nice going!"

The next guy up was a lefty and he hit a screaming line drive down the first-base line. The vice president runs over, jumps, knocks it down, tags him out and the inning is over.

We went back to the hotel. I now have this deep dilemma, an ethical dilemma. I still have the bat that he hit with. I think it was off Warren Spahn. I mean, how often do you hit off a Hall of Famer? Here is my dilemma: Do I give the bat to the vice president or keep it?

I wrestled with this, and I finally decided that, no, he'll want to keep it for his kids, his grandkids or a museum. So I said, "Vice President, here's your bat."

He said, "Thanks a lot, Ron. I really appreciate it."

The next morning we had some cops in for pictures. I was talking to the Secret Service agent outside in the hallway of our hotel. The cops came out and this huge sergeant is carrying the bat.

I said, "Hey! Where are you going with that bat?"

He said, "Oh, the vice president gave it to me."

#@!#!!   —*Ron Kaufman*

No Revolution in the Back of a Limo

Factoid: In 1990, Congressman Newt Gingrich was re-elected in the 6th district of Georgia, beating David Worley by a half of one percentage point. In 1992, running in a completely new district that had also been designated the 6th, Gingrich beat Tony Center 58-42 to win an eighth term in the House.

Georgia House Speaker Tom Murphy hated Newt Gingrich with a passion. When they got to re-districting in 1991, Murphy took the old 6th congressional district and cut it up into five pieces, so there were legitimately no parts of it left that Gingrich could run in and hope to be elected.

The time leading up to the decision of which district to run in was agonizing, filled with questions of "Should I do this? Shouldn't I do that? I really think we need to elect more Republicans, so I should take the hardest job."

I told Newt I'd been doing a lot of focus groups in his old district. I said, "This is what one of the men said, 'I don't want to listen to him because if I listen to him, he'll convince me to vote for him and I don't want to vote for him.'"

I said, "Newt, that tells me that you need as many new constituents as you can get right now, and I think the only obvious thing is for you to move to this new 6th district."

One of the things you know about Newt is that he keeps in constant telephone communication with friends and allies and always ask everybody's opinion. "What do you think? What do you think?" It was part of his "'listen and learn" doctrine.

This agony had gone on for a month. Newt kept wondering, "Should we do this? Should we do that? I can't leave my friends on the south side. This is where I came from…"

I said, "Well, you can leave and go to a brand new district because the new district is 70 percent Republican and they would like a leader. As the only Republican in Georgia, I think you could make a real impact on the north side." He wavered back and forth and kept talking to people.

I was down at the shore on Saturday morning when the phone rang at 2 a.m. It was Newt. He said, "Joe, I really have to ask you one last time, do you think I should move to the north side to this new district?"

I said, "Newt, do I have to come down there and pack the damn truck? Of course you should move."

I don't know whether that was the deciding influence or not, but he actually decided to move to the new district. We moved up north and had to go through this whole series of diplomatic statements about how he was now taking over new territory.

This was about the time the Braves won their first National League play-off series. Baseball was extraordinarily popular; we were down in the old 6th district, which was south of the airport. The new 6th district was north of Atlanta in Cobb County and in parts of north Fulton, De Kalb and Gwinnett counties. As Gingrich was making the announcement we were writing two letters: one to the old constituents, thanking them for everything they had done, and another to the new district to let people know we were on our way there. This is one of those times when we got a little too excited about the baseball play-offs and not very careful about proofreading. Instead of saying "We are moving to this new, north Atlanta district after what the speaker did to us," the letter that went out actually said, "We are moving to a new North Atlantic district because of what the speaker did to us!"

The Democrats had great fun with this, saying, "Gingrich is moving to the North Atlantic."

I had egg on my face for days. It was the worst campaign imaginable. Newt was under fire at the time because he was Minority Whip and he had a security Capitol Hill policeman. He had a car provided as well, and the car happened to be a Lincoln Continental. Dick Cheney had been Whip before him and told Gingrich, "I certainly hope you keep George, who was the Capitol Hill policeman, and keep the car, as the car is a great car." Newt did and it became his limousine, as opposed to just a car. It became a huge issue in the spring of 1992.

We were now in a fiercely competitive Republican primary campaign. Newt was the Whip in the U.S. House and he was running against the Republican Whip in the Georgia House, Herman Clark, who was running a spirited attack.

While the limousine had become a huge issue, Newt had been

out in California doing a fundraising stint during Easter recess for GOPAC. He came back on the red-eye flight before going to a Rotary breakfast in the Buckhead area.

The news media were also present because Newt always got the media in his campaigns. This was now the big story, "Would the Republican Whip survive the Georgia Whip in this newly contested territory?" There must have been ten cameras in the room at this Buckhead Rotary meeting.

We were behind the stage, and before I was introduced, I asked, "What is going on? Why is there this much coverage?"

Newt said, "I just let it be known that I was going to make an announcement this morning."

I said, "What announcement are you making?" He always did this type of thing.

Newt said, "I'm giving up the car."

"You've decided to give up the car and the driver after we've defended the car and the driver for months? You decided now you're going to give it up?"

"Yes," he answered. "I've decided that you can't conduct a revolution from the back seat of a limo."   —*Joe Gaylord*

Rhodes for Mothers in Struthers

Factoid: Jim Rhodes, in 1978, narrowly defeated Richard Celeste to win a fourth term in the Ohio governor's office by a 49-48 margin. He tried for a fifth term in 1986 but lost to Celeste by a 61-39 margin.

Ohio Governor Jim Rhodes equated everything to jobs. One huge force he saw working against jobs in Ohio was the EPA – the Environmental Protection Agency — because they were keeping Ohio's coal, which was very high-sulfur coal, from being developed to its potential.

One day during his fourth and final campaign for governor, in 1978, we went out near Youngstown, Ohio, where a power plant was having all sorts of problems because they had to put air scrubbers on their smokestacks. He was going to make a major statement about this.

It must have been a really dead night because ABC sent network cameras in for the press conference. Rhodes was at this power plant and there were about 5,000 people they had trucked in from all over the state because Ohio coal provided a lot of jobs.

Keep in mind that Rhodes was always tongue-tied when he spoke. The little town we were in was called Struthers. Rhodes got up and spoke extemporaneously for fifteen minutes about the fact that it was Christmas. He lamented over the poor mothers from Struthers because of the scrubbers. He was tongue-tied in the first place, but between all the Struthers, the mothers and the scrubbers, no one knew what he'd said by the time he was done. But that certainly didn't stop the whole place from erupting in a torrent of applause and screams from this huge crowd.

The guy from ABC finally came over to me and said, "Do you have any idea what he just said?"

I shook my head and said, "No, I don't, but you have to admit the mark of a great politician is to come into town, speak in a foreign language and have them screaming for ten minutes afterwards."

—*Steve Sandler*

Jesse Unruh Eats on Republican Money

Factoid: Jesse M. Unruh served in the California assembly from 1951 to 1969. He was speaker from 1961 to 1969. The quotable "Big Daddy" said, "If you can't drink their (lobbyists') booze, take their money, chase their women and still vote against 'em, you don't belong in politics."

Jesse M. Unruh and I were at some bipartisan political thing out in the westside of Los Angeles in the early 1970s. It was terribly boring. Pretty soon Jesse caught my eye and said, "Let's go have dinner." So we went over to Chason's, the hangout for the right-wing Republican money people.

Jesse has with him his new American Express card. Here is a guy who has been an assembly speaker and has never had a credit card in his life. He says, "I'm buying."

We go in and there is Earl Jorgensen and the whole crowd. They are watching me walk in with "Big Daddy," and I give him a how are you, good to see you. We sit down and eat up a storm.

Jesse and I are half drunk and we are arguing like all hell had broken loose at the table. The waiter comes back and whispers in his ear, like they do, "Mr. Unruh, we don't take credit cards." Jesse looked at me, and I started to laugh. I got $20 in my pocket, and we had just run up a $150 bill. I said, "Don't worry, Jesse, I'm going to bail you out with some fat-cat Republican money."

I get up and walk over to Earl Jorgensen and tell him the story. Earl laughs and gives me $200 and I go back and pay the bill.

—*Stu Spencer*

We Want Jesse, We Want Jesse

Factoid: Paul Wellstone won a second term in the Senate in 1996 when he defeated former Senator Rudy Boschwitz by a 50-41 margin. Reform Party nominee Dean Barkley got 7%.

The Jesse Ventura phenomenon began in Minnesota in 1996 when I was running for U.S. Senate and Ventura was the honorary chair of my campaign. This meant that he was going to do a couple of fundraisers, as well as walk with me in a parade or two. He agreed to walk a parade route with me on July 4th, in my hometown of Annandale. Ventura was late, as always, and he actually had to jog in three miles because of the backup. Of course, he gets there right as I take off.

About one-third of the way down the parade route, in front of Bobby Muller's house, is where they had the beer tent. I noticed an interesting thing going on. I was the candidate in my hometown, but everybody was cheering for Jesse and ignoring me. I turned to him and said, "Guess what, Jesse?"

"What?" he answered.

"The wrong guy is running for office. Next time, it's your time," I told him.

He laughed and just kind of blew it off. That, however, is when the light bulb went on that maybe he would make a good candidate, and of course, the rest is history. I convinced him to run the next year and now he's governor of the state of Minnesota.

My campaign manager Doug Friedline and I started working on Jesse in July 1997, trying to get him to think about running for governor of Minnesota. He blew us off. We kept on tag-teaming him, and every other month one of us would call and bug him or call into his talk radio show and try to get him going on the question.

Finally, on September 22, 1997, he called me and said, "Come on out to the ranch. I want to talk about this governor thing."

Doug and I went out there, outside Maple Grove, Minnesota, and worked on him for nearly an hour. Finally, he said, "Okay, you have me convinced. Now you have the tough thing; you have to convince my wife."

He called his wife, Teri.

We went out to the horse barn and Teri came out and sat there and wouldn't have anything to do with it. She thought it was the dumbest idea in the world. She was worried about the past and the privacy and him being a biker. Finally, after an unsuccessful half hour of trying to convince her, Jesse just said, "Okay, everyone be quiet."

He looked at Teri and said, "Teri, I want to find out if the American dream is still alive, where someone like me can actually become governor of the state of Minnesota. I have to try this just to see it."

In mid-January 1998 we had been trying to get Ventura to either raise money or actively do something. He was just toying with the idea on his radio show and really wasn't doing anything to show he was serious.

Ten of us, which was the formation of the campaign committee, went up to Jesse and said, "Look, we're all going to quit unless you do one of two things. You either put $10,000 of your own money into this campaign to jump-start it, so that we have some resources to work with, or you formally announce your candidacy."

Anyone who knows Jesse Ventura knows he is one of the cheapest S.O.B.s in the world. Obviously, the $10,000 from his pocket was out of the question. It was the threat of either put up some money or actually get off this little game that did the trick. Sure enough, on January 22, he announced his candidacy. We had blackmailed him to either put some money in or get off the pot!

—*Dean Barkley*

Helms Won't Repudiate 'Fine Christian Gentleman'

Factoid: Jesse Helms was elected to the U.S. Senate in 1972 when he defeated three-term Congressman Nick Galifianakis by a 54-46 margin.

Jesse Helms, to this day, never makes mistakes in dealing with the press. No matter what people think of him, he was a communicator by profession before he came to the Senate. If he says something to the press and they quote him and it sounds kind of controversial, he meant every word of it and did it on purpose. He never screws up with the press, but he does say provocative things sometimes.

In the first campaign, when there had never been a Republican elected to the Senate in North Carolina, Democrat Nick Galifianakis was running as the underdog. Around July of 1972, Helms had the bad luck of the Grand Wizard of the North Carolina Ku Klux Klan coming out and endorsing him. That was the last thing we needed.

We had been trying to prove he was not too conservative for the state and that he was not, in any way, racist. Helms had a terrific record on helping African Americans in the private sector. He hired the first black disc jockey in North Carolina.

This idiot Grand Wizard comes out and endorses Helms. Wherever Helms was campaigning, a reporter would go up to him, stick the microphone at him and say, "The Grand Wizard of the Ku Klux Klan endorsed you. Are you going to repudiate that?"

Helms replied, "Well, I don't know. What did he say?"

The reporter read him the quote that says, "I'm voting for Jesse Helms because he is a fine Christian gentleman."

Helms said, "You don't expect me to disagree with that, do you?" and he walked off!　　　　　　　　　　　　　*—Charlie Black*

Mondale Puts Down Boxing Gloves in Pennsylvania

In the 1984 primary campaign, it was like Walter Mondale thought of me as a good luck charm. We were down in Pennsylvania by 14 points. Along the way Mondale would take me behind the wing of this huge plane he had and say, "I just want you to know my whole life is hanging on your shoulders." It was a joke, but it's the way my relationship with him worked. I was only about 22 years old.

One day we were on the plane between Iowa and Pennsylvania, and he was asking me about my family. I said, "My father hasn't talked to me in 10 years. He thinks I am doing politics just to get out of real work and that it is a corrupt game."

Mondale had lost New Hampshire to Gary Hart, and ever since then he had to carry those red boxing gloves. Everywhere he went they called him "Fighting Fritz," and he said he was going to carry those boxing gloves until he beat Hart. Little did they know, it was going to be something like 13 states until he beat Hart. So every state he went to, I was carrying these boxing gloves and down we would go. We would get creamed.

We get to Pennsylvania and we're 14 points down. We had to do something really different here. I am looking around trying to get my hands on anything I can and it hits me: Senator Hart is chairman of the Three Mile Island Commission. So I'm going to get Mondale in there to stand in front of the Three Mile Island Nuclear Plant and say shut it down.

All the labor unions wanted Three Mile Island to stay open. So, if I was really lucky, and we tipped off the right guys, there would be labor unions out there picketing Mondale, saying he was turning his back on the unions. The next thing that would happen is Hart would come to the state and get asked, "Where do you stand on Three Mile Island?" He was going to have to be a mealy-mouthed politician, who couldn't say, because he was chairman of the commission.

Mondale comes in, goes to Three Mile Island and says to shut it down. The labor unions are all out there picketing him. Four hours later, Hart lands. They ask him, "Mondale is coming out for shutting down Three Mile Island, Senator. Where do you stand?" He says, "Well, you know, I really can't say because I am on the commission and we are studying it."

Hart goes from 14 points up on us to 14 points down on us, in the last 14 days of the campaign, all on Three Mile Island. Mondale wins by 14 points.

It is the first state he wins since the whole bottom drops out.

Mondale is up in the Presidential Suite of the Stratford Hotel. I am losing track of time and the polls are shut down, and I get the call that Fritz wants to see me up in his suite.

I walk up there and my dad is in the room. Fritz somehow, from the first conversation, remembered it all, got somebody to figure out where the hell my dad was and got him up there. If you go look at the tape of Fritz Mondale declaring victory in the ballroom of the Stratford Hotel, you'll see Fritz Mondale and this scrawny, old Italian guy standing behind him.

We were in the Stratford in the Presidential Suite, Mondale was turning for the door and his traveling aide says, "Sir, your gloves?" Fritz looks at him and says, "I don't need these anymore." He takes out his pen and writes on them "To Rocky Trippi, Thanks!" and he gives them to me.

My dad died in 1989, and I buried one of the gloves with him.

—Joe Trippi

CHAPTER 2

Stars in the Business

M oses, er, Charlton Heston is the best-known "star" in politics who never ran for public office. As president of the National Rifle Association, Heston appears on the stump for pro-gun candidates all over America in election years, raising thousands of dollars and guaranteeing good press coverage of the visit. A lot of gossip column blurbs ran about movie star Warren Beatty running for president in the Democratic Party primaries in 2000, but his potential candidacy never got off the ground. But, for the most part, Hollywood is active politically only with checks for liberal Democratic candidates. For all of the 1990s, Los Angeles was the most important fundraising stop for candidate and then president Clinton—not only for his campaigns, but also for the Democratic Party and, ultimately, Clinton's legal defense fund.

While most actors haven't plunged into running for elective office, it's quite another matter for sports figures. Congressman, cabinet secretary, presidential candidate and vice presidential nominee Jack Kemp was well remembered for telling his constituency in Buffalo they better keep electing him to Congress or he would come back and play quarterback for the Bills. If professional wrestling is still on the acknowledged list of real sports, then Minnesota Governor Jesse Ventura is currently the highest-ranking athlete turned state official.

Astronaut John Glenn was elected to the U.S. Senate from Ohio, but it took him three tries before he finally got lift-off. Kentucky Senator Jim Bunning pitched two no-hitters and was elected to the Baseball Hall of Fame. Wisconsin Senator Herb Kohl owns the Milwaukee Bucks basketball team. Former Supreme Court Justice Bryon White didn't pick up the nickname "Whizzer" from the court-room. He was an All-America running back at Colorado and played professional football in Pittsburgh and Detroit.

Here are some stories about people who gained fame outside of politics, then ventured into the business.

Eastwood Wins Mayor's Race in Carmel

Factoid: On April 8, 1986, Clint Eastwood unseated two-term Carmel Mayor Charlotte Townsend, winning 72-28.

In 1986 I was in the middle of a meeting of the political action committee for the Irvine Company, which is one of California's biggest landowners.

The secretary comes in and says, Clint Eastwood is on the phone for you. Well, I know that I am supposed to get a call from Eastwood, but I pretend I don't know that. I go to the phone in another room and take the call. He says, in a voice that is so recog-nizable, Eileen Padberg? I said, yes. He said, This is Clint, Clint Eastwood. That was how he always introduced himself.

He tells me he has some friends who want him to run for mayor of Carmel. The businesspeople were being screwed over by the town government and it was time to make a change. He was the one who had been designated to run for mayor because he had the name identification.

I was really excited, of course, but I didn't want to show that. He is giving me the lay of the land and tells me, "I hear that I can trust you, so will you work with me?" I said yes. He asked if I had any questions. I said, "Can I just get this off my chest right away and then we will never have to do it again?" He said, "What?" I said, "Go ahead, say it." He said, "Come on." I said, "Please, just say it once and I will never ask you again." So he said, "Okay. Make my day." I said, "Okay, I'm in."

My partner didn't even know I was talking with him. I wasn't allowed to tell anybody. I drove up to Los Angeles, and all the way in the car my heart was pounding. I sat down in the waiting room of his Warner Brothers' office, and I had my head down, because I was trying to keep my heart calm. He walked over and I didn't lift my head. I just pretended I was reading. He said, "You must be Eileen Padberg." I looked up and the first thing that came out of my mouth was, "You must be Clint Eastwood." He just smiled that silly smile.

I spent the next three hours with him. He was just a wonderful guy, and I signed on immediately and made plans to go to Carmel three weeks later and get the campaign going.

Over the next two days we decided we would do a survey just to see what the issues were in Carmel. He knew what his issues were, but I wasn't convinced they were Carmel's issues.

We did this survey and it definitely said that Eastwood couldn't win under most circumstances. I had to be the one to tell him that he couldn't win. I called him and gave him the bad news. He took it pretty well. He said, "Is there any way?" I said, "No, it's pretty clear that you can't win. We need to find another candidate. We need to find another carrier for the banner."

At about 11:30 p.m. he called me at home. "Eileen?" Yes. "This is Clint, Clint Eastwood." He said, "I wanted to talk a little bit about the survey. Have you had a chance to look at it again?" I said I had looked at it a couple of times. He said, "What if I run?" I said, "You can run, but you can't win, and think how bad it will make you look. You know, this hotshot movie star can't win a race for mayor of Carmel. What is worse, it will make me look really bad because I couldn't win this race for this hotshot movie star in this little dinky town. It makes us both look bad."

He said, ""Is there any way to win?" I told him there was probably some way. I couldn't honestly say there was no way, but it would take a lot of work. He said, "Well, I want to do it." I said okay. If you are in, then I am in.

I went to work, trying to figure out what the best way to win was. It was clear to me the survey was saying that no one took him seriously. A movie star did not impress them, because Carmel has plenty of movie stars. They figured his election would end up being another tourist attraction and would just make their city worse with tourist traffic.

We met a few days later and I said, "You have to convince these people that you are serious. That you will be a mayor that is here for every meeting, that studies, that knows what he is talking about, that cares. He said he could do that.

The opponent, Charlotte Townsend, had been mayor for four years. She was 65 years old at the time. She had been an okay mayor, but the business community was getting tired of her not allowing any additions, any improvements or things that would be good for business development. She was tired of having all the tourists come to town.

We won the Eastwood campaign because we went back to the old style of campaigns. There were probably 8,000 to 10,000 voters in the city. On a Saturday we went over with a bunch of his buddies and went through the whole voter file. We put them on labels, on three-by-five cards, and we broke the whole voter file down into three categories: yes, no and unknown. We shored up our "yes" votes. We made sure we saw all of them right away. Clint talked to almost every one of those people. The "no" votes we just tossed, and we concentrated on the "unknowns."

We broke the city down to four or five regions. We had 15 to 20 coffees in each region, and each person who volunteered to give a coffee had to invite a hundred or so names from the "unknown" list in their area.

We won the campaign by coffees. We ran one advertisement in the local *Carmel Times*, but there was no mail in the city. Mail didn't get delivered. One brochure we had at the headquarters is now a collector's item.

Clint was the perfect candidate. He did everything he was asked to do and never complained. He went to every one of those coffees. Sometimes we would have five coffees a night, and he would go to every one of them.

He would talk to everybody. He would woo them and make them understand that he was serious about being mayor. We would meet with the staff person at the end of the coffee and take out the cards and put them in the yes, no or unknown file.

By the end of the campaign we had gone through our whole

unknown file and identified every one of those voters. They were either a yes or a no. On Election Day we won overwhelmingly.

—Eileen Padberg

Elizabeth Taylor's Lucky Dress

Factoid: In 1978, John Warner lost the Republican nomination for U.S. Senate to Dick Obenshain, who had been the Virginia Republican chairman. Obenshain was killed in an airplane crash in August 1978, and the party selected Warner to take his place on the ballot.

At the beginning of the 1978 Warner Senate campaign in Virginia, I was the media guy and went down to attend John Warner's announcement event. We went down the night before and stayed in Newport News at a hotel right on the point, overlooking the harbor. There were probably 1,000 paparazzi there. Every guy from Italy and everywhere else was trying to climb over the others to get pictures of Elizabeth Taylor.

I must admit that in the time I came to know Elizabeth during this campaign, she was the greatest. She possessed classic show business talent and was an overall wonderful human being.

John and Elizabeth were staying in a suite on the top floor of this hotel. I wound up staying right next door to them because I was his consultant arranging the whole thing. Little did we know, there was a big rock concert in town that night, and the rock band was in the other suite across the hall. The night was long and loud.

We were up all night listening to these guys wailing. It finally calmed down at 4:30 a.m. At 5:30, having only one hour of sleep, I went over and knocked on the Warners' door. Out came John in his boxers, and he is obviously out of it and we can't get any coffee. So I opened up the windows and the wind starts blowing in right off the ocean. It's a nice spring day, and it's enough to get your blood going.

I literally had him propped up against the wall, starting to get his speech going and getting his mind cleared. Suddenly, somebody was tapping me on my back. I turned around and there was Elizabeth. She is standing there in her slip, holding up this dress.

25

She says, "Would you help me put on this dress?"

I said, "Sure."

She turns around and I pull the dress down over her. The dress is very tight, to say the least, and very difficult to get on. She is facing away from me, and I'm trying to get all the buttons done on the back while keeping John going with his speech. The wind continues to blow through the place.

When I finished with the buttons, she turns around and I look down and see that this dress is cut practically down to her navel. This is going to be a 6:30 a.m. press conference opening the campaign, with all the paparazzi present! I looked at her and said, "Elizabeth, it's a beautiful dress, but I just don't think you can wear it today."

She said, "But this is my lucky dress. It's the dress that John and I got married in. I have to wear this dress. Don't worry; it has a jacket. It will be fine."

I said, "Great. I'm going to call you guys in 15 minutes to give you a heads-up. You're going to come down the security elevator." I explained the whole process.

I go downstairs and discover it is a madhouse. It's chaos! I'm standing there looking around, checking to make sure everything is ready, and the campaign staff is running around. I call John and tell them to come down.

Sure enough, 10 minutes later, the elevator is opening and the flashbulbs are going and the cameras are rolling.

John steps out and Elizabeth steps out behind him. I take a look and, yes, the dress has a jacket, but it stops right at her shoulders.

That was the first stop in a six-city tour that day that ended up at the Holiday Inn in Alexandria, Virginia, where all the network news guys were waiting. This was going to be the closing press conference. Again, all the paparazzi, Sam Donaldson and everyone else was in on the action. Elizabeth had this dress on. John got up and did an admirable job giving his announcement.

The press started to say, "Let's hear what Elizabeth has to say. What does Mrs. Warner have to say about her role in the campaign? We want to know what she is going to be doing out there."

We had not planned to have her make any comments. She was prodded, so she climbed up on this little box in front of the podium, leaned over fully into all the network cameras and said, "Well, I'm just the candidate's wife."

I was dumbfounded. There was nothing that could be done. She is so sweet.

That night, I went to New York to have dinner with a friend of mine from CBS News. She looked at me and the first thing she said was, "How could you let her wear that dress?"   —*Don Ringe*

Elizabeth Taylor Revealed in Williamsburg

On an evening in late November 1978, it was finally official that John Warner had won the 1978 Senate race. He had only won it by 4,700 votes. The Republican Governor's Association was having a dinner in Williamsburg, Virginia. My wife and I were invited; we were sitting at a table with Judy Peachy and her husband, as well as some others who were associated with the Warner campaign.

Warner comes across the room to see Judy, who had been his campaign manager, to give her a big kiss and say, hey, we won. He was acting it up. Judy was sitting across from me at one of the big circular tables with very high-backed chairs, almost like a king's throne.

Something was said and I sort of reared back in my chair, not realizing that Elizabeth Taylor, Warner's wife, was standing right behind my chair. She was wearing a rather low-cut dress that had a couple of strings attached to the bodice, which had somehow gotten across the back of my chair. When I leaned back, she leaned back, and I, of course, caught the strings.

Now, I understand, though I could not see, that this was one of the great shots of all time. I mean, the guys across the table got a real good look of what Elizabeth Taylor looked like bare-chested, including John, who was mortified. She sort of yelped, and I jumped about three feet in the air. She cussed me out pretty good. But I didn't even get the pleasure of seeing what the hell I had caused.   —*Kenny Klinge*

Sonny's Got the Beat

Factoid: Former Palm Springs Mayor Sonny Bono was elected to Congress in the 44th district of California in 1994 when he received 56% of the vote against former Democratic Assemblyman Steve Clute, who got 38%.

After the June primary in 1994, Sonny Bono determined that he was not going to do any joint appearances or debates and only a very limited number of talk shows. His reason for the first two was simple. If he did not do them nobody came and it was a non-event, but when he accepted, it would generate a crowd and always some media attention. He thought we could do a limited amount at the end of the campaign and that would suffice.

Even though Bono had served as mayor of Palm Springs, he was neither an experienced candidate in the context of a congressional race, nor did he have any serious grasp of the issues. His natural instincts on the issues tended to be conservative, but with a strong dose of people concern. He spoke in very plain language that generally just made good sense.

This was not a man who spent a lot of time with "the people" even when he was mayor. His home had a gate on it, he had a driver and by and large he had been insulated for a number of years except for his maitre d' role at the restaurant, which was mostly glad-handing with fans.

I set about to persuade him that not only did we not want to decline all those invitations, we wanted to accept every one of them. I really felt this was going to be the most effective way to relate his instincts to the issues the voters were interested in.

We ended up doing a number of debates and joint appearances and many talk shows. As time went on and Sonny listened to the people, how they talked and what they were concerned about, the more confident he became and the more he was relating his language and position to what he was hearing.

Just a few days before the end of the campaign I went with him to a talk show appearance. When it was over I remarked to him what an outstanding job he had done. Old questions, new questions, issues planted by the opponent—nothing fazed him.

His response to me in typical Sonny patter was, "I got the beat. I hear the people. I know what they are saying and what they want to hear from me."

That was proven a few nights later when we had the inevitable debate. Sonny got the crowd going with him, and it was a wipeout. Bono's opponent, Steve Clute, never really understood what was happening. Bono had an uncanny ability to read an audience and immediately get into sync with the people, be it a Washington, D.C., audience of self-important types or a bunch of farmers in the Coachella Valley. —*Eddie Mahe*

Murphy Does the Old Soft Shoe on Second Base

Factoid: George Murphy was in four Broadway plays and 45 films before he was elected to the U.S. Senate in 1964, defeating Pierre Salinger by three points in California. In 1970, Murphy lost his bid for re-election to John Tunney, 54-44.

In 1970 I worked with incumbent U.S. Senator George Murphy, a former song and dance man for MGM.

Senator Murphy was 68 at the time, and I was just getting to know him, getting a sense of what kind of commercials I should do. He had a flight to catch back to Washington for a vote, and it was also "George Murphy Day" at Dodger stadium.

Dodger's owner Walter O'Malley welcomed him, and it was my job to try to impress Mr. O'Malley to have a fifth inning stretch instead of the usual seventh inning stretch. This would make it possible for the senator to make the flight back to Washington.

George had this unique ability to tap dance, to literally do the "soft shoe" at the end of every press conference. This was one of his signature moments in politics.

I hadn't been working with Murphy very long, but I took the liberty of saying, "Look, do me a favor, would you? Don't tap dance on home plate. Please. That's just not the kind of press we want."

Well, sure enough we were having a fifth inning stretch, and Murphy went out to second base with O'Malley. People were throwing pennies and beer cans, and were hooting and hollering.

He's waving to the crowd.

They give Murphy a bronze bat. He does his little thing, says a few words, takes the bat, uses it just like a dancing cane, does a little soft-shoe and comes plugging down the first-base line. I'm looking at him as though I can't believe this.

He came walking into the dugout, looked at me and said, "You said home plate; that was second base."   —*Don Ringe*

CHAPTER 3

Legends in the Campaign Business

☆ ☆ ☆

The political campaign business has always had "handlers." Mainly these were close advisers, assistants and confidantes. Through the early part of the last century, it seemed the tradition that the campaign manager for the successful presidential candidate was rewarded with nomination for attorney general. Harry Daugherty was Warren Harding's campaign manager and then his attorney general. Howard Cummings was Franklin D. Roosevelt's manager, then his attorney general. The same for Howard McGrath and Harry Truman, Herbert Brownell and Dwight Eisenhower, Robert Kennedy and his brother John F. Kennedy, and John Mitchell and Richard Nixon.

The most famous "handler" a century ago was Cleveland industrialist Mark Hanna, who signed on with William McKinley when he was an Ohio congressman and later governor. Hanna, who was the butt of the flourishing political cartoon industry, is said to have raised a record $3.5 million for McKinley's successful presidential campaign in 1896, far out-distancing the Democratic candidate, William Jennings Bryan.

But with the advent of television in the early 1960s—and its importance on the outcome of political campaigns at all levels—political consultants came into being. A new craft of political handlers, with a new range of skills and understanding of technology, took over running political campaigns, from the courthouses to the White House. In the 1976 presidential campaign, Stu Spencer of California, a full-time campaign professional, managed Gerald Ford's unsuccessful attempt to hold onto the presidency, and Hamilton Jordan, who would become White House chief of staff, managed Jimmy Carter's campaign.

Bob Squire produced television commercials for dozens of Democratic campaigns in the 1970s and 1980s, and along the way he acquired legendary status. Matt Reese, who pioneered voter identification programs and was credited with helping John F. Kennedy to an important win in the West Virginia presidential primary in 1960, was also a legend. Spencer and his partner, Bill Roberts, ran Ronald Reagan's first campaign for governor of California and grew to legendary status on the Republican side. Doug Bailey and partner John Deardourff ran virtually every important statewide campaign in the Midwest in the 1970s and 1980s for Republicans.

Here are some stories about political campaign legends, including several stories told in their own words.

When the Spirit Is With Matt, There's No One as Good

Factoid: A native of Huntington, West Virginia, Matt Reese gained national renown in 1960 when he organized the volunteer campaign that helped Massachusetts Senator John Kennedy win the West Virginia primary en route to the White House.

We were working on Attorney General Richard Bryan's gubernatorial campaign in Nevada in 1982. Bryan went on to win the campaign. He then beat Senator Chic Hecht in 1988, who was later appointed ambassador to the Bahamas, which caused Bryan to wonder who had actually won the race.

We were doing his campaign, and I had been doing most of the work on it with Keith Lee, his campaign manager, an attorney from Reno. Enough checks had been written to Matt Reese and Associates that it was time for them to see somebody other than an associate. It was time to bring the old man in.

The year 1982 was hugely challenging for us. We did 14 campaigns from the president of Venezuela to the governor of Hawaii.

I tried to be efficient with Matt's time. He had to go out to Hawaii for the governor's race, so I was going to bring him back from Honolulu to Los Angeles, and then to Las Vegas, where he would be meeting with Attorney General Bryan. I didn't realize it meant Matt would have flown all night from Hawaii to Los Angeles, worked all day in Los Angeles and then flown to Vegas.

The meeting was set up with the attorney general and his chief fundraiser, Frank Schreck; a lawyer in Las Vegas, Keith Lee; the manager, George Burger; and me. I get to the Sands Hotel and I'm checking in and see Bryan and Schreck coming across the lobby. The meeting is supposed to start in 45 minutes.

They said, "We just called Mr. Reese's room; we're here early, so he said to come on up."

Matt, God rest his soul, did not have a long attention span or a great memory for names, and I realized with horror that I hadn't prepared any briefing materials for him, so I gave my bags to a bell hop and headed up to Matt's suite. I sit down next to Matt, Bryan and Schreck; the rest of the guys in the room are across from us.

Dick Bryan, with that intensity only a sincere candidate has, is talking about the race. Matt is writing on his legal pad. He slides the legal pad over in front of me and it says, "1. What is our client's name? 2. To whom am I speaking?"

I didn't realize he was pushing from an all-night flight! I thought he was just being funny. So, to the first question, I wrote, "I thought you knew." To the second question, I wrote, "Tom Baker," the name of our guy. I slid it back across to him.

With the attorney general in mid-sentence, at full campaign rhetoric flight, Matt hurls the legal pad across the room, turns to me, points at Baker and says, "I know who he is." He points at Dick Bryan and says, "But who in God's name is this?"

I said, "Uh, Matt, this is the attorney general of Nevada, the honorable Richard Bryan."

Matt said, "Okay, son, now what are you running for? Governor or Senator?"

That Dick Bryan not only didn't fire us but remains a dear friend to this day is a measure of his enormous Christian charity.

Once Matt got focused, he was fine.

Lloyd Bentsen once said of Matt, "When that ole son-of-a-bitch is hitting on all eight cylinders, he's a sight to behold."

Ralph Murphine once said, "When the spirit is with Matt, there's no one as good. The only problem is we can't seem to get the spirit on permanent retainer." *—John Ashford*

The Loveable Matt Reese

Traveling with Matt Reese was always a trip in itself. At 6'5" and at least 350 pounds, he was packed into his airline seat like the proverbial sardine — and preferred to sit by himself. On one flight in 1979, he squeezed into his seat hopeful that the middle seat would not be occupied — but no such luck. Down the aisle came a young pregnant woman with a child about 2 in her arms, and they settled down next to Matt. A couple of rows away, I was prepared for the worst. There was no way Reese was going to get any sleep.

Then I heard his unmistakable voice: "Once upon a time there were three bears . . ." I looked back, and there was the country's most formidable Democratic political strategist with his arm around a small boy, mesmerized by the storybook they shared.

—Daryl Glenney

Manager Falls on the Sword

Factoid: In the storied race for governor in California in 1982, Los Angeles Mayor Tom Bradley won among the votes cast on Election Day, but Attorney General George Deukmejian won by a bigger margin among the absentee ballots, to win the race by less than a percentage point.

In 1982, George Deukmejian was the California attorney general, running against Tom Bradley, the mayor of Los Angeles. To put it into context, in 1980 we had had the Iranian hostage crisis, which had been resolved when Ronald Reagan brought an end to the Carter Administration. Deukmejian was Armenian, but a lot of people couldn't distinguish between an Iranian and an Armenian, so the issue of racial prejudice would be bigger for Deukmejian than for Bradley, an African American. We had some definite evidence that this would be an issue.

Deukmejian was a distinctly ethnic name while Bradley was – well who knew? And a lot of people didn't know that Bradley was African American. You didn't see a lot of photos of him in the early days of the campaign.

Bill Roberts was the campaign consultant, which we called manager in those days. He said pretty much what he thought. We had been trailing in the polls almost the entire time after the June primary.

About 10 days before the November 1982 election, Roberts gathered some of the press people in his office in Westwood. They were asking him about the campaign and he said, "At some point, the public will find out that Tom Bradley is black." That comment made the morning papers the next day. It was all over the press. Deukmejian then relieved Roberts of his duties and the campaign went forward without him in the final week.

There was much contention at the time that Roberts hadn't spoken it accidentally. However, he went to his deathbed never telling anyone that he hadn't raised the race issue intentionally. The fact is, I believe that Roberts' comment had a very significant impact on that race. Deukmejian won by only a half percent of the vote.

I believe Bill Roberts fell on the proverbial sword for Deukmejian. I don't know if they ever made peace after that event. I don't think they did. —*Steve Kinney*

The Garth Theory of Running Campaigns

Factoid: David Garth achieved his first major political victory in 1965, when his media campaign helped elect John Lindsay mayor of New York City. He started his career in the late 1950s producing sports programs at ABC-TV.

Throughout my career, I always tried to approach a new campaign the same way. The first thing I would do before I got involved with a candidate was try and get a pretty good feel for what the candidate was about – that included a thorough review of his policies, speeches, statements, positions and votes.

Sometimes a candidate's record differs from what they think their record is. If you ask any elected official how they vote, they usually come up with a very bland popular image of themselves. Sometimes their actual votes are very different from their perceptions. So the first thing I'd do as a consultant was find out who I was really consulting – what is this man or woman all about?

The next part of that self-examination is what do you have to watch out for? Are you going to be blind-sided? One of the problems that often happens in this business, especially with people who are not experienced, is that they get themselves a candidate and the next thing you know, their candidate is in trouble. All of a sudden a child appears that no one knew he had, or some woman appears that he harassed in the office.

So it's important to establish the facts. If you don't ask, you're in trouble. I always tell clients I talk to: Look, I'm going to ask you a bunch of very tough questions. The answers are going to be kept secret; I'm not going to make them public, but I want to know. I don't want to be blind-sided by a surprise. I don't want to find out something is not true that you told me or the press. Getting caught lying will get you knocked out of a campaign.

When researching an opponent, you have to have the Billy Cohn philosophy—you're gonna jab them to death, and you don't stop jabbing. There are very few times in politics when there is a knockout blow. Everybody swings from the floor, but most of the time they're pushing air.

These things just don't generally happen. Even when you have a debate, and the debate is lost and people are saying the campaign is over, two days later a poll will come out and you're not that far behind. I don't believe in the knockout punch. I believe in steady jabs.

I believe in building a campaign. If there is an area that starts to look like a trend in the opponent's record, then you start to hit that area. You don't do it in one big press release or one big press conference or one big commercial. You slowly build a case.

One of the positive uses of television is that it gives the candidate the ability to say what he or she wants to say directly. It's the one opportunity candidates have to get their message out unfiltered.

Polling is something that campaigns can't do without. However, the big mistake is letting the polls dictate the race. It's a mistake that most pollsters make. They fall in love with their own numbers. You ought to have pollsters, and the pollsters ought to be able to talk directly to the candidate. But I don't want pollsters doing strategy. I think that is a different expertise. Polling does not tell you what position to take. Polling gives you a reading of the electorate at a given moment. You find out where you are. You're the guy in the ring.

Rocky Marciano had a manager named Al Weill. And whenever they had a press conference, the press would ask Rocky when he was going to knock out his opponent. Rocky was very laid back, so Weill would jump in and give the answer. He'd say, "We'll knock him out in the third round."

One day, Red Smith asked Rocky whether he minded Weill making all these claims on his behalf. Rocky grinned and said, "The only thing I know is that when the bell rings for the first round, the last thing I see going through the ropes is Al Weill's ass."

It's the candidate's ass in the ring. The candidate has to feel comfortable by himself in the ring. You can't make him comfortable by telling him how great he is. You've got to tell him, Here's what this is about, here are the pros and the cons, now make your choice.

—David Garth

Nixon Gives Spencer Credentials

Factoid: Wyoming Governor Clifford Hansen, running for the Senate in 1966, defeated one-term Congressman Teno Roncalio, 52-48.

In 1966, I was running Cliff Hansen for the United States Senate in Wyoming. Hansen was an academic type and the steering committee was from the University of Wyoming, which was bad news to begin with. I flew into Casper for a meeting with Hansen and the committee the next day. I had all my research with me and was walking down this hallway, and around the corner comes Rosemary Woods and Pat Hillings at the Ramada Inn.

We both looked at each other, and I said, "What the hell are you doing here?" Well, Hillings was advancing for Richard Nixon. He says, "Nixon is here to talk to the state committee. Come on down and see him." I said I couldn't because I had all this research to do for an eight o'clock meeting in the morning. I told him to tell Nixon I was sorry that I couldn't make it. They had 500 Republicans there, and he gave a speech that night in the hotel, while I stayed in my room.

The next morning the 12 of us are in this little room, and I am at the head of the table talking when all of a sudden the door opens and Vice President Dick Nixon walks in and they all stand up. Dick knew a lot of them. He says, how are you doing and I said fine. He knew what I was doing in the room and he knew who they were. He turns around and says, now this guy (me) knows what the hell he is talking about. If I were you I would listen to him. Then he turned around and walked out.

Well, after that, everything I said was gospel. Nixon knew exactly what he was doing. That was a side of him that nobody knew about. He was really good. —*Stu Spencer*

CHAPTER 4

Men and Women Who Run for Public Office

☆ ☆ ☆

One has to have a lot of nerve, and a lot of ego, to go to the courthouse and tell the local elections official he or she wants to become a candidate for public office. They say, for most people, it's a life-altering experience. You're then faced with doing something 99 percent of your friends and neighbors will never do, or even think about doing. You're going to have to run a campaign for public office and face the prospect of mass public rejection. But thousands of otherwise sane human beings do it every year, and nearly half of them actually end up winning.

William F. Buckley said, in 1965, if the voters of New York City were foolish enough to elect him mayor, his first official order of business would be to demand a recount. He got 13 percent. Every election year, about 100,000 public offices, from school board and city council in Backwater, U.S.A., to Congress of the United States, are contested. A quarter of a million candidates will run, and most will be more serious about winning than Buckley was when he challenged John Lindsay and Abe Beam for mayor of the Big Apple.

One reasonably successful small-town insurance agent walked through a hotel lobby in Billings, Montana, most mornings en route to join other local businessmen for coffee. Bill Osborne often waved at the barber in the lobby barbershop and said something in passing to the customer in the barber chair. The day after he filed for public office – the story was in the morning newspaper – he walked through the lobby with a lot on his mind and forgot to wave to the barber. Those in the shop heard the barber remark that the new candidate was "too big for his britches now that he's become a politician."

The vast majority of those who take the plunge and join the ranks of office seeker do so for the very best of reasons. Most do so to make their communities better, to do a better job than those doing it now or to make a contribution to the community good through public service. And most eventually leave public service with the same ideals, though perhaps with their eyes a little more wide open. For the most part, the profile of the usual candidate is no different from the rest of us. And they have a few warts, just like all of us.

Here are some stories about people who had the guts to run for office, win, lose or draw.

The Master Turns a Phrase

Factoid: Edwin Edwards began a long career in public office in Louisiana in 1954 when he was elected to the Crowley City Council. He was re-elected to the city council in 1958.

We did Edwin Edwards' campaign in Louisiana in 1991 against David Duke, which was a fascinating campaign. My partner at the time was Bill Morgan, who lived in Baton Rouge. Morgan had contacts in the Edwards campaign, so we got hired.

Buddy Roemer was governor at the time and was considered to be kind of the new wave of modern governors – an Ivy League education along with some liberal credentials. He switched to the Republican Party, so we ended up representing Edwards. David Duke got in the race, making for a highly competitive primary election.

I'll never forget when Edwards made the announcement at the Sheraton Hotel off I-10 in Baton Rouge. There must have been 40 news cameras there. Edwards got up with no notes or anything, which was his custom, and did this rousing stump speech. When he came down from the podium to give an interview, one of the reporters asked him a question about Buddy Roemer. A lot of Republicans were upset that now he was their standard bearer.

Off the top of his head, Edwards said, "Of all the bad things that have been said about me, no one has ever said that I was wanted by either party."

A few weeks later, he was giving a speech at the Cajun Dome, an arena he helped build in Lafayette, Louisiana, and there must have been 15,000 people there. It was a perfect Edwards crowd, mainly blue-collar. He had them going and brought them to a fevered pitch.

Edwards was the master of boiling his opponents down to a phrase or two that would just hang on them. He had this group in the palm of his hand. They were cheering him. He got to talking about Roemer, and he said, "I'll tell you the difference between a boy and a man. I built the interstate highway system in Louisiana, and Buddy Roemer can't cut the grass around it."

It was a statement repeated over and over again. It showed a tremendous native political intelligence. Edwards was smart enough to know that everybody in that state would drive down a weed-choked interstate at one time or another during the campaign, and they would be reminded of Buddy Roemer's ineffectiveness. It was a brilliant statement.   —*Bill Fletcher*

Eastwood Kept His Promise

Clint Eastwood had a horrible foul mouth. I told him that he couldn't curse during the campaign for mayor of Carmel in 1986. He said, okay, I will stop, and he did. He never cursed around me or in public from then on. But election night it was just hysterical. I still laugh at this.

I had a room at a better hotel in Carmel for election night. When the polls closed we were all meeting in my room—the pollster Arnie Steinberg, lawyer Barry Fadem, onsite manager Sue Hutchison and myself. Because she was 60 years old at the time, Sue was the perfect person to send to Carmel to do the onsite work. I sent Sue to Carmel for three months to run this campaign, and she then went to work for Eastwood while he was mayor.

We all met in my room for a little toast as the polls closed. Clint knocked on the door. I opened the door and he let out a string of curse words, some that I had never heard of. He said he had been holding that in for so long. We started laughing so hard.

—*Eileen Padberg*

'Do You Have Any Idea Who Jesse Ventura Is?'

Mae Schunk is a 62-year-old schoolteacher from St. Paul who had never been involved in politics in her life. In fact, she didn't know who Jesse Ventura was.

We couldn't afford to do our own polls, but the *Minneapolis Star Tribune* did an extensive poll we read with interest. That poll showed Ventura had about a five to one, male to female, favorable rating. He was selling well with the men but was almost nonexistent with the women.

The number one issue in the poll was taxes and the surplus that had been accumulating in Minnesota. We felt we could capture this issue. The second most important issue was education. Ventura had no background on education whatsoever. He didn't know beans about education.

So we figured we needed help with women and with education. The answer, obvious to us, was a female educator on the ticket with Ventura. We went on a search to find a perfect female educator to balance the ticket.

One of our campaign volunteers, Pam Ellison, had been taught by Mae Schunk, as had one of her daughters. She thought that she might be willing to do it. Out of the blue, we called up Mrs. Schunk and asked her if she wanted to interview to run for lieutenant governor.

Mae said she went to her husband, Bill, and said, "This guy Jesse Ventura called and wants to interview me to run for lieutenant governor. Do you have any idea who Jesse Ventura is?" Bill Schunk was a wrestling fan and had some old wrestling magazines he pulled out from under the stairway that showed Jesse with the pink feathered boa.

Her reaction was, "Oh, my gosh!"

She came for the interview anyway. She was curious about this. I remember sitting there, and when Mae came in, I sat down next to Ventura. She had the grandmotherly look with gray hair, she was soft-spoken and she had been a teacher for 37 years.

I said, "That's it. I don't care what she says or what she does. This is what we need."

We called her the educational lieutenant governor; she would take care of the education policy. It sold. It did what we wanted it to do; it balanced us up, not only on gender, but also on the issue. We had the number one and number two issues covered.

—Dean Barkley

Just Handing Out Brochures, the Hard Way

Factoid: After the 1968 elections, there were 41 Republicans and 39 Democrats in the California Assembly. That was the last time the Republicans controlled that legislative body.

The California State Assembly was evenly divided in 1968, while Ronald Reagan was governor. It was extremely important to hold on to an assembly seat in Monterey County, where the Republican assemblyman had been killed in a traffic accident.

I was sent in to manage the campaign in this special election and inherited a candidate who had been selected by a Republican fact-finding committee. He was a local county supervisor, Bob Wood, who went on to have a very distinguished career. He was, however, quite green when he was running in this campaign.

Wood had this self-image of having been successful in life because he always out-worked anybody he was up against. He set himself a killer schedule, which did, in fact, almost kill him.

The consequence was that about 10 days before the election, he went brain-dead on me. He truly was not coherent and it became the job of the campaign to hide that, to not let the press see it and to not let the public see it.

One night, when we were having a campaign meeting in Monterey, we were all at a hotel and I realized Wood was operating on "emergency batteries." After the meetings were over, Wood was on his way back to his hotel room and got off the elevator on the wrong floor. He went to the room number he thought was his and the key didn't fit very well. He doesn't have a lot of patience at this point, so he just jammed the key in the lock, gave a hard twist and the door came open.

Wood went stumbling into the room, past the bathroom, and a lady sat up in bed in her nightgown with her hair in curlers. Just then, the husband came out from the bathroom in his shorts and shirt. What's going on; are they under attack or what?

The candidate was stumbling around and realizes he is in the wrong room. What does he do but reach in his coat pocket and pull out one of his brochures. He says, "Hi! I'm Bob Wood. I'm running for state assembly, and I would like to deliver one of my brochures to you."

When you get brain-dead in a campaign, you seldom recover.

He did win the election for state assembly and was later appointed to various positions in the executive branch.

—George Young

Booze, Theft, Girls, Now That's a Problem

David Walker ran for state senate in 1972 against Bob Brown, who was an incumbent out in the valley part of Minnesota. I wasn't overwhelmed with this guy, but you had a state senate candidate because you have two state House candidates, and you can raise money for all three and the DFL party had endorsed this guy.

The guy is very glib, has a campaign group, and he gets an office on Main Street in Stillwater, which is the biggest voting locale of the district. Things seem to be going fine. We do the usual fundraising and have the usual issues of education, property tax and state sales tax, the usual basket of stuff as a non-incumbent. Sometimes the incumbent hasn't done enough or has a few missed votes. So we were grinding those issues out.

One day I got a call from the party treasurer who was also operating as his Senate campaign treasurer. He tells me, "Say, can you meet me down at the office? It's pretty important."

I left my law office and went down there. He said, "Well, here is the problem. The candidate doesn't like to go out and door knock."

All right. I've had candidates like that before.

"The reason he doesn't like to go out and door knock is because he gets drunk here in the office every day by three o'clock by sitting in the front window drinking beer."

This is on Main Street. There's a big picture window, which is normally where you want the candidate's name and banner. You don't want the candidate sousing out on beer.

I replied, "Well, that's a real problem."

He explained, "That's only half of it. There is also a 16-year-old campaign worker who seems to be enamored with the 30-some-year-old candidate."

That's a problem. People are going to talk.

He continued, "And not only that, but a lot of the expenses that get run through the ledger by the candidate seem to involve what would kindly be called his personal living expenses."

We called the candidate in and had a long discussion with him. He assured us these things weren't going to happen again. They were momentary lapses and he loved to knock on doors and would soon be out there doing it. Three weeks later, the same three problems of booze, theft and girls had surfaced again. We met again and made a deal with the guy. We said, "All right. We want you to go away. Your name will stay on the ballot. We can't, at this point, endorse somebody else. The two House candidates actually have a chance and we don't want to jeopardize that, so we need you to go away. If you go away, you can continue to have the campaign expenditures that you've already put in for honored, and we just won't bother to audit the other campaign expenditures. That would not be a productive use of our time. We will never see you again."

Where upon, he said, "Great!" He and the 16-year-old took off. I don't think they were ever heard from again.

For the next six weeks of the campaign, until the November election, there was always silence when the two House candidates would ask where the Senate challenger was. I was surprised that, even though it was not a Democratic district, he got 33 percent of the vote.

—*Vance Opperman*

'My Election Proves You Can Get Anybody Elected'

Nebraska is a little odd in the way they do things. First of all they have a unicameral legislature, so there is only one legislative body. Everybody is a senator; there are no representatives. Second, it is theoretically non-partisan. But that does not stop the political parties from running slates of candidates.

In 1980, the Republican Party asked me to come out and spend a couple of days meeting one after the other with their top targeted candidates for the state senate. They were going to try to take partisan control of the legislature.

I am meeting with these people, one after another. A guy comes in and looks to be about 90 years old. He is tall and skinny, with a gaunt, weather-beaten face. He didn't really look like much, but he probably had other virtues. We started talking and it readily became clear that he didn't know much about any issues, he was not a good speaker and he was not dynamic in any way. It turned out he was a garage mechanic by trade and also looked the part. So I talked to him for maybe 15 minutes or so and then said, "Will you excuse me, Mr. (George) Fenger?"

I walked out of the room and went and found the executive director of the Nebraska Republican Party, Dave Heineman. I said, "Dave, you told me I was going to be meeting with your top candidates here. Who is this guy? He doesn't belong here." He said, "I know, I know, he is not a lot as a candidate, but…" He went on to explain that they really thought they did have some chance of winning in that district. The incumbent, Frank Lewis, who happened to be the Democratic leader in the Senate, had let his leadership role go to his head, and he had a terrible attendance record. So they thought they could use that against him and have a chance to win the race. I said, "Well, you understand this is going to be a very negative campaign if we are going to win this thing, because we don't have a lot of positive to run on here." Dave said that he understood that.

I went back and completed the interview and subsequently developed a program for the Fenger campaign. This basically consisted of some print ads and direct mail.

There was a piece I did that showed a picture of an empty desk with the incumbent senator's name plate on it, with nobody sitting there. The copy read, "Some senators vote the way their constituents want them to, some senators vote their conscience, and one senator hardly ever votes at all." Below that we had a list of the most important votes he had missed. The biggest headline on the whole thing, down on the bottom, said "Don't vote for Frank Lewis." In smaller type it said "Vote for George Fenger," and beneath that our campaign slogan, "He'll do the job."

Now, that was actually my second choice as the campaign slogan, but they rejected my first one, which was "He will show up," which I figured was about the minimum we could say, but "He'll do the job" seemed to suffice.

We let George Fenger go door to door for the whole campaign in the precincts we didn't care if we got any votes in or not. Fenger won, not by a huge margin, but he won.

The day after the election I was sitting in my office in Washington and the phone rings. I pick it up and a voice says, "This is George Fenger." I said, "Senator, how are you?" He says, "They didn't want to give me your phone number, but I got it anyway. I just wanted to call you up and tell you that my election proves one thing." I said, "Yes, what is that?" He said, "My election proves that you can get anybody elected in this country if you shut up and do what the pros tell you to."

I went back to Nebraska two to three years later to give a speech at a party meeting. George was there on the platform and gave a speech that he could no more have given at the time I met him than he could have dunked a basketball. But, clearly, the job made the man. He rose to it, he did the job, he did a good job, he became chairman of a committee eventually and I never regretted a minute of working to put him in office. —*Jay Bryant*

Running for the Legislature in Big Sky Country

Factoid: After the 1986 elections, the Montana state senate was evenly divided at 25 Democrats and 25 Republicans. The GOP controlled the house 52-48.

I was 23 years old from Alzaeda, Montana, when I decided to run for the legislature. I was a sheepherder who lived back in the woods and didn't see people too often. I was a little hardheaded and was going to do things my way, so I decided to run for office.

I knew I was Republican because when I watched things on TV, it just seemed like the Republicans were more in line with me. They were a little more hard-line, while the Democrats were a little soft.

In 1986 I filed against Hugh Abrams, who had been the Democratic state representative for about as many years as I'd been alive. My game plan was that if I just started knocking on every door and really hustling, he would switch and run for the senate because the senator who had been there a long time was retiring. I just had this hunch that he was ready to move on and that if he had a tough race, he would just go for the Senate seat and not have to run every two years.

Sure enough, he switches. I ended up with about three candidates in the Democratic primary, and I was the only Republican. I was shaking everybody's hand and attended any box social, fire fighters meeting or anything that came up.

It was getting close to the fair season when I get this letter from the Montana Republican Party. To tell you the truth, I didn't even know there was a state party.

I got this letter, which immediately impressed me. It was from the executive director, Steve Yaekel, and Wayne Philips. The note said, "We're going to be in Miles City on such and such a date, helping the candidates and preparing them with information on how to run their campaign to win the fall election."

To me, this was like a godsend. I felt like I had just won the lottery. The Democrat nominee, Earl Smith, had been president of the Woolgrowers, which was a big deal in our area, and had also been a county commissioner.

If some professional from the State Capitol was going to come down and educate me, I thought this would be a good deal. Miles City was only 150 miles away.

I load up and drive to Miles City to meet with Yaekel and Philips to learn how they're going to save me.

When I get there, they ask me if I have a voter list. I replied no, because I really didn't know what a voter list was. They then asked me if I had seen the polls from the last election. I said, "No, I really don't know what you're talking about there."

They asked, "What do you think your turnout is going to be?"

To me, *turnout* was just a word we used in the spring when we turned the cattle and sheep out. So I had to tell them I didn't know what they meant. As the discussion went on, I felt like they were trying to embarrass me because they kept bringing up things that didn't make a bit of sense to me. I didn't have a clue about what they were talking about.

Once they got through all of those questions, they asked, "Have you ordered your yard signs?"

This is where the sheepherder mentality is beginning to say I've finally had enough. I said, "What do you mean, have I ordered my yard signs?"

"Yard signs. You know what a yard sign is?"

"No," I replied.

"It's a sign you put up in the yard."

I told them I had put some posters up in businesses. They told me I had to have yard signs. He pulled out a few examples of yard signs. He had an order form for yard signs, but I said I didn't think those would work where I was from.

I put little scratch note pads in the mailboxes as I went by. They reminded me it was against the law to do that. I told them I had asked the mailman and he had told me I could do it.

They said, "You can't do that, and you have to put these yard signs up."

I said, "Steve, I appreciate your coming down here, but I just don't have the money to buy those yard signs and I don't think they'll work in my area. If you put those in the yards, nobody will see them. You already told me I can't put them up in the bar pit. So who's going to see these yard signs?"

He then stands up, points his finger at me and says, "Listen, kid. You're lucky nobody filed against you in the primary. If you don't pay attention and put up these yard signs, you're just wasting your time and ours because you can't win."

I stood up and said, "Well, I'll see you in Helena," and walked out.

When I got to Helena, we joked about that meeting. I only got 68 percent of the vote against Earl Smith. I don't remember if Earl had yard signs or not.

—*Leo Giacometto*

CHAPTER 5

Road Warrior Adventures

☆ ☆ ☆

The original definition of a political road warrior is a young person who takes an assignment to go to some strange city, usually small- to medium-sized, where they know absolutely no one, and attempts to build a street organization capable of carrying the county for their candidate in the upcoming election. They take this challenge with little or no support, little or no pay and little or no communication with the outside world. This, as you might imagine, is not easy work.

Political campaign workers, by definition, spend a lot of time in strange motel rooms, eating fast food, wearing clothes that haven't seen a washing machine in a week, working most nights and every weekend. This is not a 9-to-5 business. Most road warriors are young and single, with the stamina to keep going week after week, month after month, with little time for recuperation. For some, it's the most exciting job they'll ever have. They're on the road, they're part of the team, they're in on the action.

Every four years, hundreds of road warriors are drawn to Iowa and New Hampshire to assist some long-shot presidential hopefuls in their quest for the golden ring. They're hoping their candidate will emerge from the pack, catch lightning, and they'll be in for a long ride through the primaries, the convention and on to the White House. The road warriors who signed on early in 1976 with former Georgia Governor Jimmy Carter, a real dark horse, saw their dreams come true. The same happened in 1992 for the road warriors who signed on early with Arkansas Governor Bill Clinton. Both Carter and Clinton were just part of the pack when they started.

March Miller was a field man for the National Republican Congressional Committee in the 1980s. Like all road warriors, Miller spent a lot of time driving rental cars. In 1980, Miller pulled up in front of a restaurant in Detroit, flipped the keys to the young man standing at the curb and went inside to have lunch with a prospective congressional candidate. After lunch he went out looking for the parking valet, who was nowhere to be found. Miller went back in and asked the restaurant manager where the valet had gone. After cogitating on the question for a moment, the manager said, "Mr. Miller, we don't have any parking valets." Miller, of course, had flipped the keys to an absolute stranger who realized Christmas had come in January and drove off in the rental car.

Here are some tales from the byways and back roads of American politics, told by the road warriors who were there when it happened.

Lead Us in the Pledge of Allegiance

Factoid: Gene Chappie was first elected to Congress in 1980 in California's 1st district then, following re-districting, was elected in 1982 and 1984 in the 2nd district.

It was 1984, and I had just been hired to be Congressman Gene Chappie's press secretary and manage his re-election campaign in the 2nd district of California. At the time I had been in the United States for only two years. I'd grown up in Canada.

My first official act as Chappie's campaign manager was to fill in for him at the VFW dinner in Yreka, which is in the very northern part of the state. I show up in this hall, and it's just me facing 300 guys with crew cuts and white short-sleeve shirts. So I introduce myself and everyone is kind of annoyed that the congressman couldn't be there.

Finally, the leader of the VFW stood up, got everyone's attention and said, "We were supposed to have Congressman Gene Chappie here today as our guest, but he blew us off and sent us this young kid. Since this guy seems like a nice enough kid, we'll have him lead us in the Pledge of Allegiance to start our meeting."

My stomach was fluttering as I started to stand up. Then all of sudden I realized that I didn't know the Pledge of Allegiance. I was representing a member of the United States Congress before 300 veterans. The fact that I did not know the pledge was a potential disaster, a huge disaster.

So in a split second, I did the only thing I could think of to save the moment. I decided to fake a choking attack, and I fell down on the floor writhing in agony. I let these guys beat on my chest. They ended up calling an ambulance and hauling me away to the hospital.

I didn't have to tell anyone I didn't know the Pledge of Allegiance.

When I got back to my hotel room at 3:30 in the morning, I called my wife, woke her up and made her recite the Pledge of Allegiance to me so I could write it down and memorize it so that this never happened again.   —*David Sackett*

Running Cigars From Canada

W alter Mondale loved cigars. Somebody at the national headquarters called me while I was running Maine in the 1984 presidential primary and says it wouldn't be a bad thing if somebody went up to Canada and picked up some Cuban cigars for Fritz.

What the hell, I said, and I called up two kids. "Look, do me a favor tonight, go across the border and get some Cuban cigars and bring them down. Mondale is coming in a couple days and it would be a nice surprise." Mondale smoked Macanudos, his usual brand, and it was very seldom he wouldn't have one of those going.

These two guys go screaming across the border at about 10 o'clock at night, run to the cigar shop, buy a couple boxes of Cuban cigars, decide to go to a bar, and they get sloshed out of their minds.

It is a rural crossing up there. They start coming back at about 2:30 in the morning. They get to the border and the gate is down. One of them gets out and picks up the gate, they get in the car, drive past the gate, get out and put the gate down. They get about a mile into the United States before the sirens are screaming and the choppers are wheeling in on them.

I got this call from jail. I was saying, oh, please God, do not tell me that you told them what you were doing. Please tell me you did not say you were getting Cuban cigars for the former vice president of the United States, or that you even know who I am! They wisely did not do that.   *—Joe Trippi*

Aiming at Table Rock

Factoid: Dirk Kempthorne served one term in the U.S. Senate before returning to Idaho in 1998 to run for governor.

In September 1992, Boise Mayor Dirk Kempthorne was running against Congressman Richard Stallings for the U. S. Senate seat that was being vacated by Steve Symms.

Kempthorne, his manager Phil Reberger and I left Boise early in the morning to fly to Haley, Idaho, just outside Sun Valley where Dirk was giving a speech. I often got to sit in the right front seat of the small airplanes because I'm a licensed pilot and became an unofficial co-pilot. If something happened to the pilot, I could have landed the airplane.

So I'm sitting in the right hand seat of the Cessna 206, and as we fly out of Boise we fly by what I think is the turn-in to the canyon to land at Haley. We go four or five more miles before it dawns on the pilot that we've gone too far. I pointed out that I thought Haley was back over that last little hill, so he turned and flew back, and we landed just fine at Haley. But at the time, I thought it was an odd little incident that he wasn't quite sure where he was going.

Dirk gave his speech in Sun Valley, and later that afternoon we flew down to Twin Falls where Dirk was going to be speaking to the Jaycees. The pilot actually let me steer the plane most of the way from Haley to Twin Falls although he insisted on landing the plane.

In Twin Falls, we go do the two or three things including a fundraiser. Later in the evening, about nine o'clock, it's time to return to Boise. In September, at this time of night, it's dark out. So we load up in this 206 and start to taxi out to the runway. The pilot, who had a lot of hours, strangely could not find the taxiway, and we came upon the runway. The pilot asked the tower how much runway he had at that point. It turned out there were still 4,500 feet, plenty of room for take-off. So we started out midway on the runway, which was a little strange. There is an old pilot adage that says you don't want to leave runway behind you.

We're flying back to Boise, and I'm still sitting in the right front seat, listening to the radio communication with the Boise tower. The pilot is given a clearance to land on 27 right, and we're flying at a slight angle to that runway. We're probably 3,000 feet off the ground, five miles out from the runway threshold.

I hear the pilot given the clearance, but we fly past the angle where you would have made a 45-degree left turn to line up directly with the runway. After about a mile, I say, "There's the runway over there." He was embarrassed, but he had been transfixed on a fairly big, well-known light on the side of the mountain northeast of Boise called Table Rock. As far as I know, he was going to land on Table Rock, but I shook him out of that.

We went ahead and landed just fine back in Boise. However, I'm sure he never volunteered to fly the candidate again, nor would the candidate have considered getting back in the airplane with that pilot.

—Tony Payton

BOOK TWO

Modern Political Campaigns

☆ ☆ ☆

The first popular vote for president was reported in 1824, when "Old Hickory" Andrew Jackson was elected with a mere 41 percent of the vote. Historians report the campaign that year was tough, hard-fought, dirty and mean-spirited and only surpassed by the even tougher, meaner re-election campaign in 1828. Apparently not much has changed in American politics in 175 years.

Members of the U.S. House of Representatives ran "at large" in many states until 1842, when Congress established congressional districts for all states. Finally, the "People's House" was elected by the voters in districts, rather than statewide popularity contests. There were at the time 232 congressmen in 31 states.

Gerrymandering, a Massachusetts plot originated in 1812 when Republican Governor Elbridge Gerry signed into law redistricting legislation that ensured Republicans would be in the majority, became widespread and developed into an art form practiced even more competently today with the aid of computers. Perhaps the most artistic gerrymandering took place in North Carolina in 1992, when the legislature created the 12th congressional district that stretched 400 miles from Durham, through Greensboro, on to

Winston Salem and down to Charlotte. Precincts with a majority of black voters were strung together, often connected only by an interstate highway, to create a congressional district that was more than 50 percent black.

Members of the U.S. Senate were anointed by state legislatures until 1914, when the 17th Amendment to the Constitution was ratified. Earlier in the century, several states, starting with Oregon, conducted informal popular votes instructive to the legislative body, but the state legislators were not bound by the will of the people and often didn't send to the Senate the people's choice. Interestingly, in the first popular elections held in 1914, all 23 senators who had been appointed by their state legislatures stood for popular election and won. Incumbents have been winning most elections ever since.

New York Governor Theodore Roosevelt was elected vice president on the 1900 Republican ticket with William McKinley. He assumed the presidency when McKinley was assassinated in September 1901. And his picture was printed in the newspapers – a first for the newspaper printing technology and a first for a political figure. Future campaigns would now take into account a candidate's "looks," or image, for the first time. Being the most handsome or attractive candidate in the field doesn't guarantee success at the ballot box, but it sure isn't a detriment.

A New York City radio station ran the first paid advertising in 1922, a 10-minute sales pitch for a suburban apartment house. It didn't take the politicians long to see the benefit of radio, but the biggest boost came when President Franklin Roosevelt launched his fireside chats in 1933, just eight days after he was inaugurated on March 4. His first topic was the Depression-era bank crisis. It was the first time a sitting president took his message over the heads of Congress and the press and directly to the people, a practice still pursued today by the occupant of the Oval Office.

When General Dwight Eisenhower ran for president in 1952, about 10 percent of the homes in America had television sets. Ike's campaign did, however, put up the first TV political ads, and the best was the noteworthy cartoon produced by Walt Disney, with marching elephants waving Ike banners and the voice-over repeating "Ike for President." Eisenhower's opponent, Adlai Stevenson, bought a 30-minute television show that ran in the *I Love Lucy* time slot and thousands of viewers sent hate mail.

The first significant attack on television was President Lyndon Johnson's "daisy girl" commercial against Senator Barry Goldwater in 1964. Though the ad didn't mention Goldwater by name, everybody knew the intent, to put fear in voters' minds that the Republican couldn't be trusted in the nuclear age. Few remember Johnson's campaign ran a host of other attack ads that drove Goldwater down to just 39 percent of the popular vote. Negative television campaigns were off and running and show few signs of easing up.

Since the advent of the modern political campaign in the 1960s, the biggest single change has been speed. Campaigns were still clip-clopping along 40 years ago, but today's version is operated at a hyper-sonic rate. It often took two weeks to produce a new television commercial in the 1960s, and at least a week if you put the pedal to the metal. Shots were made on film; the film had to be processed in some faraway lab. Editing was done with razor blades. It was slow and tedious work. Today, a new TV spot can be produced in studio on very expensive high-tech equipment, satellite fed to the TV station and broadcast in an hour. Public opinion research is another area campaigns have improved in a timely manner. It used to take 10 days to field a survey, program the data for input, input the data, print out a round of tabulations, analyze the data and get it in the hands of the client, by which time the information was dated and sometimes of little value. Today, it's a two- or three-hour process. Interviews are conducted at 7 p.m. and by 10 p.m. the same evening the data is on the campaign manager's computer, having arrived via the Internet.

Lists of voters have always been used in campaigns for mailing lists to supporters and the undecideds. They're used for telephone voter identification – are you with us or against us? And the lists are priceless for turning out your supporters on Election Day. Even a quarter of a century ago, voters' names were individually typed on three-by-five cards and manipulated in shoeboxes. In the average congressional campaign of the early 1970s, it was an all-day job for two or three people just to keep the shoeboxes in order and the cards sorted appropriately. Today, a computer hums out hundreds of personally addressed letters by the hour, the tax letter to the first voter, the education letter to the second, the environment letter to the third and so on. Campaigns today are a lot less hands-on work for campaign staff and volunteers, and a lot more sterile too.

Today's candidate, and his or her campaign team, has to be ready to run very hard and very fast or face losing to the opponent who has mastered the technology of the business at a higher level. These are stories about the art of the campaign in the new age.

CHAPTER 6

Tapping Public Opinion

☆ ☆ ☆

Newspapers in the early 1800s reported the results of "straw polls" and claimed they were the pulse of the public. The first such poll was printed in 1824, and for the next 100 years, newspapers and magazines were the primary source of polling information – almost all the results of straw polls that might or might not have any degree of accuracy. *Literary Digest's* straw poll in 1936 that predicted Alf Landon would oust Franklin Roosevelt from the presidency was one of the best-known examples of straw poll accuracy, or inaccuracy, as the case was. But that same year the American Institute of Public Opinion was founded by George Gallup, and their poll accurately reported that Roosevelt would be re-elected handily. Thus, the political campaign polling that we know today was born.

No self-respecting campaign manager today would launch a campaign for high public office without first fielding a public opinion survey. Surveys reveal a lot of information, besides the head-to-head ballot question, that is useful to the campaign strategist. If the manager is handling an incumbent congressman, the first thing he wants to know is how tough to beat his candidate will be and how strong the potential challenger might be. The traditional "who will you be voting for" question tells the strategist very little meaningful information nine months before Election Day.

Literally hundreds of surveys are being conducted every day across America, many of them for the television networks and major news organizations. Then there are all the surveys being conducted by colleges and universities, many times with the interviews done by rank amateurs, er, political science students. Travel companies conduct surveys to see where we want to go on our next vacation; financial institutions conduct surveys to see if we care about their new checking account offer; car companies conduct surveys to see which make and model we'd rather be seen driving; and energy companies conduct surveys to see if we'll buy their justification for higher rates. And that's just the tip of the iceberg.

Surveys used to be conducted door to door in sample neighborhoods. All the polling pros thought the accuracy was pretty good, but it was expensive and took a lot longer than telephone surveys. But with all the political pollsters competing with storm window salesmen for phone time in households, it's become very difficult to get the great unwashed to participate.

Here are some stories from professional pollsters and consultants who insist on looking at cross tabs before asking directions to the bathroom.

Perpich Takes His Own Poll at the Mall

Factoid: Minnesota Governor Rudy Perpich was nominated for a second term in 1986 when he defeated primary challenger George Latimer, 57-41. Perpich beat Republican Cal Ludeman, 57-43, in the general election.

Minnesota Governor Rudy Perpich was running for re-election in 1986 against a primary challenger, the very colorful mayor of St. Paul, George Latimer. We had just done a poll right before St. Patrick's Day, though the governor didn't believe in polls. The poll showed Perpich was widely disliked and that his chance of winning against Latimer was very slim. He was 5 percent lower than any Republican you could mention in the polls.

We took this information into the governor and said, "Rudy, there is some bad news in this poll. It is early March, though, so we haven't had a political convention. They haven't heard of your great accomplishments. However, we want you to concentrate."

The reason for this poll was to get Perpich to concentrate on the election process, which, of course, he never did. It was very difficult to get him to focus. He looked at the poll, threw his hands up and said, "Well, I'm not worried. I take my own poll."

I replied, "Oh, what poll is that, governor?"

"I go in the malls and go to the shoe stores. I see these mothers, and they're buying new shoes for the youngest kid. Well, there you are," he responded.

There was a deafening silence. I almost felt like I was in a Three Stooges movie and I'm the only one not laughing, so I did.

I said, "Governor, it doesn't seem to me to be responsive to this poll."

He replied, "Well, don't you get it? When mothers are buying new shoes for the youngest kid, it means times are good. They are not passing down shoes to the youngest kid. When times are good, incumbents win."

He always had some little thing like that, which by the way proved to be true, as most of these did.

Later in the summer, I said, "You know, Rudy, I think we're going to have some problems in the parts of the 2nd and 7th congressional districts that primarily depend on agriculture."

We were in my office, and Rudy said, "Well, come here for a minute. Look down there at the Mississippi River. See that river?"

I said I did.

"It's pretty high, isn't it?" he asked.

I agreed.

He said, "No problem."

The same Three Stooges movie flashes by.

He continued, "The river is pretty full, and there are no water problems. Therefore, the farmers will be happy. Happy farmers vote for incumbents."

They did, too, as it turned out.

I took away from that that you could measure your chances of re-election by the water level of the Mississippi River or by checking the number of multiple-child families where the mother is buying new shoes for the youngest kid. It worked like a charm.

In 1985 Terry Montgomery and I had to go meet Perpich one time at five o'clock in the morning, at the parking lot of the *St. Paul*

Pioneer Press. Montgomery, who was the chief of staff for the governor, alerted me to get over to the newspaper office. Perpich was going to punch out the person who wrote an unflattering article about his daughter, who at that time was 17 years of age.

The article was about how Mary Sue allegedly had a state trooper drive her on a couple of shopping trips to downtown St. Paul. The Perpiches didn't own a car here in the cities because of state law, which required Rudy to have security with him at all times. The teenage daughter availed herself of that and drove down to one or two department stores in St. Paul.

The paper got hold of it and made it sound as though a taxpayer-provided security officer was squiring her around in a limo.

We prevailed in the situation, however. We explained to Rudy that my job of getting him re-elected would be tougher. He said these were awful, terrible, vicious, mean people. We agreed with him.

We informed him that if he punched this guy out, it would end up on the front page of the newspaper and they would sell a lot more issues of the paper, making a lot more money. Well, he could see that would be a bad thing.

Rudy was a big guy. He kept himself in tremendous physical shape. He would have made a considerable dent in the reporter's face. In retrospect, maybe he should have.   —*Vance Opperman*

'Get Serious Day' in Montana

Factoid: Conrad Burns, a well-known farm broadcaster, surprised two-term Senator John Melcher in Montana in 1988, winning by a 52-48 margin.

In the Montana 1988 Senate race, the candidates were incumbent John Melcher and Conrad Burns, a Yellowstone County commissioner who was challenging him. Our tracking in late September and the early part of October showed there was still quite a gap of 55/35 in the ballot, sometimes 52/37, all in favor of Melcher.

During the October 13 debate between Vice President George Bush and Massachusetts Governor Mike Dukakis, moderator Bernard Shaw asked Dukakis how he would feel about the death penalty if his wife Kitty Dukakis were raped and murdered. In our opinion and the opinion of many analysts, Dukakis's unemotional answer to that question caused a lot of people to decide whom they were going to elect for president.

A night or two later, the tracking in the Montana Senate race showed a substantial narrowing. Conrad Burns was still not ahead but had narrowed it down to a four- or five-point margin. The point we concluded was that after the Bush and Dukakis debate, anybody still on the fence said to themselves, "Oh, I now know who I'm going to vote for for president." They then had the luxury of looking to the next race to say, "Now let's take a closer look at the candidates for Senate." It was at that point people started taking a closer look at Burns and Melcher. People on the fence now started looking at Burns seriously for the first time.

In polling, we say there is a decision-making time, which we refer to as "get serious day." When you ask people questions, they don't have anything at stake, regardless of how they answer the question, and life still goes on for them. However, if someone is undecided, they can still say Melcher one day and Burns the next because they know they don't really have to make a decision until November.

Two or three weeks before election, there comes a time when people stop bouncing around and make a decision on whom they will vote for. The timing of the Bush and Dukakis debate was important because it released voters from putting that "get serious" energy into the presidential decision and allowed them to focus on their decision for the Senate race.

Even though Burns never really led in the three-day rolling average in the nightly tracking surveys, we could see a momentum building. He actually led only one single night, the Thursday night before the election, our last night of surveying, but the momentum had been established from the "get serious day" to the election, and he won by four points.   *—Gary Lawrence*

CHAPTER 7

Digging Up Dirt on the Opponent

☆ ☆ ☆

There's an old adage in the political business that more campaigns are won in the library than on the field of battle. Every year dozens of campaigns dig up some little piece of information about the opponent, play that trump card in the last couple of weeks before the election and skate on to victory. It happens all the time.

The Gore campaign almost pulled off the old trick when a Democratic activist in Maine leaked to the press the sordid details of George W. Bush's drunk driving conviction from September 24, 1976, in Kennebunkport. The information was given to a Fox News local reporter in Maine who aired the story four days before the election. More than a few Republican pollsters will say the story let enough air out of Bush's campaign in the final weekend that the Republican's small lead of three or four points evaporated into a statistical dead heat.

In the campaign business, a manager will often commission a thorough opposition research report done on his own candidate—first to learn what the other side will learn when they start digging through all the old information, but then to prepare the appropriate defense and response when the attack is finally launched by the opponent. There are always a few squeamish candidates who refuse to invest any resources in learning about the opponent's untold background, saying they're committed to running a high-road campaign. That's a nice, optimistic attitude if you're going to win big, no matter what. But if you're in a street fight, you need every advantage you can get, starting with knowing everything possible about the opponent.

Here are some true stories, as told by some of the sleuths who make a living digging up dirt on candidates of the other persuasion.

Enjoying a Little Snort

Factoid: Democrats lost partisan control of the Virginia State Senate for the first time in the 1997 elections.

One of the more outspoken members of the Virginia State Senate, Bill Fears, represented the Eastern Shore of Virginia. In 1991, Virginia was considering legislation that would lower the blood alcohol content limit for being under the influence from a rating of .10 to .08. During the debate on the Senate floor, Fears got up and said, "You've taken all the sport out of drinking and driving. Let's not do any more damage than we've already done in this state to people who enjoy a little snort once in a while."

In that speech, he also recalled that during his days as a World War II bomber pilot, he found it easier to fly after a few drinks.

That speech was used against him in his re-election campaign that fall and was instrumental in his being defeated by Republican Tommy Norment of Williamsburg.   *—Terry Cooper*

Hiring a Detective

Factoid: Bob Packwood, running for a fourth term in the U.S. Senate in 1986, received 63% of the vote in the general election, defeating Rick Bauman.

In 1986 when Bob Packwood was running for re-election and Congressman Jim Weaver was going to run against him, there were rumors that Weaver was going to San Francisco to secretly receive illegal drug treatments to fight some condition that was plaguing him.

We had this discussion in the campaign steering committee meeting about how we would go about documenting this. The candidate got up and suggested that we hire a private detective and have him followed. A couple of us said we thought that this was a dumb idea, but Packwood was very insistent about hiring a private detective. I got up and said this was going to lead to big trouble.

The campaign chairman finally said he would take care of the private detective. After the meeting, I went over to him to express my concern. He just smiled and said, "No, I'm not going to hire anyone, but he thinks it's going to be done."

—Bob Moore

CHAPTER 8

Raising Money to Pay the Bills

☆ ☆ ☆

More money is spent by McDonald's advertising the Big Mac with fries than is spent by political campaigns in a given year. More money is spent advertising beer each year than is spent on political campaigns. Hey, more money is spent on pornography each year than is spent on political campaigns. With that inventory, some would say there's still too much money spent on political campaigns, though others would say they're just doing a better job of fundraising in some other avenues of the economy.

There's an old rule of thumb in the campaign business that says you probably need to spend at least four dollars on your campaign for every vote you need to win. If it's going to take 100,000 votes to get 51 percent in the election, then start thinking you'll need at least $400,000 to run a competitive campaign. Things never cost less, so perhaps you'll need more than that. The wise candidate is thinking hard about how he or she might get 100,000 voters to see things their way, and all the while they're thinking equally hard about where 400 big ones are going to come from.

A recent study suggested than only 4 percent of the people in this nation are involved in politics either as a volunteer or as a financial contributor. Obviously more people would rather go bowling than participate in campaigns. In a very hotly contested election in an average congressional district where 100,001 votes will win, your campaign will work very hard to get 4,000 contributors who will write checks that average $100. This is not easy work. But every successful money man will say there really is just one secret to political fundraising. Ask. You have to ask for the money.

Some fundraising is expensive and some is not so expensive. A typical campaign will spend up to 25 percent of the entire budget on the cost of raising the dollars. Direct mail for money is an expensive method of fundraising. So is telephone solicitation. Big dinners have a large overhead. Every year there are stories about the campaign that spent $25,000 for invitations, the hall, the decorations, a good band, great hors d'oeuvres, but only brought in $15,000 at the gate. This is not called fundraising, its entertainment.

Jon Corzine gave everyone a lesson on how to raise money on the cheap. Corzine spent $65 million – that's right, $65 million – out of his own pocket en route to buying the Senate election in New Jersey in 2000. Even with that huge expenditure, Corzine scraped out a 51-47 win over Republican Bob Franks. The only guy that came close to spending that much personal money was Ross Perot in his ill-fated 1992 presidential campaign. But in 2001, Michael Bloomberg rose to the top of the big-spenders list, spending $75 million from his own pocket to be elected mayor of New York City.

Here are some true-life stories from professionals who learned a long time ago the secret of asking for the order.

They Won't Say He Couldn't Raise His Hat

The rap they put on me when I was DNC chairman, in addition to being this wild-eyed liberal from Massachusetts, was, "He couldn't raise his hat." The party had a $2 million deficit. We lost the White House, we didn't have the Senate, and so it was not an easy time raising money. I'm one of those guys who finds it embarrassing to pass the box in church. It is not my cup of tea.

But now I had the chairman's job, and fundraising is an important part of this. I put on my game face and did what I had to do. I tried as best I could while I was in Washington to put aside an hour or two in the afternoon, just making money calls.

One day I put in a call to Joan Kroc, who I had never met before. Within a couple of days she returned my call. Joan was the widow of Ray Kroc, founder of McDonald's. She owned the San Diego Padres baseball team.

We had some introductory small talk and I tell her about the Victory Fund, which is basically the non-federal money to help shore up the state parties. But she is very issue oriented. One of the things she was concerned about was the whole nuclear proliferation issue and the party situation. It was a pretty good conversation.

Near the end of it she said, "I thought I could only give $1,000 personally and $5,000 to the party." I said, "This is non-federal money and a person arguably could give up to a million dollars, whatever he or she chose to give." My saying a million dollars was a figure of speech.

At the end of the conversation she said to me, "Paul, would a million dollars be helpful from me?"

I almost fell off my chair.

I remember it was a front-page story in *USA Today* about Joan Kroc contributing a million dollars to the Democratic National Party.

I thought, well, the guys said he couldn't raise his hat. They won't say that again.   *—Paul Kirk*

Reagan Letter Pays for Entire 1984 Campaign

In 1984 President Ronald Reagan didn't decide to officially declare his candidacy until after the beginning of the New Year. He wanted to postpone any primary fundraising efforts until he had completed the State of the Union Address and started his business for the New Year. As his fundraisers, we were chomping at the bit to get started in 1983. We thought the end of the world would come because we wouldn't be able to raise our money until six months prior to the convention. At the time I was the finance director at the RNC and there wasn't really any official Ronald Reagan finance director. It was a coalition of his top advisers working on the political end and some of us, including the chairman of the party, Frank Fahrenkopf, and the general chairman, Senator Paul Laxalt, who were spearheading this.

We finally got the green light to launch a fundraising drive. Reagan, being president, didn't have time to go out and do a lot of fundraising events. That wasn't his style to begin with. He rarely did the typical fundraising that we know of today, the cocktail parties, the receptions and the dinners. But he was the consummate letter writer and communicator, and his direct-mail letters always yielded the highest return, because it was Ronald Reagan. Emmy Lewis had met Reagan in 1964 and was a "Goldwater Girl" who could capture Reagan's voice and personality in the direct-mail letters we sent.

In early 1984 we pooled all the RNC donor files, the congressional committee file, the Citizens for the Republic file, which was Reagan's old political action committee, and a few others. We put together about two and a half million names of contributors to these various entities. It was legal because the Reagan campaign committee paid a fair market value for the rental of those lists. We did one big mailing. It was dropped in late March and early April; that one mailing yielded somewhere in the neighborhood of $13 million.

Keep in mind that in 1984, the spending limit in the primary was $20.2 million. That was all that could be spent. The fundraising limit was, of course, a bit higher, because you had compliance fund dollars that could be raised, and as in all presidential campaigns under the federal election campaign act, there is a fundraising offset where you can apply 20 percent of the fund to the cost of the fundraising and that doesn't apply toward the spending limits.

Our jobs were over—our usefulness to the president came to a quick end because of that single letter. We did one additional follow-up mailing, and altogether about $16 million was raised in that campaign from individual donors. He got a match of $10.1 million, and Reagan was the first presidential candidate since the enactment of the Federal Election Campaign Act who qualified for the maximum matching amount. At the end of the day he spent about $25.9 million. Walter Mondale spent $26.3 million in his primary, Gary Hart spent $14.5 million and John Glenn spent $12.1 million. So they had raised a Democrat total of $52.9 million during the primary.

Ronald Reagan didn't really have a reason to spend a whole lot of money, but it was all done with no events. Reagan did a few 10-minute handshakes with old finance committee members from his California days, but it basically all was done through the mail with one letter.

I remember the letter was on a very bland-looking piece of paper with a Reagan letterhead. It was four pages in length with a response device and that was it.

This illustrates not only the power of the candidate in attracting dollars, but also that when Reagan wrote a letter it was received as a genuine letter. The potential contributor understood the power of his thoughts and words. Reagan wanted to do two or three big things during his presidency. People respond better to that than to a bunch of little things.   —*Phil Smith*

Raising the Money in 10 Minutes

The chairman of the Republican State Committee in New Jersey in 1967 was a man named Webster B. Todd, whose daughter, Christy Todd Whitman, became governor and was head of the Environmental Protection Agency in Washington. Web Todd's wife, Eleanor Todd, was at the same time the Republican National Committeewoman from New Jersey.

Todd called me one day and asked me to come over to New Jersey. He said that as party chairman he would like to do all he could to help elect a Republican legislature that year. The odd number years are the years in which New Jersey elects all of its state officials. The Democrats had a two to one majority in both houses of the New Jersey legislature.

As Todd and I talked, I said, "What would you think about our doing an advertising campaign directed at the Democratic legislature, which would be an umbrella campaign for the individual campaigns of individual legislators?"

He said, "That sounds like a good idea. Why don't you come up with some good ideas for me and then we'll see if we can raise the money to do it?"

I went back to my office in New York and called a friend of mine, Mel McDougall, who was the creative director at BBD & O (Batton, Barston, Durston and Osborn), one of the leading advertising agencies in the world at that time. I said, "Mel, I think there's something that might be interesting to you that we could do together."

We put our heads together and decided that television was out of the question in New Jersey, and radio was probably more expensive because most of that would have to come from New York or Philadelphia. A series of full-page newspaper ads run in all the major daily papers in New Jersey might be a way to implement Todd's ideas.

We spent some time putting together a series of full-page newspaper ads, most of which had some element of humor in them. One that I remember well, featured an almost full-scale picture of a rhinoceros with the caption, "This horse was made in Trenton." It was an effort to point out that when you turn problems over to the Democrats in the legislature, they could turn even a horse into a rhinoceros.

We took the ads to show to Web Todd. He seemed to like them and said, "I will assemble a group of businessmen to see if they like them. If they do, maybe they can put up the money for it."

On a chosen night, Mel McDougall and I showed up at a private men's club in downtown Newark to present these ads. At the meeting were the leading bankers and industrialists in New Jersey, a group of eight to 10 men. Prominent among the group were Philip Hoffman, then chairman of the board of Johnson & Johnson, and the president of Johnson & Johnson, Richard Sellers. It was the cream of the crop of Republican industrialists and business leaders in New Jersey.

Mel and I proceeded to present this campaign, and it was very difficult to get any sense whether the men thought this was a great idea or a really bad one. They were stone-faced during the meeting, with several of them smoking large cigars, filling the room with cigar smoke.

We kept going and finally ended our presentation. Their faces were absolutely blank. Todd, who clearly also couldn't read their reactions, said, "Well, fellas, what did you think of this ad campaign?"

After a moment of pause, Philip Hoffman put his cigar on the table, turned to Webster Todd and said, "Web, I've got to tell you this is the best damn thing you've ever done for the party."

He then reached into his pocket, pulled out a checkbook and said, "I'm going to write you a check tonight for $25,000 because I think this is the right thing for us to be doing."

He turned to Dick Sellers, the president of Johnson & Johnson, and his employee, and said, "Dick, how about you?"

Sellers, who had no real choice, said, "I'm in for $10,000."

Quickly, all the men in the room followed suit. I'm sure many of them felt either personal pressure or some business responsibility to follow Hoffman's lead. Within a matter of 10 minutes, they had raised nearly $100,000 with which to put this campaign in the papers.

—John Deardourff

Raising the Money at the Non-fundraiser

Factoid: In a special congressional election in the Washington 7ᵗʰ district in 1977 – brought about by the resignation of Brock Adams, who had been confirmed as secretary of transportation – Republican Jack Cunningham beat Marvin Durning by a 54-45 margin.

Early in 1977, President Jimmy Carter named Washington district 7 Congressman Brock Adams secretary of transportation. George Bush had been ambassador to China and was back in the United States. He agreed to do this fundraiser for the Republican candidate, Jack Cunningham, in the Washington State special election.

It was hoped the fundraiser would raise most of the money for this little election. One of Bush's close friends and advisers, Della Reese, in Seattle, was the person in charge of the event.

About a week before the big dinner, we were told that Bush had cancelled it. Amidst great consternation, everyone wondered how we were going to raise the money we needed for this race. They decided to move ahead and very creatively sent out letters stating that, due to scheduling problems, the event had been cancelled but to please send your money anyway. Then you won't have to come eat another bad chicken dinner.

Consequently, they raised more than they would have otherwise because there were very few overhead expenses. It ended up being a wildly successful fundraiser.

About a week later, I met George Bush for the first time. Bush had been chairman of the RNC, and he was back visiting old friends. He came in and asked me why we'd cancelled the fundraising dinner in Seattle.

A little taken aback, I told him that we hadn't cancelled it, but he had. He said, "No, no, Della called me and told me the campaign had cancelled it." Obviously, she had determined that it wasn't going to be successful and pulled the plug on it, telling each side that the other had cancelled.

As a result, they raised more money without doing the fundraiser. Former President Bush may not get the credit, but other campaigns have followed the idea of a "non-fundraiser fundraiser" and offered people a chance to send their money without having to come to another dinner and eat bad chicken.　　*—Ladonna Lee*

You Say a Thousand From Whom?

Factoid: College professor Newt Gingrich was elected to Congress in 1978 when he defeated Democrat Virginia Sheppard, 54-46, in the 6th district of Georgia.

In 1978, at a Republican Party event in Douglasville, Georgia, Newt Gingrich tells me that one thing we have to do while we are there is get this check from one of the Smith brothers. There were three or four Smith brothers, and they owned the car dealerships in Douglasville. Newt said he'd talked to Joe Smith and he would give him a thousand bucks.

Newt is working the crowd, and he points over to this guy and tells me to go get the thousand dollars from him. So I wander over to the guy and say, "Mr. Smith, Newt asked me to pick up the thousand dollars from you." The guy says okay, pulls out his checkbook, writes the check and hands it to me.

Pleased as punch, I walk back to Newt and proudly show him the check. However, it's the wrong Smith. I had just asked the wrong guy! But he didn't even blink an eye. He just pulled out his checkbook and wrote the check. I was embarrassed, and Newt went and got the other check from the other brother.　　*—Carlyle Gregory*

Giving the Money Back in Massachusetts

Factoid: John Kerry won a third term in the U.S. Senate in 1996 when he defeated Massachusetts Governor Bill Weld by a 52-45 margin.

In Bill Weld's U.S. Senate race in 1996 against John Kerry, for which I was the finance director, we raised $8 million in 11 months. It was an amazing success story.

Many people in Washington had advised us that to raise PAC money, you needed an expert. It wasn't something we knew anything about. We'd never done it before. So we hired PAC fundraiser Steve Gordon and pretty well filled up his dance card.

The problem was over the difficulty of travel. He was used to calling to set up a meeting. He'd phone a prospect and say, "What about a meeting next Thursday?" They'd say, "Sure, fine." And they were off and running. We were, of course, constantly dragging our feet over every scheduling request. *The Boston Globe* wrote an article every time Bill Weld got on an airplane. So we aggravated Steve to no end, and he and I fought like cats and dogs throughout the campaign.

Federal election rules require that you collect from each donor who gives $200 or more their occupation and employer, along with their address. You have to make your best effort to obtain this personal information so it can be reported on the FEC forms. If you don't make your best effort within two weeks of accepting the money, then you're supposed to send the contribution back.

There may not be a campaign on earth that actually does this except for us, the ill-fated Weld campaign. In 1996, we ended up having a computer snafu. We hadn't called a group of donors to ask them for their employment information. Therefore, we determined that we had not used our best effort to obtain the necessary information within the required two weeks.

So we refunded $75,000 to donors because we felt we hadn't dotted the I's and crossed the T's correctly. It was a very sad day for the campaign when we did it, but we felt strongly that it was the right thing to do. Of course, when you go to those extremes, no one ever audits you.

—*Martha Chayet*

Extra for Roquefort for Cory Non-dinner

Factoid: Ken Cory was elected to the California Assembly in 1966 and served four terms. In 1974, he was elected state controller and served three terms until 1987.

In 1974, then state Assemblyman Ken Cory was running for state controller in California. Cory mailed out an invitation for a $100-per-person dinner. However, you didn't come to anything.

Most of the lobbyists and everyone else needed an invitation to go to something. It was $100 for a phantom dinner, but what was particularly ingenious about it is, if you wanted Roquefort dressing, it was another $2.50. Cory, by the way, was elected.

—Harvey Englander

CHAPTER 9

Winning in the Streets

☆ ☆ ☆

B efore television, before phone banks, when campaigns were flush with volunteers, there was a better way to win votes and influence people. It was called street organization. Oh, campaigns today still try to recreate those antiques from the past, where you had block captains and precinct chairs, and dozens of interested advocates working the different constituencies. You could fill a headquarters with 50 volunteers every day to stuff envelopes and call their friends and neighbors; you could put together a team of a thousand people to staff the polls on Election Day. Those were the days. And we're just talking 25 years ago.

In that kinder and gentler time, the campaign volunteer corps was top-heavy with women, many with children at home. But today, all those women who filled the volunteer ranks a quarter of a century ago are gainfully employed and way too busy for anything as interesting as politics. Go into your local campaign headquarters in September and October of an election year now and the average age of the volunteers is 69. They're all retired, and stuffing envelopes beats watching daytime TV.

For the past quarter of a century, campaigns at many levels have relied, not on street organization to deliver the message, but on television commercials and radio spots, with some direct-mail flyers mixed in the final weeks. Many campaigns were won or lost in the air wars. But things are changing, and fast. With cable and satellite

77

television taking a bigger and bigger share of television viewers, it's tougher to break through with a political message on TV. When the air wars started a quarter of a century ago, there were just the big three networks to contend with. Any idiot could put together a decent TV buy then. Today, even a rocket scientist couldn't figure out all the ins and outs of TV viewing habits.

Winning in the streets with people may be back in vogue. It may be easier, cheaper and a lot more effective to get your message out using street walkers and door knockers, even if you have to pay them. These new-age door knockers will be armed with Palm Pilots that tell them who lives where, how many registered voters live with you and perhaps your dog's name. But what goes around comes around, they say.

Here are some stories from professionals who understand how to put together street organizations in the country, in the suburbs and in the cities.

Taking a Soaking for the Mayor

Factoid: Kevin White was elected mayor of Boston four times. In 1967 and 1971 he beat Loise Day Hicks in the general election. In 1975 and 1979 he defeated Joseph Timiley.

My first political job was with Boston Mayor Kevin White when he was running against Louise Day Hicks in 1971. I was 20 years old.

The first job they gave me to do was to get signatures for re-election in this Irish-Catholic community. I went and knocked on the first door, they answered the door and I asked, "Would you like to sign for Kevin White for re-election as mayor?" She said, "Yes, I love Kevin," so she signed it. At the next door, I got, "Oh, Kevin, yes, I like Kevin, he's good." The third door was empty and the fourth door was empty and the fifth person was outside watering her lawn. So I walked up to her and was thinking, this is the easiest job ever. I said, "Would you like to sign up for the re-election of Kevin White?" She put the hose right in my face, soaked me and said, "I wouldn't sign for that no-good son-of-a-bitch."

The first thing I did, I graduated to become a precinct captain and sent other people out to get the signatures.   —*Tom King*

Dad Dies, But Do We Still Have a Deal?

Paul Nace, who was Matt Reese's partner, was doing a "Right to Work Campaign" in Missouri in 1978. The tradition in St. Louis is to hire different organizations in the community to do political work. One of the organizations was a family that owned a number of funeral homes in the black community. Interestingly, churches and funeral homes are centers of politics in black neighborhoods. The family comes in and says they are going to put up signs, get out literature, and do this and that—they have a whole program. Reese said we will pay you this much, but we are coming down here next week to check out how it's going.

So the next week comes around and Nace flies in to check things out. Well, there are no house signs, and no leaflets had been distributed, nothing. He walks into this meeting, and he is sitting there and he says, I told you I would check, and we went here and here and here, and nothing is happening. All of a sudden he sees the guy he is yelling at get very angry and the guy drops dead of a heart attack. Nace is totally beside himself, thinking, I have just killed this poor man. So everyone is coming around and Nace is saying, Oh, God, what have I done?

After the body has been removed and things quiet down, they are walking out and the son comes up to Nace and says, "Do we still have a deal?"   —*Anonymous*

CHAPTER 10

Making the Classic
TV Commercial

☆ ☆ ☆

Many political commercials, voters would agree, are boring, offensive and obnoxious. Interestingly, a lot of those lackluster commercials end up doing a pretty good job for the candidate paying to put them on the air. They may not knock your socks off like the commercials aired every day by the soft drink or beer manufacturers who are locked in market-share wars, but they are putting points on the board for the politician. But every election year, several political commercials will rise above the others to attain the standing of a classic.

Bob Goodman, a TV producer from Baltimore, made a spot for Malcolm Wallop when he first ran for the U.S. Senate in Wyoming in 1976, showing cowboys taking a government-mandated porta-potty out on the roundup. It was a classic that has been copied several times. A local advertising agency in Anchorage made a spot for Arliss Sturgulewski in 1986 using a half-dozen first graders trying to pronounce her difficult name unsuccessfully. The spot concluded with "Let's just call her governor." It's on all the demo reels of great spots.

Every candidate starts the campaign believing he or she can win if they just come up with that dynamite spot that grabs the voters by the shoulders and shakes them silly. Ninety-nine times out of a hundred, that's not reality, or at least it's not what's needed to put together a winning campaign. Voters can either be entertained by "cute" spots, or they can get vital information through those lackluster spots we see so often on the air. Studies suggest that TV spots with the candidate "talking to the camera" are often the most effective way to communicate a believable message to voters. Voters will feel they know more about the candidate if the message comes directly from his or her mouth.

Here are some stories from professionals who made a few of those classic TV commercials.

Looking for Dee Huddleston

Factoid: Mitch McConnell won the 1984 Kentucky Senate race, beating incumbent Democrat Dee Huddleston by just 5,269 votes.

This is the story of the "Bloodhounds" commercial. The year was 1984 and Mitch McConnell was then the county executive, or county judge, as they say in Louisville, Kentucky. McConnell is relentlessly focused, not terribly personable, but he is willing to do whatever it takes to win, without question.

We started quite early in the campaign, in January, on the air with 30-second, 60-second and even two-minute spots. McConnell raised a significant amount of money. We'd done ads that were mostly positive.

Early in August, pollster Lance Tarrance walked into the Jefferson County Courthouse into McConnell's office and plopped down his survey on the table. He proceeded to tell Mitch that they were still 44 points down in the head-to-head numbers against U.S. Senator Dee Huddleston, who was the good old boy. McConnell rarely shows emotion, but he really flinched. Lance, who usually has no shortage of ideas, said they'd pretty much tried everything on the positive side, even some contrast, and nothing was working. It was a fairly brief and dispirited meeting. We didn't know what to say, so we went back to New York.

Roger Ailes, the media consultant, was very depressed. He thought of Mitch as kind of his pet project. He liked the fact that Mitch was the underdog. We took the polling data and research, and he confesses that he didn't have any huge insight from the book, but while he was watching TV he saw a dog commercial.

He came in the next morning and said, "Dogs." He and I developed the premise of bloodhounds looking for Huddleston. Huddleston didn't have a terrible attendance record for those times, but we decided that attendance was the only thing that might work. We convinced McConnell that we wanted to question his opponent's attendance.

We wanted to do a very simple graphic spot that set the problem up and laid the facts out. Then we wanted to do a backwoods Kentucky hunter trying to find Dee Huddleston because he was missing. This was a concept that just didn't work on the McConnell side of the brain. It was completely alien to him and a very tough sale. But when you're 44 points down, you think, "What the hell?"

So we went through the process – and I'm sure we must have typed 30 to 35 versions of the script before we got one they liked. They finally signed off on it. We did the quick, graphic shot, which was up for five days, and then we shot the second ad, "Bloodhounds," near Washington, D.C. We made several mistakes shooting "Bloodhounds." The first mistake was that we actually hired a trainer with four bloodhounds for $2,500. We forgot to specify that they all be the same gender because basically every moment that the dogs weren't in front of the cameras, they were humping. Bloodhounds, despite their somewhat slothful appearance, are very strong and very heavy. They spent a good part of the 18-hour day either humping or trying to hump or sniffing the wrong place.

With those two commercials – the graphic spot and the bloodhounds ad – McConnell moved 17 points in the polls in 10 days, which may be the biggest move I've ever seen in a campaign survey. We were still about 27 points down, but that started the ball rolling.

"Bloodhounds" became the symbol of the campaign and received enormous earned media value. It got run over and over again on TV news and became a real novelty. Editorial cartoons would feature McConnell dogs baying at the house. Huddleston didn't answer the claim for weeks. So every week from then on, we began to inch our way closer and closer.

"Bloodhounds" went up in late August, and then for eight weeks we kept moving like a rocket on different issues. But two weeks out we were stalling, and we didn't know how to close out those final eight points. We decided to go back to the dogs.

This time we were much smarter. We got either gay or same-sex bloodhounds. We were really organized. Two weeks from Election Day we go to Morristown, New Jersey. However, we had neglected in our scouting to notice one important thing: Morristown was the headquarters for the Seeing Eye Dog Foundation.

The whole town was full of people training their golden retrievers and German shepherds how to work with a blind person. We show up with these four wild bloodhounds and cause enormous havoc throughout town. It was driving their dogs and our dogs wild as we went down the sidewalk.

"Bloodhounds 2" had a new element, and that was to include Huddleston in the ad. We did a casting call in New York for people looking like Huddleston. Then we had a professional makeup artist paint a very heavy mask on our new Huddleston lookalike to make him look real. We found an out-of-work Shakespearean actor and took him out to Morristown to film this commercial. We had these four bloodhounds and this crazy actor who was constantly muttering. People thought he was acting, but he was actually just crazy.

This poor actor was doing wind sprints for 12 hours through mud, down streams and through restaurants. As soon as we started shooting the outdoors stuff, it started to rain a very fine mist. You couldn't see it on the cameras, which helped. However, it made everything wet, including our Dee Huddleston mask. After a few minutes of rain, it began to slide right off his cheekbones. We were in such desperate time trouble that we would shove it back into position, glue it and keep shooting.

In the end, "Bloodhounds 2" was what finally pushed McConnell over and got him that 44th point. 　　　　　　—*Larry McCarthy*

Filming Mr. Yankee in Brooklyn

Factoid: The former U.S. attorney for the southern district of New York, Rudy Giuliani, was elected New York City's 107th mayor in 1993.

David Garth likes to go out and interview a lot of people. In a given campaign, he may interview 80 people, even if you are only going to make 10 or 12 spots out of that. First you get the stories made, then you find the nuggets you have in mind. With Garth, you always have the camera rolling.

One of the things we had to do with the Rudy Giuliani mayoral campaign in 1993 was to humanize the man. New Yorkers already knew he was tough enough. We were out filming with him doing education spots, letting him talk about education. At the end of the shoot, we were in his old neighborhood in Queens. He was leaning against the hood of the car giving his education talk, and afterwards we began to wind down.

As we were winding down, Rudy began talking about growing up as a kid in Brooklyn, being a Yankees fan. He was the only Yankees fan in Brooklyn. Our camera always stays on, so the cameraman had the camera on at this time. He added how his father would dress him up in this little Yankees uniform and send him out to play with the kids, and they would throw him in the mud. Everybody else around this neighborhood was a Dodger fan.

When the campaign began, that was the first commercial we put on. The funny thing about this was that nobody could figure it out. They would wonder what on earth he was doing and also wonder who cared? He was so relaxed while doing the spot, though, telling this little story, and people were not expecting this.

The reason we did the spot was because he was so real in it. When he is not focused on a goal, Rudy is a very entertaining person to be around. He has great stories about his prosecutions, but you never see that in his public persona; you only see that when he is really relaxed, but it is real and authentic. That was "found gold." We did not even have to edit it.

The one little problem we had was the camera began to slip and the cameraman had to pull it back up. Consequently, we could not close the spot with Rudy's face. Rather, we covered five seconds of sound from the story with a picture of Rudy and then later came back to him. The TV spot ended up setting the perfect tone because it made people look at him and see him in a way they hadn't thought about before. —*Richard Bryers*

Bentsen Social Security Spot Widely Used

Factoid: Lloyd Bentsen won a third term in the U.S. Senate in 1982 when he beat Republican Congressman Jim Collins, 59-41.

*N*ewsweek ran my picture after I made a Social Security spot for the 1982 campaign for Lloyd Bentsen. My scripts bothered me; I just wasn't impressed with them. Bentsen was chairman of the Senate finance committee and was very hard to nail down. I heard he was going to be in San Antonio the next day, so I set up a meeting with him and drove from Austin to San Antonio.

I was doodling on a napkin in the bar at the Hyatt Hotel when all of a sudden a television spot came to me, in its entirety. I didn't know if it was the alcohol or creativity. Now, about that time a young college student who worked for Bentsen as a driver walked by. He was with another young intern from the University of Texas. They saw me and knew I was good for a couple of free beers, so they came over.

I said, "Boys, I need a favor." I showed them my napkin and said, "Try to find me a house sitting off a blacktop road with a gravel driveway leading to it, with a mailbox in the foreground. If you can find one with a windmill in the back I would like that even more. Somewhere out of town, in ranchland, close enough to get there within a half hour." They said, "Yes, sir."

Early the next morning they called and said they had my place. I said, "I can't get there until 11. Are you sure?" And they agreed. I told them I needed an elderly, weatherbeaten woman for the commercial, but I would like to see a couple. They said they would do it.

I really didn't believe I would do this television spot, because it was all so happenstance. We usually spent days scouting locations and would work on everything to get it just right. Now I had two college kids who had never done a television spot out freelancing for me, for free beer.

I get out there at about 11:30. Damned if it isn't the perfect white-framed prairie house, with a creaking windmill behind it, a gravel driveway with a big curve in it and some mesquite growing around the house. But no mailbox.

I said, "Boys, I don't have a mailbox." They said, "Now, just a minute." Here comes a pickup truck and in the back of it is a mailbox that obviously had just been uprooted from someone's lawn. It had dirt around the bottom of it and somebody's name on it. I told them it's a federal offense to steal a mailbox. They said, "Oh, we'll take it back and it will be better than when we got it." Then they started painting the mailbox silver. The paint was still wet.

They brought me two women, and damned if they weren't two sisters; they had lined faces that looked like they had been facing a West Texas wind for about 50 years. They wore house dresses. I just had to flip a coin. I gave the one I didn't use a hundred bucks and I gave the one I did use two hundred dollars. All she had to do was walk from the house to the mailbox, open the mailbox, look in the mailbox and then look down the road.

What she was looking for was her Social Security check, to see if it had come. When she realizes the Social Security check didn't come, she's worried. She hangs her head, leaves the mailbox open and walks back to the house. That is the entire spot. Of course, the camera goes into the empty mailbox, pans down the empty road and then shows the old woman's face. She wipes the sweat off her brow with her sleeve.

The spot went something like this: What if the checks stopped? What if the Republicans finally won their battle against Social Security? The only thing standing between them and your Social Security check is a few Democrats who care, like Lloyd Bentsen. That was it. We ended up running it in about 30 states, and we changed it for every Democratic senator.

The Democrats nearly took back the Senate in 1982, after being knocked out in 1980 in the Reagan revolution. I don't know if the mailbox spot had anything to do with it, but it was given a lot of credit for boosting the Democrats on one issue.

It is still on my reel, and it is still on most people's reels as one of the best local spots ever produced. It was produced on Margaritas, Long Star Beer and the inspiration of two college kids, the way things happen in our business. —*Ray Strother*

Inhofe Wins Senate Special
With Dancing Convicts

Factoid: In the 1994 special U.S. Senate election in Oklahoma, Congressman Jim Inhofe beat Congressman Dave McCurdy by a 55-40 margin.

A decent, hard-nosed, right-wing guy like Jim Inhofe became an acceptable alternative to Dave McCurdy, a big political candidate, because we used humor to take the edge off. And McCurdy was so perfect, he expected to win.

When we put on the dancing ballerina ad, it was an overnight success. And the success was not really the result of what it was selling. What it was selling was the insanity of Bill Clinton's crime bill. The bill had typical government waste and put all these additional policemen on the street. It also had stupid government programs like dance lessons for felons in it.

Because the dancing convicts ad was witty and attention-getting, it said something about Inhofe that people didn't know. Nobody thought Inhofe was witty, but he is. Nobody thought Jim would ever approve something like that, but he did. I think what it said about Inhofe was more important than what it said about the specific issue involved. What I wanted to do was make Clinton look bad, which was easy in 1994, while tying McCurdy to Clinton. We set the mousetrap.

The dancing convicts ad was the most instrumental ad in turning around Inhofe's image. We wanted voters to see that this guy was really someone you could live with, that he brought some joy and humor to the race, and he's not out there saying mean and nasty things about McCurdy, which people expected.

McCurdy's numbers began to fall through the floor when we ran two or three ads in a row that positioned him as blood brother to Bill Clinton. Later when he saw that this was a mistake, he quickly said he hardly knew Clinton.

From day one I knew I had footage of Dave McCurdy nominating Bill Clinton at the Democratic National Convention. You don't get much closer to the president than that. Plus I had footage of him jogging with Clinton.

We let him have two or three unanswered weeks of building his case that he hardly knew Clinton. Then we sprang the trap. The trap was a single ad that showed Dave McCurdy introducing Clinton, calling him his "good friend." We had all these great crowd shots of the convention with people holding posters saying things like "lesbian rights," which is not really a popular issue in Oklahoma. By the end of the 30 seconds, you know that this guy has lied to you about his relationship with Clinton.

The ad is the lead news story the next day. All of a sudden, McCurdy plummets in the polls. As he plummets, we begin to run a positive ad about Inhofe's background. McCurdy self-destructs.

The next ad was a Pinocchio ad with McCurdy's face. Not only did his nose grow, but his eyes got darker, his eyebrows got bushier and his ears got pointy. The background gradually went to red flames, as in the flames of hell.

Mike Royko, a syndicated columnist with the *Chicago Tribune*, wrote an entire column about the ad, saying I was turning this decent man into the devil. In general appearance, it was a nice humorous ad, but it told the audience that this man had not been truthful about a lot of things. The distorted picture of McCurdy with the big nose, bushy eyebrows and pointy ears ran in four-color on the front page of *USA Today*.

As a result, McCurdy lost his confidence. He could no longer give a speech. He stammered when he talked. He didn't even dress as well as he had before. This ad took the wind out of some very proud sails.

We believed there was a high likelihood of a last-minute dirty attack, so we needed to have something special ready to go.

One big difference between the candidates was that every weekend, almost without fail, Inhofe was on that plane flying back to Oklahoma. He would spend the weekend visiting with the people he represented, then fly back to Washington on Monday to go to work. McCurdy, on the other hand, had seldom come back to Oklahoma. He sold his house, moved his family to northern Virginia and became a Washington guy. Inhofe remained an Oklahoma guy.

Somewhere during the campaign, someone doing research found a little recording of McCurdy giving a speech in Virginia, where he had lived. He said in his own words something like, "My constituents back in Oklahoma think a big Saturday night is sitting on the back porch with a six pack of beer watching the bug zapper." He was making a joke, but when I heard it, what flashed through my mind was what this guy must think of Oklahoma to say those words. He was out of touch with his home state.

We wanted an ad with a family sitting on a porch. We had enormous trouble casting it because I wanted actors who looked kind of dumb to fit McCurdy's description of what Oklahomans looked like. You can cross over the line very easily and end up making it stupid and irritating, which will backfire on you. I cast this mother and father and two kids all independently from a casting company, but I wasn't really sold on them.

We built this set in a studio in Tulsa, and we had this old bug zapper that a prop guy made for us. We had these fake bugs that would crash into it and fry – very loudly. Everything looked good, but I still wasn't happy with the casting.

The morning we were going to shoot, I drove up to the studio, and as fate would have it there was this old beat-up junk car sitting out front along with the nice cars of the crew members. As I walked by it, a gray-haired man with a beard down to his belly and a pony-tail down to his waist leaned out to catch my attention. He had this overweight, gray-haired wife alongside him and two kids in the back. They appeared to have mental disorders. They didn't, but they looked like they might.

As I started to walk into the studio, this guy asked if I knew Mr. Davis. I said that was me. He said that someone had told them a commercial was going to happen, and he might make $50 for the family if they could appear in it.

I started to tell him we'd already cast it, then I stooped and looked into that car, and I tell you it was perfection. I offered them $50 apiece if they'd do it. The father was in heaven. So I nicely get rid of the other people, and we bring them onto the set. The kids would stare at the bug zapper until I literally had tears rolling down my cheeks. I would do my directing tricks, but I didn't need to do much because they were so perfect for this.

We have this ad ready to go maybe six to eight weeks before the election. From an advertising standpoint, I loved the ad. I didn't see any downside to running it. Inhofe was very nervous about it, however. He took it to Jay Brothers, who was doing the media buying, to see what he thought of it. To his credit, Jay told Jim it was the best ad he'd ever seen and that he would run it the next day if he could.

I'd sold the ad from day one as our "let's hold it until we need it" ad. So I was stuck with that. I couldn't go back on my original theory. As we got closer and closer to Election Day, we could see that we had turned the corner and were going to win. The country was doing well for Republicans. Jim Inhofe was going to be the next U.S. senator.

So then we had a decision. Should we run the ad or should it go down in history as the great ad that never ran? We still have it in the can if there is a big surprise on Friday afternoon before Election Day, to deflect any last-minute attack that might come up.

But no last-minute effort came up. I was quite distraught that this was never going to run. On Monday, I was at my mother's house watching Rush Limbaugh.

Toward the end of the show, Rush says, "I'm going to commercial, then I'm going to give you your marching orders for tomorrow. So don't shut your TV off. I'm also going to show you our favorite ad of this political season."

He came back from commercial break and said, "This is an ad for Jim Inhofe of Oklahoma." I'm entirely shocked, and I don't know how he's even seen any of our ads, but I figure it's the ballerina ad. Then Rush goes on to say, "I think this is the greatest ad, but I don't think it even ran on TV because they didn't need it, but I love it." Then he proceeds to run the bug zapper ad, the entire 30-second ad, on national television. I'm about to die, but I'm also wondering how in the hell he got that ad. Only four copies of that ad were ever made. They were numbered and closely guarded.

The program ends, and I'm still watching. The first ad that airs locally after the Limbaugh show is the bug zapper ad. I'm floored. This is Monday night before the election. I don't know who to call or what to do.

I'm in charge of this media effort, and I don't know anything about this. I continue watching TV, and the ad runs during Leno and during Letterman. It turns out that Inhofe himself had dialed in those media changes. Of course, he had no idea that Limbaugh would run it. To this day, I think it was a little gift to me. —*Fred Davis*

CHAPTER 11

Television and Radio Spots That Work

☆ ☆ ☆

The typical congressional campaign outside of major metropolitan areas will, on average, produce and air from half a dozen to a dozen TV commercials during the final 60 days of a campaign. Statewide campaigns for governor or senator might produce twice that number, while campaigns for president will produce 40 or 50 different spots.

But all of the spots, whether you're running for the White House or the courthouse, have some of the same purposes. Usually, the first phase in the TV plan is an introduction of the candidate. Candidate Smith has a nice family, even a nice dog, they have been successful in some endeavor that provides credentials for the candidacy and they'll make a good public servant because they are — fill in the blank — honest, smart, capable of accomplishment, whatever. The second phase is to explain where Smith stands on issues important to the office. Smith is for or against taxes, for or against crime, for or against a cleaner environment, etc. Actually no candidate has ever run a TV spot saying they were for more crime and dirtier air.

The Smith campaign then seeks to contrast their stands on public issues with the positions of the scoundrel who had the gall to become the opposition. Some see these types of ads as attack, while campaigns say they are just bringing to the voters' attention the "differences" between the candidates. Voters have a right, they say, to know the truth.

Toward the end, Smith's campaign might film a "man on the street" commercial, with several typical citizens – usually volunteers right out of the headquarters — speaking into the camera about what a wonderful public servant Smith would be. Campaign strategists believe that showing typical voters supporting their candidate creates a sense of momentum. Hey, if those nice people are for Smith, maybe everybody's for Smith. Finally, in the last few days, Smith will appear "face on camera" and ask for the vote on Election Day. Strategists believe typical voters want to see the candidate actually ask for the order. Sometimes this will be the only time the candidate appears on camera, thus proving to the voters that he or she is capable of speaking in coherent sentences. Little do they know that the spot they're seeing is the result of 55 "takes."

Here are some stories from political TV producers telling, in their own words, how they go about the business of winning campaigns on the tube.

Old Gingrich Film Proves Useful

Factoid: Tennessee 6th district Congressman Bart Gordon faced Republican challenger Steve Gill in 1994, narrowly winning by just 2,174 votes. In a 1996 re-run, Gordon won handily by a 54-42 margin.

Republican challenger Steve Gill, an attorney who is now on the radio in Nashville, ran two successive times against Congressman Mark Gordon in Tennessee's 6th district. We've worked for Gordon since 1984, but 1994 and 1996 were his two toughest elections.

Newt Gingrich in mid-1994 was not a name many people were familiar with, though even back then he was a master at raising money. Gingrich came to Nashville and held a fundraiser for Gill at the Ryman Auditorium where the Grand Ole Opry was born.

At the time, John Rowley, who is now my partner, was then an employee no one really knew. We bought a ticket to the fundraiser and Rowley went in with a handheld video camera and recorded the whole thing. In August of 1994, Gill stood on the stage with a sort of forced jocularity that often erupts at these things and said,

"People ask me why I want to go to Washington to work with this guy." That line meant nothing in 1994, but in 1996 it was different.

We held onto that video footage the whole time, and 10 days before the '96 election, we made a spot called the "Pea Pod" using these great production studios we have in Nashville. We did a drawing of a vine with a pea pod on it. We had Newt Gingrich's and Steve Gill's head pop out of it. The voice-over said, "Newt Gingrich and Steve Gill – two peas in a pod." Then we tied them both together on some controversial issues.

Two-thirds of the way through we run this footage of Gill saying, "People ask me why I want to go to Washington to work with this guy." There was just a beat of silence, then this female voice says, "Good question." It was a devastating ad right at the end.

—Bill Fletcher

Sherwood Sure Would Appreciate Your Vote

Factoid: Beverly Sherwood won a seat in the Virginia House of Delegates in 1993 when she defeated R.C. "Buzz" Sandy in the 29th district, 62-38.

In 1993, I was helping Beverly Sherwood run for the State House of Delegates in the 29th district of Virginia. Beverly had been involved in some local political things but was not well known. We knew that we needed name identification in a big way. This was a state representative district in Winchester, so we decided to do a radio commercial for the local radio station and back it up with some direct mail.

I am looking for a name identification device, something I can do that will give "memorability" to the name. You go through the various kinds of things you can do like a rhyme or a pun. You start thinking about what can make this name memorable.

The radio commercial is a man on the street, and the interviewer says to the man, Do you think Beverly Sherwood would make a good state representative? The man on the street responds by saying, she sure would, whereupon the interviewer says, what did you say? And the man says, "Beverly Sherwood." By picking up on that theme and repeating that pun three or four more times, the commercial ended with Beverly's voice saying, "Would I appreciate your vote on Election Day? I sure would."

The name identification solution was literally solved overnight. The day after the spot went on the air, Beverly herself went into one of the local hotels to arrange a room for a meeting. She went up to the desk and said to the clerk, "Hi, I am Beverly Sherwood," and the clerk said, "Oh, sure would!" It had reached the hotel clerks in one day.

She won the race and is still serving today in the Virginia legislature.   —*Jay Bryant*

Ventura's TV Puts Him Over the Top

Bill Hillsman, a very creative ad man, did Senator Paul Wellstone's campaigns. People wonder where the action figure of Jesse Ventura came from. It came from the combination of Norman Schwartzkopf's head with Robin's body (from Batman and Robin). Hillsman had to make the first two TV ads without Ventura appearing in the spots.

Since we only got the money five days before the election, we did not have time to make the ads using Jesse on camera. We needed a surrogate, a stand-in for the real Ventura. He had been a WWF wrestling figure in the past, so we created the surrogate, which was the Jesse Ventura action figure with the little kid. That received an Emmy for being one of the best ads in the country in 1998.

Hillsman did three ads for the campaign. The first one was with the cute little kid, and the second one was announcing our 72-hour road to victory with the little action figure driving the RV.

We also did a "thinker" ad, the Rodin pose, which was the best ad. Jesse had to come in for half a day to do the shoot. It was filmed on Friday before the election, and we all saw it Friday night. Ventura's daughter, Jade, just went crazy about it because it looked like her dad was posed naked.

On Friday night, I did our marketing test. I took a copy of that ad around to show to six different females, from a conservative preacher's wife to a typical soccer mom. The overwhelming reaction was, "I want to see it again." Every time they saw it, they liked it better and better.

On Halloween night, we sat down at two o'clock in the morning to decide whether or not to go with the "thinker" advertisement. It was very controversial, but it really did what we wanted it to do. Jesse said, "Oh, what the hell–what do we have to lose?"

By that point in time, we knew we had momentum going, so this would either kill us or put us over the top. That ad won us the election.   *—Dean Barkley*

Dog Spot Won't Hunt in Missouri

Factoid: Democrat George Westfall was elected county executive of St. Louis County in 1990 when he defeated H.C. Milford, 55-45.

George R. "Buzz" Westfall was running for county executive in St. Louis County, Missouri, in 1990. We had this negative advertisement citing the incompetent county executive who voted to spend $50,000 for a dog museum and then voted to cut funding for prosecutors. We did this ad that played off the song "How Much Is That Doggie in the Window,?" and we had dogs jumping through hoops, playing jump rope, all from old footage.

St. Louis Magazine named it the best commercial in Missouri and Illinois. Everybody loved the spot, but the survey numbers did not move an inch.

So we put out a similar message, just a straight-copy ad, no cute dogs, that said the incumbent voted for a dog museum and then the next day voted to cut prosecutors. How can we trust him to be our county executive, etc. The numbers went through the roof. The cleverest commercials aren't always the best for moving the campaign forward.   *—Tom King*

Making a TV Spot About a Bull's Operation

Factoid: Iowa Governor Bob Ray was elected five times, in 1968, 1970 and 1972 to two-year terms and in 1974 and 1978 to four-

year terms. In his last election in 1978, he defeated Democrat Jerome Fitzgerald, 58-41.

We did the campaign for Iowa Governor Bob Ray in 1978 when he was running for re-election. We had agreed that the best way for incumbents to run was to run a positive campaign.

Ray said, "I want to run on my record; I'm proud of my record. I think I've done a lot of things for the people of Iowa." He said, "One of the things I think would really be good, even in the Des Moines market, but certainly in all the smaller TV markets, is that we've built a magnificent veterinary medical school at Iowa State. It is the top of the line. The farmers and the whole agricultural industry in our state and the Middle West have benefited from this. I'd like for you to go up there and film something that represents that achievement. I'm particularly proud of the new surgical facilities that have been created there. I'll call the head of the school and we'll set that up so you guys can go there and film that."

We drove up to the university on a day when they were having a major operation. We go into this stainless steel facility, and we don't know what is going on—we just knew they had made arrangements for us to film that day. We go into this large room and in the center is a surgical table.

We set up our lights and cameras, and they tell us when we're ready the doctors will come in and the operation can proceed. We tell them we are now ready anytime they are, at which point the surgical table is lowered by elevator down to a lower level. The animal is placed on this stainless-steel table and then raised back up to where we are.

It's as though the entire thing has been choreographed. The animal rises up into the room at the same time six or seven doctors and nurses all come in. They've scrubbed and they're in their surgical gowns, with their masks and hats. What emerges is this gigantic bull, which must have weighed two tons. It turns out the operation is going to repair the bull's penis.

This is a grand champion bull, which has been so overworked that it is no longer able to function properly, and these doctors are going to do a major repair on this prize bull. This is what we've been sent to film.

I say to the cameraman, "Obviously, we are not going to have a bull's penis on camera here. You've got to shoot this from the other side of the bull. The doctors can be doing whatever they're doing, and we'll just describe this as a routine surgical procedure."

It was all I could do to restrain the crew, who were in hysterics about this. Most of them were city guys from New York, and they were just having quite a time. —*John Deardourff*

CHAPTER 12

Debates Don't Usually Matter

☆ ☆ ☆

Very few debates between candidates at all levels make any difference in the outcome of the election. There are a few exceptions, but 19 times out of 20, a political debate produces no winner and no loser. And, on top of that, debates between candidates for any office beneath the presidency usually have such a small audience that even if there was a debate winner, nobody would know.

President Gerald Ford stepped in it on October 6, 1976, in San Francisco, in the second debate with Jimmy Carter when he denied that Eastern Europe was under Soviet domination. Carter was the winner because Ford lost it. The 2000 debates between Al Gore and George Bush are better examples of debates with not much lasting outcome. Other than Gore's huffing and puffing and Bush's occasional malapropisms, it's hard to remember anything meaningful about those three debates. Historians still point to the 1960 debate between Vice President Richard Nixon and Senator John F. Kennedy. The winner or loser mantel is clouded because, they say, TV viewers scored the debate for Kennedy, but radio listeners, who were still a large share of the total audience at that time, gave it to Nixon.

But the press demands that candidates for office at all levels stand forthright for debates. The press is a lot more interested in debates than candidates or their supporters are because the reporters and TV faces are usually included in the panel, which invariably tries to play "stump the candidate" with inane questions of little interest to the general public.

Here are some stories about candidates for local and statewide office in debates.

Still in Fighting Trim at 80

Factoid: North Dakotan Quentin Burdick was elected to a sixth term in the U.S. Senate in 1988, when he defeated Republican challenger Earl Strinden, 59-39.

Quentin Burdick was first elected to the U.S. Senate from North Dakota in 1960. A Fargo lawyer, he had been elected to the U.S. House two years earlier. After a tough race in 1960 that Burdick won by less than a percentage point, he was easily elected for the next four terms.

In 1988 Earl Strinden, an aggressive political figure, challenged the 80-year-old Burdick. Strinden, 20 years younger than the senior senator, had been the state House majority leader for 12 years and had served in the state legislature for 22 years.

Strinden took after Burdick with a passion. His main campaign theme was that the elderly Burdick should "Come home, Quentin. It's time to come home." Burdick, though, prided himself in his physical fitness and was said to even practice judo at a high level. Some suggested he might have earned a black belt.

On the night of the live debate, the host invited the two candidates to shake hands before the debate got under way. Strinden immediately popped out from behind his lectern and marched boldly across the stage to confront Burdick face to face, obviously forgetting that Burdick was a judo expert. As Strinden moved forward and extended his hand, Burdick took it and deftly tossed him off the podium.   *—Don Ringe*

A Carpetbagger by Choice

Factoid: Congressman George E. Brown defeated Republican Howard Snider in 1972 by a 56-43 margin in the 38th district in California. Brown had been elected to Congress for four terms in the nearby 29th district, and then ran unsuccessfully for U.S. Senate in 1970.

We were doing a campaign in the 38th district of California, after the 1970 census and the re-districting. George Brown had been a congressman for four terms in the 29th district, from 1964 to 1970. Because of the way the lines were drawn, Brown, as a Democrat, would be required to leave his present home and move a few miles across the line into the district from which he wanted to run for office.

We were doing the work for Howard Snider, Brown's Republican opponent. We had this carpetbagging issue, and we were going to nail the guy with it. The polls showed that the people did not want someone from outside their district coming in to run for office.

We were waiting for just the right time to pull the trigger on that issue. September or early October, during the debate, was the right time to spring it. Our guy gets it all ready and when it comes to the opportune time, he accuses Brown of being a carpetbagger and all the things that go with it.

Brown waited patiently for his turn, and in one sentence he completely turned off the carpetbagging issue. He said, "I would just like to ask the audience, why wouldn't I want to live among the people I plan to represent?"   —*Gary Lawrence*

BOOK THREE

The Myths and Reality of Campaign Strategy

☆ ☆ ☆

S uppose for a moment you are a businessperson who decides to open a retail store selling television sets. Your business plan calls for a grand opening on January 1, but you intend to shut down the business on the evening of the first Tuesday in November. You're only going to be in business for a little more than 10 months.

Now to make matters more interesting still, say your business plan calls for achieving a 51 percent market share – but you're only going to sell those TV sets on the last day. A real going-out-of-business sale.

To complicate the problem a little more, your cousin Vinny has opened a retail store across the street, also selling TV sets. He, too, understands that success will be measured by getting 51 percent of the market share. In the business schools, they call this competition.

To make this all work, you'll need financing, which is called fundraising in the political business. You'll certainly need some advertising. You'll probably want to identify a bunch of customers before the big sale day, which is called voter identification in the political world, and you'll want to call them on the day of the big sale to remind them that this is the big event, not unlike voter turnout in political campaigns. You might sell a few TV sets before the close of business in November, a process in the political business known as absentee balloting.

When all the dust settles on that first Tuesday after the first Monday in November, only one is going to be successful. The other loses his shirt, so to speak. What determines who wins and who loses? It could be any number of things, like location or the compelling nature of the advertising. Maybe one store has a hotter brand of television sets, maybe one store got a better source of financing, maybe one store had a better sales staff.

To put the wrap on the fable, we learn that Vinny hired a business consultant back at the beginning who helped him write a better business plan. As a consequence, Vinny convinced a larger share of the television buying public that he had better sets, he was in a more convenient location, buyers would like his friendly staff better, and buyers could get sets delivered with no money down and no payments for six months – a much better deal than they could get across the street. Vinny, it turns out, had a better strategy.

Vinny and his consultant had done a survey of the television buying public and carved out a 51 percent market share by getting a larger percentage of the new, young households to buy Vinny's sets, because they were attracted to the "no money down" and "no payments for six months" proposition. Vinny's television advertising didn't spring this attractive offer on the buying public until late in October, when it was too late for you (at the store across the street) to come up with a more appealing offer.

Political campaign strategists are the gurus, or wizards, who think about things like 51 percent market share. Several words or phrases are descriptive of campaign strategy. *Positioning* is a word often used to describe the process of getting a candidate positioned in the voters' minds so that 51 percent is attainable.

Some strategists believe there are basically nine different reasons why voters pick and choose particular candidates to support. Determining which of the nine is most important to a candidate is why they pay wizards the big bucks. The biggest reason most people vote for a candidate is simple partisanship. Half of the American electorate is strongly partisan, with about a quarter of the voters on the Democratic side and a quarter on the Republican side. An elderly patron down a dirt road in rural Louisiana described partisanship like this: "My daddy voted for the Democrats, my granddaddy voted for the Democrats and my great granddaddy voted for the Democrats because Abraham Lincoln was a Republican, and we're not changing now."

Voters with a lot less partisan bent pick candidates for reasons other than the party label. Some make their ballot choices based on philosophy. While liberal tracks fairly closely with Democrats and conservative tracks fairly closely with Republicans, there are some differences. Single-issue voters are the next biggest block, with some voters choosing their candidates strictly because of their stand on a specific issue, like abortion, guns or environment, to name a few. Members of certain coalitions also tend to support the same kinds of candidates. Examples would be labor groups, which typically vote for Democrats more than Republicans, while business groups such as the chamber of commerce tend to vote for Republicans more than Democrats.

Campaigns put together large street organizations with the sole purpose of having volunteers knock on doors and saying, "I'm working for Mary Smith for state representative. I hope you'll read this information about her and think about voting for Mary. She'll be great in the state House." Thousands of votes are won each election by the campaign with the best street organization.

Some voters simply vote for or against candidates because they either like them better or dislike them more. Usually these opinions are the results of paid media.

Finally, some candidates simply buy elections. And we're not talking about the way they still do it in some counties in the South, with $10 bills. In 2000 Jon Corzine of New Jersey bought an election for U.S. Senate. He ran enough advertising on television, radio, newspaper, billboards and anything else they could slap his face on, and finally 51 percent of the voters in New Jersey said, "That's enough. We give up. We're going to vote for you." Corzine's $65 million overwhelmed Republican Bob Franks, but he also overwhelmed nearly 1.3 million voters.

After all the heavy thinking is done creating a winning strategy, the high-priced wizards will admit that most days they'd rather be lucky than good. *Buena suerte.*

CHAPTER 13

Strategies That Seem to Work

☆ ☆ ☆

A month, six months or a year before the election, the campaign strategist figures out the three or four certain things that have to take place during the course of the campaign, and if they do, then their candidate has a very good chance of winning. The events come to pass and lo and behold the candidate wins, and the strategist is seen as a genius. Or a very lucky fortuneteller.

One of the things a strategist must always gauge is the depth of the political tide running for or against one party or the other. Almost every election year, voters tend to vote a little more for the Republicans or a little more for the Democrats. In presidential election years, for instance, voters tend to be more sharply partisan. If you're a Democrat in a presidential year, there's a very good chance you'll be voting a straight party ticket. Same on the Republican side. But in non-presidential years, other things come into play. Are voters going to throw the rascals out? In those times, perhaps it's not so good to be an incumbent. Or maybe voters are happy with the status quo. In that case, perhaps it's good to be in office seeking re-election. Strategists know there is always a tide running, one way or the other.

In the post Watergate elections of 1974, the Republicans lost a net of 48 seats in the House of Representatives, driving their number from 192 down to 144. In 1994, the Democrats lost a net of 54 seats in the House, from 258 down to 204, and lost the majority for the first time since the elections of 1952. Those were tsunami waves, for sure.

Here are some stories revealing strategies that were successful in real campaigns.

The Winning Strategy on a Bar Napkin

Factoid: Reform Party candidate Jesse Ventura was elected governor of Minnesota in 1998 with 38% of the vote. St. Paul Mayor Norm Coleman, the Republican, got 34% and DFL candidate Hubert Humphrey III got 28%.

The first big public event that Jesse Ventura went to was the Minneapolis St. Patrick's Day parade. A CBS news crew was in town and looking for something to do, and they wanted to look into this Jesse Ventura thing. This TV crew followed us on the parade. We printed up 12,000 pieces of literature for a parade that is six blocks long in Minneapolis. We came out with the "Jesse buck," where we had the big dollar bill with Jesse Ventura's picture in the middle, with our reform agenda on the back.

Ventura was on a convertible and people were crowding up during the parade, asking him to sign the buck. We ran out of literature four blocks into that parade. The CBS crew was impressed at the overwhelming recognition and support Ventura was getting.

Before the St. Patrick's Day parade, Doug Friedline, Ventura and myself sat down at Famous Dave's Restaurant in Maple Grove and plotted out our campaign strategy on the back of a bar napkin. We said we had to get him into double-digits support, about 20 percent, without spending any money by the primary.

We had to get Ventura into all the debates, which was a critical thing. We knew if he wasn't included in the debates, Ventura would be dead. We had to get the public money that was available to major party candidates. Since we were a major party, there was a $350,000 pot of gold for us if we met the criteria.

We also had to figure out how to raise enough money to do a last-minute media blitz to really get him over the top.

We knew we had to get a 10 percent higher voter turnout than they expected. We knew we needed a 60 percent turnout in order to win. We had to expand the electorate.

We needed to target the young voters, to get them interested in the election. We used black and ugly green colors, kind of anti-establishment colors, in our campaign materials. We also sold T-shirts that read "Retaliate in 98." It was those anti-establishment black T-shirts that did it; we sold 20,000 at the state fair. The sales of the T-shirts raised the money we needed to get the public money. We actually had the key to how to accomplish all this on the back of a bar napkin. That was our great campaign strategy.

—Dean Barkley

Veterinarian Versus Lobbyist in Colorado

Factoid: Colorado Congressman Wayne Allard was elected to the U.S. Senate in 1996, beating Democrat Ted Strickland by a 51-46 margin.

In the 1996 race for U.S. Senate in Colorado, Congressman Wayne Allard had been representing eastern Colorado. He's a very conservative, two-term member of Congress, and he wasn't very well known outside his district. A hotshot by the name of Ted Strickland was opposing him. Strickland is a well-known name in Colorado. He was well tied in with Governor Romer's crowd as well as with the business crowd. He had very strong environmental credentials at a time when the environment was a tough issue. On paper, we were on the wrong side of that campaign.

In putting together the campaign, Walt Klein, Allard's consultant, made sure we looked at all the fundamentals. We did one of those candidates A and B series in an early survey. Without using their names or party affiliations, we polled people: If based on this description, would you be more likely to vote for candidate A or candidate B?

Before he had been in Congress, Wayne Allard was a veterinarian. Strickland had been a lawyer and lobbyist. On the candidate A/B series, these things popped out fairly significantly.

On Denver television, the campaign spent more than half the money we were going to spend on TV advertising throughout the campaign, in the month of September putting forth this simple message: "Who would you rather have as your U.S. senator – a veterinarian or a lawyer/lobbyist?"

It was a very simple, black-and-white spot. We beat that message into the ground. The race was actually over by the time that spot got off the air. Strickland never got traction again. He attacked us. Allard had a very harsh position on abortion. Allard had a very harsh position on the death penalty.

But none of the attacks ever stuck. Looking at the "verbatims" in October, a month after the spot was on the air, respondents were asked, "Why are you voting this way?" and the answer was, "I'd rather have a veterinarian than a lobbyist."   —*David Sackett*

The Stangeland Plan

Factoid: Arlan Stangeland was elected to U.S. House of Representatives in a special election in Minnesota's 7th district in 1977. He defeated Michael Sullivan, the DFL nominee, 58-37.

We did Arlan Stangeland's campaigns for three or four elections. Arlan was the kind of guy for which an 800-vote margin was a major win. He was always right on the edge, and most of it he earned himself.

In 1982, Stangeland was really in bad shape. We weren't going to win. I asked Arlan what he thought was the one thing people around there really wanted. He thought about it for a while, and then he said, "They probably want $8 a bushel soybeans. But that's not going to happen. You know what they really want? They want to keep the Great Lakes from freezing over because when they do, they have to sell their crops right after the harvest when the prices are the lowest. If they could keep the lakes from freezing, they could wait until the prices went up, then sell the crop at the height of the market."

I asked how he thought we could possibly solve that problem. He told me how the Russians were fooling around with these icebreakers. In order to get into their ice-locked harbors, they would put an icebreaker up front and three or four ships behind it, and they would just push through the ice into their Arctic ports. We weren't able to do that because we didn't have icebreakers that powerful.

So Arlan came up with what was called the Stangeland Plan. It consisted of our buying two huge Russian icebreakers in order to build an ice-free port in Duluth. Part of the plan included putting up grain storage facilities in special parts of the Great Lakes so that farmers would be able to sell their corn, barley and soybeans when the markets were right. And we had farmers saying, "That's what we need. We need people in Washington who think like that."

Stangeland won the election by about 5,000 votes, which was a landslide for him. People kind of knew the plan would never happen, but it was nice of Stangeland to think of it.

The next thing you know, the Stangeland Plan is in front of the Senate Agriculture Committee, and one of the ag subcommittees is looking at it and a bill is written.

We know that it's impossible. This is not going to happen. If it did happen, the stuff they shipped out of there would cost about $3 million a bushel. Not only would you have to break ice in Lake Superior, but you'd also have to break ice all the way up the St. Lawrence River.

It got tabled, but it was an interesting example of life following art.

—Steve Sandler

CHAPTER 14

Dynamic Events That
Re-deal the Cards

☆ ☆ ☆

There's an old saying in politics that you have to play the hand
you're dealt. The candidate is who he or she is, and not a lot
can be done to change it. The political tide is running for or against
your candidate, and nothing can be done to change it. The important issues of the day are pretty much cast in steel, and not much
can be done to change it. You play the hand you're dealt.

Occasionally, however, some event takes place and the cards get
reshuffled. Everybody gets to play a new hand. State Senator Sid
Morrison was challenging five-term Congressman Mike
McCormick in Washington's 4ᵗʰ district in 1980. Morrison's
campaign was tramping along until May 18, when the Mount St.
Helens volcano erupted, knocking off 1,314 feet of the mountain's
summit and spreading volcanic ash several inches thick throughout
the district. The following Sunday, the Morrison campaign's volunteers had shoveled ash out of many church parking lots. The ash
"marked" the skins on eastern Washington's famous apple crop.
Morrison was on radio stations throughout the district telling farmers how to deal with the disaster. And Morrison was able to get the
state apple board to make a special designation for Mount St.
Helens apples. He was dealt a new hand and played it very well, en
route to beating McCormick 57-43 in November.

On a bigger stage in 1980, President Jimmy Carter had virtually
no control over the hostage-taking in Iran. That he couldn't get the

hostages released before the election proved to the American people that Carter lacked effectiveness. He didn't play his hand very well, and Ronald Reagan was elected president.

Here are some stories about campaigns that went through dynamic events.

Lindsay Goes to Harlem When King Is Slain

Factoid: Republican John V. Lindsay was elected four times, from 1958 to 1964, in the 17th congressional district of New York. He was twice elected mayor of New York City, in 1965 and 1969. He ran unsuccessfully for president as a Democrat in 1972 and unsuccessfully for the U.S. Senate in 1980.

John Lindsay, love him or hate him, had come from the silk stocking district, a very wealthy area of New York City. Due to the 1965 mayoral campaign, he had decided to get out and mingle to see how the rest of the city lived. He was genuinely shocked by what he found, and he badly wanted to make it better.

This meant going to communities that really had had no representation, such as the Irish and Italian neighborhoods. The black and Hispanic communities with growing populations had never had much help from elected officials. Schools were bad and neighborhoods didn't get sanitation service.

Services that were normally taken for granted in the rest of New York City just didn't happen in those neighborhoods. Lindsay worked very hard in those disenfranchised communities to do what government should do, which is to provide the same level of service to everybody.

By the time we entered the second Lindsay mayoral campaign, we knew we were in trouble. And when we took the polls, I don't think Lindsay had 30 percent of the vote. When you asked people open-ended questions, they'd talk about the school strike. They'd talk about the garbage. They'd talk about all the mistakes Lindsay had made.

We then had a choice to make about the kind of campaign we were going to run. Money was fairly limited because Lindsay had lost the Republican primary, so in the general election he ran on the Liberal Party line, which didn't have a large number of members.

I'll never forget when Martin Luther King was assassinated on April 4, 1968. Lindsay was attending the theater with his wife. When he got the word, he immediately called me and asked me to come get him. I went to the theater to pick him up and we went back to Gracie Mansion, where we picked up Pat Veccio, Lindsay's bodyguard, and Harry O'Donnell. Then we drove up to Harlem.

That night Harlem was just writhing with action. Fires had been started and mobs of people crammed the street. The cops stayed on the side streets. There was no direct confrontation, but you could tell the tension was building.

I got out of the car with Lindsay and Veccio. We looked down the street, and as far as you could see across 125th Street people were walking toward the East River.

I said to myself, "This is it. Give yourself to God, because your ass is going to stay in the street." Lindsay just stood up and spread his arms and expressed that he knew what they were feeling. He had such credibility. If it had been anyone else, they would have thrown him in the flipping river. With John Lindsay, they didn't do that. They started to mingle around fighting over who would protect the mayor. Things finally settled down. For me, it was a frightening experience.

Racial tension was an ongoing crisis nationally. Lindsay had been working very diligently on race relations and improving opportunities for the black community. The assassination of Martin Luther King was the spark that set off the conflagration. In most major cities, there were problems, but people in New York sensed that Lindsay had done a great service.

Actually, I'm not sure Lindsay would have won re-election without the riots around the country. It was really a strange thing to see. The problems happened almost everywhere else, but not here. And it didn't happen in New York because of John Lindsay.

The idea that Lindsay could win re-election on the Liberal Party line was impossible. Unthinkable. Well, he did it. It's not easy. It's not usual. But it is possible. People cling to shibboleths. This is America; anything's possible.   —*David Garth*

White Beats Clinton on Car Tags and Cubans

Factoid: In 1980, Republican Frank White upset incumbent Arkansas Governor Bill Clinton, 52-45.

In 1978, Arkansas Attorney General Bill Clinton was elected governor of Arkansas. At that time, his wife, Hillary Rodham, refused to take the last name of her husband. He was featured on the front cover of *Parade* magazine as the future United States president.

A one-time Democrat, Frank White was a back-slapping, good old boy Navy Academy graduate and Air Force pilot who later had worked as a stockbroker gambler. White became a Republican and filed for governor in 1980 against Clinton. White didn't have a whole lot of money and had no idea what he was doing, but he didn't know what he couldn't do either.

Pollster Lance Tarrance and I concocted this survey mechanism to identify yellow-dog Democrats who might be interested in conservative issues, but were particularly interested in the very high level of unemployment at the end of the Carter administration. Unemployment was about 14 percent in the state of Arkansas.

Clinton had raised the cost of car tags in Arkansas, and though it was a very small tax, it was something Arkansans could relate to because it was cash out of their pockets and they didn't have any cash. Secondly, Clinton had agreed with President Carter to house all of the Cuban refugees in Arkansas. The Cubans, not happy to be locked up in prison-like conditions, were rioting and burning the facility, which got a lot of press attention.

Clinton didn't look all that hot in the polls, but certainly well enough to beat White. At some point, Clinton allegedly punched out his adviser, Dick Morris, because Morris brought him a poll he didn't like. While it was only an allegation, not a proven fact, the fisticuff story went through the Arkansas political and press community.

White went on the air with the Cubans and the car tags television ads, linking both to the unemployment and inflation rate. We were able to convince the Reagan campaign to make an appearance in Arkansas, which was very helpful to White. Incidentally, White actually ran ahead of Clinton by about 30,000 votes.   —*Bill Lee*

CHAPTER 15

The Art of Counter-punching

☆ ☆ ☆

Many hard-fought campaigns in the modern age, since the 1960s, have found it necessary to survive through successful counter-punching. Candidate A smacks candidate B with a negative TV commercial. Candidate B returns fire – a counter-punch. Candidate A then counters candidate B's counter-punch with a counter-punch of his or her own. And so on and so forth.

It's in these exchanges, mostly through negative advertising on television or radio, that close campaigns are won, or, as the case may be, lost. The best counter-puncher is often the only candidate left standing at the bloody, bitter end.

There are several rules of engagement to consider in the art of counter-punching. When attacked by the opponent, a very good option is often to do absolutely nothing. But snap judgments have to be made. Is the opponent's attack going to stick? State Senator Ron Twilegar attacked Congressman Larry Craig on the abortion issue in their Senate race in Idaho in 1990. Twilegar's TV commercial, showing coat hangers swirling around a dry cleaner's clothes rack, was so poorly done even Twilegar's own supporters howled for him to get the ad off the air. Craig, who had two response ads in the can on the abortion issue, chose not to air either ad and won handily with 61 percent.

The second option when under attack is to deny the charge. Congressman Gary Condit was under attack from the press in the disappearance of intern Chandra Levy. You'd have to have spent the summer of 2001 in Mongolia not to be aware that the press suspected Condit of foul play, or at least being guilty of not telling all he knew. His defense: deny, deny, deny.

The third option, when faced with attack, is to admit that the charge is true but explain effectively that it's not what it seems. It's true I voted for that pay raise in the Senate in 1991, but it's not what it seems. The choices were to vote "yes" on a pay raise and eliminate honoraria, where special-interest groups were paying off politicians, or vote "no" on a pay raise and leave the honoraria process in place. It was one or the other.

And the last option, often the weapon of choice these days, is to counter-punch. Make no mention of the opponent's attack, but launch an attack on the opponent for an act even more egregious.

These are stories about the art of counter-punching in the political arena.

Giving Dukakis a Hard Time in Massachusetts

Factoid: In the 1988 presidential election, Vice President George Bush carried 40 states en route to defeating Massachusetts Governor Michael Dukakis. However, Dukakis won in his home state, 53-45.

In the 1988 general election, my job was to go to Boston and drive Governor Michael Dukakis nuts. I tend to overachieve. It is really unusual for actions in any one state to drive the campaign; it is usually the other way around.

We did little things. The Bush office in Boston was in a strategic corner around from the back of the State House. It is right on the road Dukakis had to drive down when he went to his governor's office. The Bush campaign, in 1988, had one billboard in the entire country. It was in downtown Boston and ensured that anytime Dukakis went to work at the State Capitol, he had to see this big Bush sign.

We did a couple of interesting things. I believe the rationale for the Dukakis presidency was the so-called "Massachusetts miracle." If you take a miracle and make it a myth, there is no rationale for a Dukakis presidency. This is what Al Gore tried to do to George W. Bush in 2000, but they found out the Bush miracle in Texas was real. This is why it never worked.

The first stage was that the north and central American Greek Orthodox Church had their annual dinner that year in Boston. I wanted to have the vice president come to Boston several times to do events. As you can imagine, the campaign was reluctant to bring any Republican to Boston for any reason, let alone running against the governor of the state.

I convinced the campaign to let the vice president speak at this church meeting. Dukakis spoke at lunch and Bush spoke after Dukakis. Dukakis was Greek Orthodox, but he was not in good relations with the church because of some of his stands.

Bush, however, had a great relationship with Archbishop Iakovos. The archbishop had a personal political affection for Bush, as did many of the members of the church.

Dukakis came in and got a tepid response. I made sure the press was there. Bush came in a couple hours later and people were standing on chairs, waving their handkerchiefs. It was a big story, not just that he was warmly received by the church members, but in comparison to the tepid response for Dukakis. For me, the key was bringing him into Boston.

Using that as my wedge, the next thing we did was work to get the Boston Police Officer's Union to endorse the vice president. One of our theories was that Dukakis was a legitimate liberal. Part of that philosophy was that he was soft on crime. Who best to make that point than his home police department?

After we spent many hours with the Boston Police Officer's Union, they had a big vote on endorsements. They endorsed the vice president, despite the fact Senator Kennedy and Boston Mayor Ray Flynn lobbied them. The next day, the vice president came in to accept the endorsement.

That picture of him with the police officers played across the entire country. It was a great event, even though it was just the local police officers' endorsement. It made the point we were trying to make all along that those who know Dukakis best realize he is a liberal on crime. It was a huge success.

Three days later, just to give him one more tickle, we had the Springfield police endorse Bush also. The idea was to drive him crazy one more time in his home state.

The most remembered part of all this was the problem of cleaning up Boston Harbor. The truth is, Dukakis was just a stubborn governor, and because he wouldn't do a couple of things he was supposed to do he lost the federal funding to clean up the harbor. Boston Harbor is one of the most famous and most scenic harbors in America. We just wanted to make the point, by using the harbor as a backdrop, that Dukakis was not a good manager of the environment.

A good friend of mine, Patrick Percell, was the publisher of the *Boston Herald*. The newspaper was going to do a poll. I told him the vice president was coming in to Boston. He was the only person I told. At this point, we were about 12 points behind in national surveys. I could sense it starting to come around.

I felt the polling was closer in Massachusetts than it was nationally. Perhaps it was close enough to be in single digits. We made a deal that the newspaper would print the results of their poll and it would come out the day of Bush's visit.

We decided that if the poll was a favorable one for Bush, I'd have him walk off the plane carrying the front page of the *Boston Herald*, which would give the *Herald* great national press. He thought it was a pretty good deal. I promised Percell an interview with the vice president either way.

I'll never forget waiting for the first run of the newspaper to come out that morning. When it did, it carried the headline "Poll shocker: Bush ties Dukakis in Massachusetts." The poll showed us dead even. The vice president walked off the plane holding that headline up, and it made a huge national story.

We went up Boston Harbor in the boat and did it again. Very seldom are you lucky enough to be in a state where you can do things that actually impact a national campaign. I've loved the *Boston Herald* ever since. —*Ron Kaufman*

Coverdell Wins Second Senate Term With 'Soap Lady'

Factoid: Paul Coverdell was elected to a second term in the U.S. Senate in 1998 when he defeated Democrat Michael Coles, 52-45.

Senator Paul Coverdell in 1998 was running against Michael

Coles, founder of the Great American Cookie Company, which was worth about $50 million. Coles was a very attractive candidate, a great speaker and a great philanthropist. He'd been quoted in the press as saying he'd be willing to spend whatever it took to win this race.

Coverdell was internally known in Washington as hard-working, he had a great position in leadership and he worked for all the right things. But he wasn't a very good external politician. He had a squeaky voice and this quirky style that reminded everyone of Dana Carvey on *Saturday Night Live* doing George Bush.

Coles had the money and Coverdell had a record. The Coverdell team narrowed down the top 10 vulnerable areas. This is six months before anyone is even printing bumper stickers. The campaign team came up with a response to every one of Coverdell's vulnerabilities on our list. We had the details of how we were going to respond. We got to the point where Coverdell wanted to see the actual scripts of the ad responses.

We decided that even though the campaign was far better financed than a vast majority of campaigns, we did not have the money to go out and shoot 30 response ads, edit them and have them in the can.

So the idea we came up with was called the Soap Lady. The Soap Lady concept was very controversial internally and not entirely supported by the senator.

Now, keep in mind that our opponent was not from Georgia. He was from Brooklyn, New York, and you just can't take the Brooklyn out of someone. Our hope was that the more we tied Coles to Brooklyn, the less people would like him in Georgia.

We found a wonderful little old lady with leathery suntanned skin who wore bright orange lipstick and flashy clothes. We basically implied that this was Coles's mother, and for every charge they would hit Coverdell with, she'd respond to it. The whole premise was that she was going to wash out Michael Coles's mouth with soap every time he tried to go after Paul Coverdell.

If we thought it through more, she could become even funnier and more outrageous as the election went on. We presented this idea to the team, and they pretty well liked the approach. The senator very reluctantly went along with it.

Coverdell shows it to his wife, Nancy, and she absolutely hates the ad. Somehow, about this time, Coles hits us with some sort of attack. So what do we have ready? The Soap Lady.

Coverdell had a very precise way of speaking. He called Marty Ryall, the campaign manager, and left him a message that Marty later played for me, after we'd run the spot for one day. The message said, "Marty, it's Paul. Nancy doesn't like the Soap Lady. I don't like the Soap Lady. The Soap Lady goes." And he hung up.

Marty and I were both distraught because we'd put a lot of effort into this series of ads. But we pulled the Soap Lady on Saturday.

Coverdell was one of the hardest-working candidates in the world. He'd be on a private plane at five o'clock in the morning on Saturday. He would hit 10 different cities with well-organized events in each city. He would shake the hand of every person in attendance at each stop. And every person came away thinking he was their best friend.

The very next day after we pulled the ad, he called both Ryall and me. He told us that wherever he went, people were bringing him bars of soap to autograph. People loved the Soap Lady. People told him he was a genius for having the Soap Lady – this was a brilliant way of getting out his response in a pleasant, lighthearted way. From that moment on, the Soap Lady overrode Nancy's complaints. It was a huge success in that campaign.   —*Fred Davis*

CHAPTER 16

When the Opponent Buys Ink by the Barrel

☆ ☆ ☆

No matter which side of the partisan spectrum your campaign is coming from, you're absolutely convinced the press is against you and for the other guy. This goes back even further than the advent of yellow journalism when Joseph Pulitzer's *New York World* battled it out with William Randolph Hearst's *New York Journal* to see who could inflame Americans the quickest with their overblown reporting on the Spanish American War. For the first three-fourths of America's history , newspapers were the sole source of news for the citizenry. No TV, no radio, no Internet. And while there have been telephones for more than a century, nobody figured out push-polling until about 15 years ago.

Newspapers eventually gave way to reasonable reporting, at least on most front pages around the country. Two holdouts were the *Manchester Union Leader* in New Hampshire and the *Las Vegas Sun*, where the publishers continued, until just a few years ago, to editorialize on the top fold of page one. Publisher Hank Greenspun, in the *Sun*, attacked Republican gubernatorial candidate Ed Fike with scathing front-page editorials and accompanying slanted stories on page one for the entire month before the 1970 election in Nevada. Greenspun's trumped up charges embarrassed most legitimate newspaper editors, but Fike lost to Mike O'Callaghan, 48-44.

The national press corps ganged up on Ollie North when he challenged Virginia Senator Chuck Robb in 1994. The press regurgitated all of the Iran Contra charges day after day through the last month of the campaign, while Robb sat idly by and won narrowly, 46-43. The country hadn't seen a press feeding frenzy like that since the endless attacks on Senator Dan Quayle following his nomination as vice president in 1988.

Today, most professionals in the campaign business would agree that the press – the print version, along with television reporting and radio news – doesn't hold much sway over campaigns, except on rare occasions. Here are some stories where the press played a role in the outcome of elections.

'Textual Deviant' Makes the Plain Dealer

Factoid: Vice President Hubert Humphrey narrowly lost Ohio to Richard Nixon in 1968. Nixon got 45% — and 24 electoral votes — to Humphrey's 43%. George Wallace got 12%.

Vice President Hubert Humphrey, in 1968, was going to be addressing the Downtown Club in Cleveland, Ohio, the next day. I was doing the press briefing, and there was room for 70 to 100 members of the press to come in to get their Secret Service accreditation.

I handed out the text of his speech for the next day. I gave the rules: nothing for attribution, we aren't going to give you this or that, and we'll take questions at such and such a time. It was the usual ground rules.

One reporter stands up and says, "Will he be sticking to the text?"

I said, "Well, you know, he's a textual deviant."

They all laughed. I was really using the good stuff.

I get back to the Cleveland Sheraton, feeling pretty good about the day, and somebody comes in and says, "Have you seen the bulldog edition of the Cleveland *Plain Dealer*?" On the front page in a box is the "textual deviant" story and it obviously looks like a typo.

I went down to the cigar store and bought all the papers they had. There must have been 25 or 30 of them. I hid them under the bed in my hotel room. Norman Sherman, Humphrey's press secretary, came up to the room laughing about the story. Meanwhile I'm in the bathroom throwing up.

I was so upset about it that I did something I've never done before. I called the publisher, Thomas Vale, and probably got him out of bed. He said, "Who is this?" I said, "It doesn't matter because if we don't get this taken care of, I ain't going to be anybody tomorrow. I'll be dead. There's a box in bold on the front page and it violates the rules we agreed to."

He said, "I don't even have the paper here."

"You gotta call somebody because that's got to go".

He must not have wanted to be wakened again because it was gone the next morning in the regular edition. The Secret Service was all over the hotel looking for a newspaper to give the vice president in his suite that night. I had them all under my bed.

—D.J. Leary

Keeping Giuliani Cool With the Press

Factoid: In the closest mayoral race in New York City history, in 1989, David Dinkins edged Rudy Giuliani to become the city's first black mayor. In a re-run in 1993, Giuliani won by 45,000 votes.

Rudy Giuliani made a second try for mayor in New York City after he had run for mayor in 1989 and lost. He had entered the 1989 campaign very well known and was a popular attorney from the district of New York, with a lot of high-profile prosecutions.

But he was a very bad candidate in 1989, going through a primary against Ron Lauder, who spent several million dollars tearing him down. He didn't handle himself very well with the press. As U.S. attorney for the southern district, he had gotten pretty good press because he could control the flow of information. Reporters were nice to him because they knew they would get information from him.

As soon as he stepped out of the prosecutor role and into the role of candidate, the press in New York was not that kind. Giuliani ran and performed very badly as a candidate, and crime was increasing. There were a lot of racial tensions in the city.

Four years later, in 1993, the number of murders in the city had gone up dramatically. We had a pogrom in Crown Heights, a Jewish community, where they were under siege for three days. The police really did nothing to stop the violence and rioting in the streets. A similar incident occurred up in a Dominican neighborhood in which a cop shot a drug dealer and people rioted. Mayor Dinkins still did not back the cops; rather, he backed the rioters. Now we had the right climate for Giuliani's message.

But still we had the problem that he was not a very good candidate. When I first came onto the campaign, David Garth said he wanted me to work with Giuliani. He said I needed to keep him level so we could get out there and win the race on an issue.

In my first experience with Giuliani, a reporter was calling him about some lame issue regarding a contract for a parking garage. Giuliani had prosecuted this company for a contract they had reached with the Koch administration that involved bribery. He prosecuted the company, they cleared out all the officers and now they were coming back for another contract with the city. After they had cleaned out, there was a letter from Giuliani saying, now you've cleaned up the mess, we don't see any impairment in getting a contract. This reporter was calling up about that letter because Mayor Dinkins was saying Giuliani was giving the okay for the contract. It was a nothing issue.

I sat down with Rudy and explained what the reporter would ask him and what his responses should be. I gave him the questions, and he answered them. We went back over it again, and then he called up the reporter. The reporter asked the first question and all that preparation went right down the tubes. Rudy had a total meltdown on the guy, complete with cursing. I was stunned.

My job was to alert Garth when we had a problem on the campaign. I called him up immediately and told him Giuliani could not deal with this guy and had a complete meltdown. Consequently, we had a sit-down with Rudy and told him he should not let his emotions get involved.

The end result of that first experience with a reporter was that I had to spend the rest of the campaign traveling with Rudy every day. He is a very hard-working guy, going 20 hours a day, then usually getting a little catnap. He is the same way as a mayor. He visits the neighborhoods and takes little catnaps in the van.

When I traveled with him 20 hours a day, I never knew what

question was going to come up, and I had to have him prepared. The one critical factor in our campaign was that people knew the tough side of him already, and we had to show the other sides of him as a person. Every day in the campaign van when we traveled around, we went through the day's headlines, what the reporters were going to ask him and what his responses should be. We would let him vent in the van to ensure that when he did get hit, he was in good shape. He performed very well for the rest of the campaign.

—*Richard Bryers*

Graves Loses Race, Wins Law Suit

The battle for the mayor of Lexington, Kentucky, in 1977 was being fought by T-shirt slogans between the two campaigns. Joe Graves, my candidate, used the slogan that said "We dig Graves." I thought that was less than uplifting. The other candidate was Jimmy Amato, and his slogan on their T-shirts was, "Not a slogan, Amato."

But it all changed within two weeks of the election when the local newspaper, the *Lexington Herald Leader*, which was heavily biased to the Democrat candidate, came out with nine attacks against Graves.

We could defend three of the allegations, three were a toss-up and we really didn't want to go into the other three. We took the three we could defend, and that was the highlight of the news conference on Monday.

On the Sunday before that news conference, we bought a quarter-page ad in the newspaper with the headline saying, "One thousand dollar reward for information leading to the conviction for slander or evidence showing direct collusion between the campaign of Jimmy Amato and the editors of the *Lexington Herald Leader.*"

The thousand-dollar ad became the dominating news story on all the electronic media all day Monday before our news conference. I knew we were making progress when the reporter who had written the story showed up with his lawyer at our news conference.

One day later, the editor called me and asked me to pull off our suit. He said they would not make any further mention of the nine charges. I said, "I expect you not to make any further mention of the nine charges. As for the suit, we'll hold that in abeyance until after the campaign to make sure you behave."

Graves lost the campaign narrowly.

About 18 months later, I was in Washington when I received a call at 11 o'clock at night. Someone on the other end was shouting, "We won, we won!"

I said, "Won what?"

They said, "The jury just came out and awarded Joe Graves $144,000 for his libel suit against the local newspapers."

I said, "You have to be kidding me. He wasn't supposed to file that suit. You can't have a libel suit against the newspaper from a political campaign." I had forgotten to tell them not to, though, and they had gone ahead and filed it.   —*Buddy Bishop*

'He Was Responsible for My Panties'

Factoid: In 1978, Nevada Attorney General Bob List, running against Lieutenant Governor Bob Rose, was elected governor by a 57-40 margin.

In 1977, I went to work as the assistant campaign manager and press secretary for the Bob List for Governor campaign in Nevada. It was my very first big act in politics. This was February 1978, when he was going to make the formal announcement of his candidacy. We were going to start in Las Vegas, then go up to Reno, then conclude in Carson City. We went to Elko that day as well.

I go down on Sunday night to Las Vegas, and I'm all excited. I asked our advertising consultant what he expected the press turnout to be. He said, "I thought you called the press." So I spent a desperate Sunday night leaving voice mail messages about our press conference at nine o'clock the next morning.

I don't sleep at all that night, knowing that no one is going to show up for this Monday morning press conference. And it's all my fault.

We get up, and we're hustling and bustling to get ready to go. There is Bob, his wife, Kathy, his son Hank, his daughter Suzanne and his youngest daughter Michelle, who was about 5 at the time. We get to the site, and lo and behold, there is press waiting for us at the location. I'm greatly relieved.

Things are going well. Cameras are rolling. List is up on the podium making a passionate case of why he should be the next governor of the great state of Nevada.

Little Michelle is just standing there beside her daddy, sort of hopping from one foot to another as if she's wondering what's going on. For some reason, she suddenly reaches down and pulls her dress up over her head. The kicker is that she isn't wearing any panties that morning.

I just nearly faint. I thought for sure her mother was going to faint when she glanced over.

So from that point forward, it was my responsibility to make sure Michelle had underwear on before every event.

Twenty years later, Suzanne is getting married. My wife and I fly to Nevada for the wedding. I had not seen Michelle since she was 10 or 11 years old. She was now a beautiful young lady. She came up to me and proudly introduced me to her beau of the moment. "This is Bill Phillips, and he was always responsible for my panties," she says. That was the glorious beginning to my political work.

—Bill Phillips

Governor Says 'Shoot to Kill'

On the 1987 Fourth of July holiday, everyone, including New Mexico Governor Garry Carruthers, went off to celebrate the holiday. I came home after having more than a few drinks that evening. I arrived about midnight at my apartment and went to sleep.

About two o'clock in the morning the phone rings. It's a reporter from one of the Albuquerque television stations. She says, "Selma, this is Karen McDaniel from Channel 7. Can you tell me the latest on what's going on?" Not knowing what she was talking about, but not wanting her to know that I didn't know, I said, "No, I haven't heard anything recently, but I'll tell you what, give me your telephone number. I'll make a few phone calls and get right back to you."

After hanging up, I quickly went over to my answering machine, which I had not checked when I'd come home. There were like 35 messages, so I started playing them. Several of them were from the corrections secretary, Lane McCotter. "Selma, I need your help. We've had an incident at the prison, and I need you to call me." In addition to his calls were several from the media as well.

I immediately called the prison and found that seven of the most violent criminals who had ever been imprisoned in the Santa Fe facility had escaped. Once I at least knew what the situation was, I called Karen McDaniel back to tell her I was heading to the prison and would let her know more after I'd been briefed. I quickly got in the shower and sobered up, and then drove to the prison. The governor had been up in Farmington celebrating with his family. They took a state plane up and flew him back. By the time he got to the prison, it was three or four o'clock in the morning. By that time, I'd already had a briefing with reporters to update them on the situation. At least I was coherent enough to tell them what was going on.

When the governor came down, he received a briefing from the corrections staff. He'd also had a little bit too much to drink and was as fuzzy as I was. We were told that these were rapists, murderers – extremely violent criminals. We knew that people were in danger out there. So Carruthers leaned over and in a soft voice asked me, "What do you think? Should I issue a shoot-to-kill order?" I said, "Sure, why not? Just go ahead."

In a news conference afterwards, he said, "People should be very cautious if they encounter these criminals. In fact, you should shoot to kill if you see them."

The next day in the paper when we were all sobered up, we read this. Carruthers was so upset at himself for this reaction. He asked why I let him do it. I told him it was the advice everyone was giving us. We did get some favorable coverage out of it, so it wasn't just a negative thing.

But the biggest result of the whole deal was that Carruthers swore he would quit drinking for the rest of his administration. And he never had another drop to drink until he completed his term as governor.   —*Selma Sierra*

A Media Moment for Governor Mike Leavitt

Factoid: Utah Governor Mike Leavitt won a second term in 2000 when he defeated Democrat Bill Orton, 56-42.

The Mike Leavitt for Governor campaign field staff decided it would be a great opportunity to show Leavitt's support of small business by attending the opening of a Krispy Kreme in Provo, Utah, and, of course, scoring some fresh donuts. They took the campaign motor home and pulled into the store parking area at 6 a.m. The grand opening was slated for 7 a.m.

No one realized how big a hit Krispy Kreme was going to be in Utah. I got a call a little after 6 a.m. from the organization director saying there were lines of people circling the store and cars backed up for blocks. It was suggested that I should call the governor at home, wake him up and have him drive to Provo (over an hour away) to show his support for donuts and shake some hands. I was not quite convinced this was the thing to do.

However, when I turned on the news, all of the morning shows were covering this grand opening. Somehow the campaign motor home was positioned so that it was in all the television news shots. One reporter knocked on the door of the motor home to find out what time the governor would be there.

While the governor was never called upon to eat some fresh donuts, the lieutenant governor, Olene Walker, after getting her early wake-up call, showed up in time to sign Krispy Kreme hats with excuse notes for all the kids who had skipped school to stand in line for donuts.

It was one of the best news events of the entire campaign.

—*Allyson Bell*

Life Magazine Gives Reagan a Jab

When we first had Ronald Reagan on the road as a more serious candidate in 1966, *Life* magazine sent Shana Alexander, a chief feature columnist, out to do a story on him. She wrote a story that was obviously not based on facts. It was the worst example I ever saw of false news reporting. As an example, she said he showed up at this event with pancake makeup, but in reality Reagan never wore makeup at all, not even in the movies. That was just his natural complexion.

Reagan was telling me he was going to call the chief editorial writer at *Life* magazine. I advised him to wait and talk to Bill Roberts, the campaign manager, before he did anything like that.

Most candidates are afraid to make a move without checking with the manager and are intimidated by something as large as *Life* magazine. Not Ronald Reagan, though. He picked up the phone, called them and laid it on the line. I believe the magazine wrote a retraction.

—George Young

BOOK FOUR

Winning the Big Enchilada

☆ ☆ ☆

Running for president of the United States is nothing. Thousands of people have announced their candidacy for the highest office in the land over the years. Everybody does it, it seems. Winning, though, is another matter. While historians may list George W. Bush as the 43rd president, only 37 have actually run for the office and been elected.

We tend to forget that even the founding father of our nation was inaugurated only after winning a contested election. They didn't just hand the keys to the country over to George Washington. Ultimately, they called his election "unanimous," but Washington got only 46 percent of the Electoral College vote, defeating John Adams, who got 23 percent. That made Adams the vice president, and he was elected president eight years later. Four years after that, Thomas Jefferson and Aaron Burr were tied at 73 each in the Electoral College, but the issue was settled in the House of Representatives after 36 ballots, giving Jefferson the presidency in 1801.

The first president to be inaugurated even though he received fewer votes was John Quincy Adams in 1824. This was the first election in which popular votes were tallied and mattered in the outcome. Andrew Jackson led in the election with 43 percent of the popular vote and got 99 electoral votes, while Adams got only 30 percent of the popular vote and 84 in the Electoral College. Two others, Henry Clay and William Crawford, got 78 electoral votes between them. Because Jackson received less than the majority, the election went to the House of Representatives, where Clay was the speaker. Clay threw his support to Adams and made him president. Adams then named Clay secretary of state, which was not met with applause all around. Jackson resigned from the Senate, pledging to defeat Adams in 1828, which is exactly what he did.

In 1876, Rutherford B. Hayes lost the popular vote narrowly to Democrat Samuel Tilden but ended up winning the Electoral College by a single vote, 185-184. The outcome in three states, Florida, Louisiana and South Carolina, was contested. A congressional committee settled the three disputes on straight party line votes of eight to seven, and Hayes, a Republican, was declared the winner in all three states, giving him the one-vote victory. Nobody knows who really won.

Republican William Howard Taft had been elected president in 1908 and was running for re-election in 1912. Theodore Roosevelt, who had served two terms as a Republican president from 1901 to 1909, was running under the Bull Moose banner and got 30 percent of the popular vote, becoming the first third-party candidate to seriously alter the outcome in a modern election. Democrat Woodrow Wilson's 45 percent of the popular vote and 435 in the Electoral College made him president.

The only other third-party candidate to alter the outcome of an election was H. Ross Perot in 1992. Perot got 19 percent of the popular vote, allowing Democrat Bill Clinton to defeat incumbent George Bush, 43 percent to 38 percent.

Several milestones have altered the way presidential elections are run. The first was in 1824, when they started counting popular votes. The Electoral College, of course, has been in place since the beginning, though state legislatures determined each state's electoral vote until popular votes were counted. The 12th amendment to the Constitution, adopted in 1804, left the Electoral College pretty much as it is today.

The first meaningful federal election law was in place for the

1976 election between Gerald Ford and Jimmy Carter. The 1974 law was enacted, as much as anything, because of the abuses unearthed during the Watergate investigation. Prior to that, a number of laws were enacted, but most proved unenforceable and were routinely overlooked. Everything was pretty much a free-for-all. The 1974 law set up the mechanism for public reporting and matching funds for presidential candidates. It also set fundraising and expenditure limits for primaries and general elections. But limits were obliterated in 1996 when the Clinton-Gore campaign plowed new ground allowing the Democratic Party to spend millions openly supporting their re-election effort. And, in 2004, the Supreme Court ruling on McCain-Feingold once again changed the rules on political giving.

On the communications front, Dwight Eisenhower and Adlai Stevenson launched modern presidential campaigns in 1952 with the first use of television commercials. And, in 1960, Vice President Richard Nixon and Senator John F. Kennedy debated on TV, a first for presidential nominees. Compared to the campaigns of the 1950s and 1960s, campaigns today are operated at warp speed with overnight production of new TV commercials fed by satellite to any television market in the nation. Survey results are available to strategists on a daily basis with information just a couple of hours out of the field; the Internet provides for instant communications with campaign workers throughout the 50 states. Candidates routinely jet across the country to access the local news cycle in all four times zones on a daily basis.

Today's winners are often those who respond to tough situations the quickest, utilize the technology more efficiently and faster, and jump on newly emerging issues in minutes rather than days. Presidential campaigns have come a long, long way from the platform on the back of a railroad car whistlestopping across the Midwest.

CHAPTER 17

The New Hampshire Primary and Iowa Caucus

☆ ☆ ☆

The first New Hampshire presidential primary, of record, was held on the second Tuesday in March 1916. There are some reports that the Republicans held a primary in 1912, but the results have long since been lost. In the early primaries, ballots carried lists of delegates, rather than candidates' names. For instance, in the 1920 primary, New Hampshire Republicans voted for a slate of delegates committed to Leonard Wood, who had ridden with Teddy Roosevelt's Rough Riders. Wood didn't get far in the Republican convention, where the nomination went to Calvin Coolidge.

New Hampshire, which after 1916 was always the first primary, voted for delegate slates until 1952, when state legislators decided voters wanted to see real candidate names on the ballot. They thought it would create more interest among voters, which would lead to a higher turnout on Election Day. In that first modern primary, General Dwight Eisenhower defeated Ohio Senator Robert Taft in the Republican primary, 57-43. Eisenhower, who never sat foot in the state during the campaign, later hired New Hampshire Governor Sherman Adams as his chief of staff. On the Democratic side, Tennessee Senator Estes Kefauver upset President Harry Truman, 55-45, encouraging Truman not to seek re-election.

Iowa held its one and only presidential primary on April 10, 1916, but backed out of the early primary business until the state established the first early caucus in 1972. Maine Senator Edmund

Muskie lost to "uncommitted" by three-tenths of a percentage point, 35.8 to 35.5, and the press wrote him off as having done worse than expected. South Dakota Senator George McGovern, though, started to catch "Big Mo" with 22.6 percent of the caucus attendees. Go figure. On the Republican side in 1972, President Richard Nixon ran virtually unopposed in Iowa.

Here are some stories from professionals who have been through the snow and cold of Iowa and New Hampshire.

Bush Edges Reagan in 1980 Iowa Caucus

Factoid: George Bush, in an upset, edged Ronald Reagan in the 1980 Iowa presidential caucus. Bush got 31.6% of the caucus attendees, while Reagan got 29.5%. Howard Baker was third with 15.3%, followed by John Connally with 9.3%.

I was the legislative campaign director of the Iowa GOP, not directly involved in the presidential caucuses, but I was helping out. Steve Roberts was state chairman and Lloyd McGee was executive director. The organization director, the person primarily responsible for staffing, organizing and reporting the caucuses, was a very confident young man by the name of Lou Bongignore.

In the Hotel Fort Des Moines, we were trying a new system of reporting. There were close to 5,000 precincts in the state of Iowa. We had phone banks with volunteers who were taking calls from a designated person in each of the 5,000 precincts. They would fill in a little IBM card with the outcome in that particular precinct. The person had some sort of I.D. they would have to give to theoretically secure it.

This was 1980, and desktop computers and computing capabilities were not what they are today. We had three Apple computers. We had bought this system that had card readers, and the results were to be printed out. We had a huge scoreboard and somebody would run over and post the county's total. There were ninety-nine counties for each of the candidates.

Ronald Reagan was front-line, George Bush was coming on strong and there were five other candidates: Illinois Congressman

John Anderson, former Texas Governor John Connally, Tennessee Senator Howard Baker, Illinois Congressman Phil Crane and Kansas Senator Bob Dole.

It was bedlam in those early caucus years, as compared to the 20 years since then. Hundreds of international reporters and the TV networks wanted to show footage at 10 p.m., of course.

Unfortunately, the whole system broke down. The card readers wouldn't cooperate. The state chairman was in another room somewhere doing interviews and schmoozing with donors. The executive director was doing the same thing.

So it was just Lou and I with all the international media there and all the campaigns wondering what on earth is going on. We couldn't find our bosses, and all the volunteers and other field people were just looking at us. Lou said, "Well, I'm going to have to announce to the press that the system broke down and we'll never know who won."

I said, "You can't do that!"

Lou and I made the decision that we'd say the system broke down and that we had a back-up, but it would be a few hours before the final tally was known.

Bush was slightly ahead in our highly inaccurate hand count, so there was already a hint in the air that the Bush campaign would announce a victory.

Lou and I disappeared into the state party headquarters, into a large conference room with a long table. We had 99 piles of cards, one for each county. We just stacked them all up and started counting the cards by hand. By then, the state chairman had been made aware of the crisis and was prepared.

At midday the following day, he announced the results that Bush had won. To this day, nobody is certain we didn't make the results up! We did not make them up, I can assure you.

I'm reasonably confident we were roughly right because the Reagan people were so well organized and were doing parallel counts. They pretty much knew before we did who won and what the percentages were. They accepted the results that Bush won, and it was an upset.

—Tim Hyde

On the Run From the Press in New Hampshire

Factoid: Californian Ronald Reagan got nearly 50% in the 1980 Republican presidential primary in New Hampshire. George Bush got 23%, followed by Howard Baker 12%, John Anderson 10% and Phil Crane 2%.

Ronald Reagan came out of the 1976 elections as the front-runner for the 1980 Republican nomination after President Gerald Ford lost the general election to Jimmy Carter. Even though we ran a great race in 1976, factions developed in the campaign, such as tensions between John Sears and the Californians surrounding Reagan, like Ed Meese, Mike Deaver, Lyn Nofziger and a few others.

When the 1980 Reagan campaign was formed in late 1978 and early 1979, they negotiated a structure that left Sears in charge, with Jim Lake, myself and the three Californians in important positions, along with Dick Wirthlin, the pollster, and two or three other people.

As we went through 1979, the tensions were bad, though it didn't break out into the open. Nofziger had a goal of trying to work Deaver out of the campaign over time. Lake and I thought it was a pretty tall order to run Deaver out of the Reagan campaign; however that was what he wanted to do. There were some issues of performance, among other things, that Sears thought was legitimate, so he enlisted Lake to help him.

On the Saturday after Thanksgiving of 1979, we all showed up at Reagan's house with Deaver and presented our case to Reagan about how Deaver was screwing up the campaign.

To Deaver's credit, about one hour into this, he saw how serious we were. He then withdrew rather than defend himself or fight us. The following day, Meese, who was still there as a policy person in the campaign, made it very plain to Sears and the rest of us that he was mad about it and would figure out some way to get us.

We flew around the country trying to do our job, with Reagan still the front-runner. We screwed up Iowa by not putting in enough time there.

In those days, there were five weeks between the Iowa caucuses and the New Hampshire primary, thus we had five weeks to try to right the campaign and get Reagan back on track. Lake and I spent a lot of time in New Hampshire, while Sears devoted most of his time to figuring out how to get us back in the race. During this whole time, Meese was scheming behind our backs and developing analysis to go to the Reagans to tell them how screwed up we were.

Working the campaign was very intense at this point, with us working seven days a week. Everybody was hyper, but we knew it didn't matter who had been in charge if we lost New Hampshire.

Several national newspaper reports wrote that at the height of the campaign the Reagan campaign was extremely effective. We had two great debates, with the national debate being famous. It was obvious by Sunday before the election that Reagan was going to win New Hampshire. He ended up winning it by a huge margin, 50 to 23, over Bush.

For Election Day we had reserved rooms at the Manchester Holiday Inn for the election night party. We jumped on a bus around 11 o'clock in the morning with Reagan, and he went around to work some polling places. He visited close to half a dozen polling places around Manchester, shaking hands with people. We pulled up at the Holiday Inn around 1:30 p.m. Sears had stayed at the hotel. I was on the bus with Reagan, Lake was on the press bus behind us, and Reagan turned to me and said, "Where's John?"

I replied, "He's up at the hotel."

Reagan asked me to find Sears and said he wanted to see Sears, Lake, and me.

I agreed to find him and added that we would be over as soon as we could.

Some other things had occurred that weekend that made us realize we might be in jeopardy, but nobody thought we would get executed before the primary was over. But when Reagan asked to see us, we knew something was up.

I grabbed Jim, and we went and got John and proceeded up to Reagan's suite 20 minutes later. The three of us entered the room and found Reagan and Bill Casey. Casey had actually been brought into the campaign by Sears during the fall of 1979 to help out with some things such as fundraising and organization. Reagan and the Californians didn't know who Casey was until then. Obviously, he raised himself to the occasion very well.

We came into the room and Casey and Reagan were sitting

around the coffee table. At the other end of the suite, 50 feet away, was Nancy Reagan. I knew we were doomed at that moment because Nancy Reagan was always at the table, sitting beside the governor, anytime he had a meeting.

We sat down and Reagan said, "Obviously, we've been having some difficulties here, and I think I'm in the position to settle them. I want you to read this."

He hands Sears a one-page paper to read. Sears reads it and hands it back to Reagan and doesn't say anything.

Reagan just looks at him. Nobody says anything for about ten seconds, which can seem like an eternity in that kind of setting. From the corner, Nancy says, "Well, John?"

He turns and looks at her and replies, "I'm not surprised."

At that point, Reagan hands me the paper. I'm smart enough to know it's a press release saying Sears was fired.

Lake and I had previously told Reagan that would be a mistake. We put our chips on the table with Sears and said not to fire Sears, as we would go too. We had said they shouldn't fire Sears because of what it would do to the campaign.

After Reagan handed me the paper, I put it face down on the coffee table. I said, "Governor, I just want you to know before I read this that I resign from the campaign."

I picked it up and read it, and right there in the second paragraph it said that I resigned. My comments had been redundant.

I gave it to Lake, who said he resigned too. Of course, the first paragraph had been about Sears's resignation. None of us were surprised and nobody raised their voice.

Reagan said, "I appreciate what you guys have done, but I need to make a change. I can't have all this conflict on the campaign. I'm asking Bill to take over. I think he's set for the time being for the transition. I hope you will cooperate with him."

We didn't say much of anything.

Nancy Reagan again tries to press Sears, asking, What are you going to say? What are you going to do about this?

Sears says, "I don't know. It depends on how you all act."

We left, but we knew we didn't have very long to talk about it, perhaps only five minutes. As soon as they put that release out, the press would swarm us.

The fact is we didn't want to sink Reagan. We had devoted many years to trying to get Reagan elected president. Even if we thought he was wrong to fire us, we weren't going to jump out there and start to badmouth him. We wanted to be professional, so the point was to see how they treated us. We would wait to see what they said.

We decided we had to get out of town and avoid the press until we could see how the Reagans handled it. We rushed to our rooms, crammed our things in our suitcases, took our assistants, and within 20 minutes we were on our way to Boston.

Sometime during that next hour, they put the release out and they had Pete Hannaford handle the press. Reporters loved Sears, but they also liked Jim and me; the reporters were just beating the crap out of them, repeatedly asking, "Why did you do this? How could you do this to them?"

We hightailed to Boston to check into a Howard Johnson hotel. We didn't have cell phones in those days, so we couldn't call from the car. We arrived at the Howard Johnson's and called the office, as well as our friends remaining in the campaign, to see how this was being handled. So far, they had handled it on the basis of disagreements, personality conflicts, and had not badmouthed us.

Our friends in Washington already knew the press had staked out the Boston airport, as well as the Washington airport, under the assumption we'd be flying from Boston to Washington. So we decided to stay at the Holiday Inn rather than Howard Johnson's that night, figuring people were not likely to find us there.

We sat there and watched the New Hampshire returns on the networks and grabbed something to eat.

Late at night, Reagan won big and everyone was happy. We planned to fly back early the next morning. However, we found out through our friends that the airport was staked out and the press was dying to get us involved in the story.

Instead of going to the airport, we checked out the next morning. As I went down to the lobby to check us out, Garrick Utley, who was with NBC in those days, was wandering around in the lobby. We waited another 20 minutes till Utley was gone, and then we jumped in our car and went down to Providence, Rhode Island.

This time we checked into the Hilton in Providence, which is close to the airport. We hung out there the rest of the day. The Reagan people were still pretty disciplined and did not badmouth us. So we decided we would play ball and be kind, and be for Reagan. We had some of our friends in D.C. set up a national press conference on Thursday.

Over 100 reporters were in attendance. With the press being the press, they were pulling for us to badmouth Reagan. However, we didn't. We told them we were happy he had won New Hampshire, we hoped he would be the nominee, and we thought he was the best guy for president. Yes, we told them we'd had some disagreements over strategy, but we didn't get into much detail for about 45 minutes, then we left.

For 36 hours we felt like criminals on the run. We tried to do the right thing; we didn't talk to the press until we had everything figured out.   *—Charlie Black*

Mondale Tops Cranston in Maine, Iowa Straw Polls

The whole Walter Mondale campaign in 1983 was built on the inevitable fact that he was going to be the nominee and couldn't be beat. Senator Alan Cranston, of California, made a big part of his strategy to beat Mondale in the straw votes. Out of nowhere he beat Mondale in the Wisconsin straw vote.

Mondale made some kind of vow that we would never lose another straw vote and if he did, he just shouldn't be running for office.

I was sent up to Maine to run the straw vote in that state. I get up there and we know who all the usual delegates are. We call them, and they are all for Cranston. They were the only guys up there.

We were down 49 to 29. I found this clause in the rules that said if a town hadn't held a caucus you could still call the caucus, you just had to post it with seven days' notice. You can call an emergency caucus to elect delegates as long as it happens 30 days before the convention.

A large number of very small towns in Maine had never held a caucus. We brought a lot of bodies in to work this. We posted a caucus notice under a station wagon parked in front of the sheriff's office. One guy later told me the way he won his town was, once the Cranston people were identified as the volunteer firemen, he pulled the fire alarm to make sure the Cranston guys were all running off that way, while the Mondale people quickly elected delegates and sent them up to the state convention.

In one day, we posted in all these towns where no one even knew we were there. There was a caucus at Charlie's house, or wherever, and the only people in town who knew were the three Mondale people we had already identified. In the two or three towns where Cranston people figured out what we were doing, they were pulling all kinds of stuff. We ended up electing enough delegates in that one day to go to the convention to beat Cranston.

These straw votes were huge and expensive. In Maine we spent something like half a million dollars on 800 people going to the state convention.

There is a great scene where Mondale flies in on a chopper to this dinky pre-delegate town and the whole town has never seen a chopper before. They are just pouring out of the homes and stores to see who is arriving.

You couldn't tell who was more dumbfounded, the people in the town to see the former vice president, or Mondale, wondering why he was doing this.

In Iowa, when we got there, the same thing happened. Cranston had gotten there ahead of us and bought all the damn tickets. There was no way around it this time. There were no ways to exploit the rules to get your guys elected. But Cranston had a problem. He had more tickets than he could get rid of. At the time we didn't know that part.

What we did was bus a bunch of people to about two miles away from the convention center. They had no tickets or anything. The guys on the ground for Mondale decorated the buses up in Cranston signs and then pulled the buses up to the Cranston tent, outside the hall. One of the guys from our staff was on the bus, wearing Cranston colors and buttons and saying, "Iowa City Cranston delegates, come up and get your tickets." They would all get off and go into the Cranston tent and at the Cranston booth they would give them their tickets. Then they would go in and switch to

Mondale colors. We pulled up with about 10 to 15 buses. When their real buses started showing up, they were out of tickets.

That is how Mondale won the Iowa straw vote. To this day the Cranston people I still run into on a campaign are like, you bastard.

—*Joe Trippi*

'Onward Christian Soldiers' in Iowa

Factoid: In the January 1988 Republican Caucus in Iowa, Senator Bob Dole got 37%, Pat Robertson 25%, Vice President George Bush 19%, Congressman Jack Kemp 11% and Pierre du Pont 7%.

You'd think we would have learned our lesson in Michigan in 1986, but a year later, Iowa has their straw poll. If you pay five dollars, you get to vote for whomever you wish. It's very apparent that this is a fundraiser for the state party. It had no bearing on delegate selection whatsoever, but the media was there.

The vice president was on his way in. Lee Atwater, the campaign manager, was on the plane with him. Lee calls from the air and asks me what it looks like. I tell him that Senator Bob Dole is all over the place. My guess was that we were going to be second because I didn't think there was any way we could beat Dole. He asked about Pat Robertson and I told him there was no sign of him. They had no signs, no banners, nothing.

Atwater told me they'd be landing in about 10 minutes and asked me to meet them outside the door to the building. I went to the appointed place. It was pretty chilly. The land in Iowa is very flat, except it dropped off to a slope in the distance. I'm standing there, waiting for the vice president's motorcade. I'm thinking to myself that this is going to be a disappointment since we're probably going to come in second.

Suddenly I hear singing off in the distance. I can't quite figure out what it is as I strain my ears. The music slowly gets louder. All of a sudden, I saw the biggest crowd I'd ever seen in my life. They came up over that little rise singing "Onward Christian Soldiers."

Pat Robertson won the straw poll. Dole came in second and Bush came in third.

I was invited to go back to Washington on Air Force Two. It was the only time in my life that I didn't want to ride on it. I'm sitting as far back as I could get, in the darkest corner I could find.

Here comes Atwater. He says, "Bill, the man wants to see you."

I thought, "Well, it's been a brilliant political career. I started out in small-town local politics in Nevada, and here I am working at the national level. It's coming to an abrupt end, but I gave it all I could."

It was the longest walk I ever made. I walked up to the front and stepped into the front cabin where the vice president stays. He was sitting at the table and asked me to sit in the chair facing him. Mrs. Bush was sitting on the other side working on one of those rugs that she always worked on in the plane. His chief of staff, Craig Fuller, was sitting there doing something. Atwater disappeared as I sat down.

"Bill, I just want to tell you that we appreciate everything you've done," the vice president says. "Don't let today bother you. We're going to have peaks and we're going to have valleys. Today was a valley. But we're going to win this thing and we wanted you to know that."

I jumped up because I was ready to get out of there. I couldn't believe what a gracious thing he had just done. Mrs. Bush looked up from her rug and asked, "Bill, when are you heading back to Iowa?"

"Tomorrow," I said, and I did. The next day I was back in Iowa recouping our losses.
—*Bill Phillips*

CHAPTER 18

Political Party Conventions

☆ ☆ ☆

In December 1831, the National Republican Party, a short-lived group that soon became the Whigs, convened in Philadelphia for the first national convention for a major political party. They selected Senator Henry Clay of Kentucky as their nominee. They knew the Democrats would be re-nominating popular President Andrew Jackson, which is exactly what happened in Baltimore five months later. Clay was selected as the most anti-Jackson candidate they could find. No matter, though. Jackson won re-election handily in 1832, winning 56 percent of the popular vote and 77 percent of the electoral votes. Clay, by the way, ran for president three times, and though he was never successful, he's given credit for the line: "I'd rather be right than president." But that was the start of the national political convention process.

The first Republican Party convention, in 1856, convened in Philadelphia and John C. Fremont of California was nominated for president. The first plank in the platform addressed keeping the union intact; the second plank advocated the end of slavery. In the 1860 Republican convention in Chicago, Abraham Lincoln surprised the field by finishing second on the first ballot and was nominated on the third ballot.

For the Democrats in 1860, it was a different and more difficult matter. The Democrats convened in Charleston, South Carolina, in April and, after 11 days and 57 ballots, adjourned without a nominee. In those days, the Democrats required two-thirds support to win the nomination, which effectively gave veto power to Southern states. By the end of the convention, most Southern delegations had walked out, but Illinois Senator Stephen Douglas still could not muster two-thirds support. The Democrats reconvened in Baltimore two months later and Douglas was nominated. Southern Democrats ran two other candidates for president, which allowed Lincoln to win the presidency fairly easily, though with less than a majority in the popular vote. Lincoln was inaugurated in March 1961, and shots were fired at Ft. Sumter, South Carolina, two months later. The Civil War was on.

William Jennings Bryan was a 36-year-old Illinois Congressman when he showed up at the Democratic National Convention in Chicago in 1896. When he gave what is arguably the most famous speech ever given at a convention, delegates quickly drafted him for the nomination. "You shall not press down upon the brow of labor this crown of thorns, you shall not crucify mankind on a cross of gold," Bryan intoned. Though he ran two other times for president, the greatest orator of his time was never successful.

The Democrats met in New York City in 1924 and after 16 days and 103 ballots, finally named John W. Davis of West Virginia as their nominee. It was easily the longest convention and the most ballots ever required. The Republicans re-nominated President Calvin Coolidge, who won 56 percent of the popular vote with the slogan "Keep cool with Coolidge."

The most recent contested convention came in 1952 in Chicago, when the Democrats took three ballots to nominate Illinois Governor Adlai Stevenson. The Republicans thought they had a contested convention in 1976 in Kansas City, but President Gerald Ford won a first ballot victory over Ronald Reagan, 1,187 to 1,070.

Here are some stories from the professionals who have fought their way to the conventions.

Kirk Elected DNC Chair, DLC Formed

After Walter Mondale's failed presidential election in 1984, Paul Kirk decided to run for chairman of the Democratic National Committee in 1985. He had had it with losing so badly to the Republicans. He asked if I would help him run for chairman. Kirk, from Boston, launches the campaign, but he is Senator Ted

Kennedy's guy. People didn't know Kirk. The establishment and the DNC didn't really know him personally, so he was just known as Kennedy's guy.

Kirk had been the national political director for Kennedy's failed challenge to President Jimmy Carter in 1980. Nobody was going to elect Kennedy's guy after the Mondale thing, especially the Democratic governors. The governors were behind a "stop Kirk" movement that surfaced at a meeting in Kansas City, on December 10, 1984.

They were trying to draft a candidate against him and had come up with Scott Matheson, the governor of Utah. The moderate conservative wing of the party started to rise up saying, "We can't have a liberal chairman after we just lost 49 states."

Nobody was giving Kirk a break, not giving him a chance. So it was a hard, tough campaign. Ultimately they get Terry Sanford, the president of Duke University and former North Carolina governor, as their candidate. At the time there was no such thing as Democratic Leadership Council. But Kirk pulls it off in this hard-fought race.

He is walking up to accept the chairmanship of the party and Chuck Robb, the governor of Virginia, and two other Southern governors inform him they are forming another group, which then became the DLC. Welcome to the party leadership, Mr. Chairman.

—*Brian Lunde*

The Low-water Mark for the Republicans

The 1974 election followed President Richard Nixon's resignation and President Gerald Ford's pardon of President Nixon. The results of the 1974 election were disastrous. The Republicans had lost a net of 48 House seats. We actually ended up politically worse off than we had been in 1964 for many reasons.

After the election, I caught up with one of the significant Republican research firms in the country, Market Opinion Research, and Bob Teeter. Even though we never had a lot of money, we scraped up enough to do a national survey. George Bush had left the RNC and Mary Louise Smith, of Iowa, became chairman. I was named executive director at the RNC.

When we got it done, Teeter said it would be better if Dick Thaxton and I came to Detroit to see the data, rather than him bringing the data in to Washington. In that national survey, on the self-identified party ID question, only 18 percent self-identified as Republican, which was less than half of the people who in fact were registered Republicans. People who had even registered Republicans were unwilling to acknowledge they were Republicans.

As Teeter said at the time, "We are no longer the minority party, we are now a minor party, much like in Canada, because when you drop below 20 percent, you are no longer a minority party, you are then a minor party."

We never brought the survey data to Washington for fear it would leak out to the press. The only person we talked to about the horrible shape we were in was Mary Louise Smith. A newspaper article about it could have been quite destructive. If a newspaper had printed that only 18 percent of the voters in America claimed to be Republicans, we believed we would have died as a party.

At Thanksgiving time, right after the 1974 election, I closed the building down for a month because I could afford to pay their salaries, but I couldn't afford to pay the overhead expenses of the building. We had no money. All those costs and traveling were too much, so the cheapest solution was to close down the building. We were down to about 85 employees.

Fortunately, Rod Smith, the finance director, had tucked away about $100,000, which was just enough to put out the first mailing for the membership, which was then $15 per year. People responded, fortunately, which was enough to get us back in business.

—Eddie Mahe

Rev. Billy Graham: 'We Can't Say That'

Factoid: The Republican National Convention in 1980 was held in Detroit, where Ronald Reagan and George Bush were nominated. It's the only time, since 1856, that the GOP has held its convention in Detroit.

As the program director for the 1980 Republican National

Convention in Detroit, we brought in lots of entertainment, and instead of the Monday night featured speech we had a Monday night theme show. We made a lot of changes within the convention itself in an attempt to show a broad-base appeal to the Republican Party.

One of my jobs was to make sure that every word spoken at the podium during the four-day convention was not misinterpreted and was giving out the message we needed to give. I had asked Tully Plesser of New York to be my reader, to make sure nothing would be said that could be misinterpreted.

He came to me shortly before the session started one day and said, "I think we have a problem here. Look at Billy Graham's invocation."

I looked at his invocation, and in it he said, "Dear Lord, please keep our hostages in Iran."

Tully said, "I know what he is saying here, and you know what he is saying, but is American going to know what he is saying? Now, who gets to go tell Rev. Graham that he should change his invocation?"

Since I was in charge of the program, I was nominated. Rev. Graham was very gracious and responded, "Oh, my goodness! We can't say that."   —*Ken Rietz*

CHAPTER 19

Presidential Debates Often Have Consequences

☆ ☆ ☆

On September 26, 1960, Vice President Richard Nixon and Massachusetts Senator John F. Kennedy sat down in the WBBM studio in Chicago for the very first presidential debate between party nominees. Not only was this the first presidential debate ever, but it was also the first debate on television and carried on radio. The debate is remembered, particularly, because of Nixon's swarthy appearance. He looked like he hadn't shaved in three days. Pollsters the next day asked television viewers who they thought had won, and the charismatic Kennedy was the easy winner. Interestingly, those listening on radio said it was a draw and the *New York Times* actually scored it for Nixon on classic debate points – like answering the questions. Sporting a clean shave and makeup, Nixon faced Kennedy in three more debates that year, which is still the record for the most debates.

The first radio debate between two presidential candidates occurred in Oregon in 1948, where Tom Dewey and Harold Stassen were competing in the Republican primary election. On May 17, 1948, at KEX radio in Portland, Dewey and Stassen each gave 20-minute opening statements followed by eight-minute rebuttals on one topic – should the Communist Party be outlawed in the United States? Historians say the radio audience that night was huge. They also say Dewey seemed to have the upper hand in the debate.

In 1956 in Miami, former Illinois Governor Adlai Stevenson and

Tennessee Senator Estes Kefauver appeared in the first televised debate between presidential candidates in a primary campaign.

Unlike the hundreds of debates that take place at the local and statewide level each election year for every office from dog catcher to U.S. senator, presidential debates, with their increased attention and national reporting, would appear to have more significance in the final outcome of the elections. Here are some tales from presidential debates, told by those who were there, as well as some presidential advance tales.

The Great Nashua Debate Strategy

Factoid: George Bush won the 1980 Iowa caucus with 31.6%, followed by Ronald Reagan with 29.5%. Others were Howard Baker at 15.3% and John Connally at 9.3%.

We lost Iowa in late January of 1980, when George Bush upset Ronald Reagan. We stayed up all night in Des Moines trying to count votes, as you didn't know in those days until five or six o'clock in the morning what the final count was. It looked as though Bush had beaten us by close to two thousand votes. We stayed up all night and John Sears, Jim Lake and I went to the airport to fly to Chicago at eight o'clock in the morning. At the airport, we ran into George W. Bush, who had been there with his father.

I didn't know him very well, but he was a casual friend of mine, so I congratulated him, as did the others. We told him his father was a big player now. We had a real nice conversation with him.

We flew to Chicago and checked into the Hyatt Hotel near O'Hare Airport. We sat in one of our rooms and discussed, "What are we going to do now? How do we come back from this in New Hampshire?" We thought out some tactics.

One thing we settled on was that we knew Reagan didn't debate enough. Perhaps the best thing to happen, since Bush was now the new front-runner, was to get a one-on-one debate with Reagan versus Bush. We liked that contrast. It is always hard to break out of the pack in a six- or seven-candidate debate, so we talked for a couple hours on how we were going to get a one-on-one with Bush.

There was no reason Bush would want to do it. Jim Lake was very knowledgeable about New Hampshire; he had worked New Hampshire in 1976 and had stayed up there the whole time during the campaign. Jim said the only way this was going to work was if it was the Bush people's idea and not ours.

He called up former New Hampshire Governor Hugh Gregg, who had been the Reagan chairman in 1976 and was now the Bush chairman in 1980, and talked it through with him. He told him congratulations and said his man was a big player now. He explained how we were on the road and told him what we were going to do. Gregg somehow coaxed the conversation down to, "I guess we're going to have Reagan debate at least once or twice, but it's okay because he'll be insulated by a bunch of other candidates."

Lake somehow led Hugh into saying, "You know, the race is down to Bush and Reagan. Maybe we ought to have a two-man debate."

Lake replied, "Oh, I don't know if we could do that, Hugh." However, he had planted the seed.

Within a day or so, Gregg talked to Jerry (Gerald) Carmen about it, who was Reagan's New Hampshire manager. Of course, we had briefed Carmen on this. Playing along, Jerry said, "Well, I don't know if we want to do that."

Within a week, Gregg had gone to the *Nashua Telegraph* newspaper—where he was very close to the owners—and asked for a favor, a pro-Bush favor. He lined them up to be a sponsor of the proposed two-man debate.

The Bush people proposed a Bush/Reagan debate sponsored by the *Nashua Telegraph* to be held on Saturday night, the last weekend before the election. We pooh-poohed around for a couple of days, then reluctantly accepted.

This two-man debate was cooked up by Sears and Lake. Sears is the smartest strategist I've ever known; he is always a few steps ahead of everybody else. When we concocted this, he figured out other steps and moves in the chess game that ultimately would make a huge difference.

We go along and announce this two-man debate. The other candidates in the race, Howard Baker, Phil Crane, John Anderson, John Connally and Bob Dole, protested. They said, "You can't have a debate that excludes everybody."

On the Wednesday night prior to the Nashua debate it was announced that the local Public Broadcasting Station would televise the debate.

The other candidates started protesting that they ought to be included in this debate. Of course, Sears had assigned us to talk to each of them to make sure they knew, starting Thursday, they needed to be demanding to the press to get into the debate.

At this point, everybody knew Reagan had closed the gap; however, the race was still close. The press was treating this as a very competitive Reagan/Bush race. Thursday and Friday, they bought into all the guys protesting about how they were being excluded from the debate. Finally, it was set for Saturday night at Nashua High School.

On Saturday morning, Sears called all the other candidates, including John Connally, who was in Minnesota. Sears had invited all of them to come to Nashua High School where Reagan was going to invite them to join the debate.

About mid-morning, Reagan issued a statement in the form of a letter to Bush indicating these guys had a point, it was a fair race and they should be allowed in the debate. Bush and Jim Baker took the bait and replied, "Absolutely not. You agreed to a two-man debate and we're holding you to it."

All Saturday afternoon, the press was really working the debate. Reagan was demanding the other candidates be in the debate.

Around 6:30 on the Saturday night of the 7 o'clock debate, in the band room of the Nashua High School, we had Reagan, Dole, Baker, Anderson and Crane. Bush was still saying they couldn't go into the debate. They are all furious at this point.

Reagan is really mad and turns around and looks at Sears and Senator Paul Laxalt, who is in the room with us, and says, "If Bush doesn't agree to this, I'm not going to go through with the debate. I'm not going to go on stage without them."

Sears says, "Well, Governor, you probably shouldn't do that. You can't look like you're running from anything."

Laxalt says, "No, Ronnie, you have to go through with the debate."

"I want to talk to Bush," Reagan replied.

I volunteered and ran across the school to the Bush holding room and asked to see Baker for a minute. I told him Governor Reagan wanted to speak with Mr. Bush, explaining he would be happy to come down to their room to talk to him.

Baker said, "No, we are not talking. We will be on stage for the debate in twenty minutes. We hope you are by yourself."

I took the message back and Reagan was very mad that Bush would not even meet with him. He turned around to Laxalt and said, "Paul, you go down there and talk to Bush personally. I want him to hear from you, personally, that I want to meet with him."

Paul hesitates for a moment and the other guy standing there in the band room with us was Gordon Humphrey, co-chairman in New Hampshire. He was a U.S. senator who campaigned very hard for Reagan. It just so happened I knew George Bush couldn't stand Gordon Humphrey. Therefore, when Laxalt hesitated for a minute, I said, "Governor, how about this? Since it is Gordon's state, why don't you (Humphrey) go ask Bush to come down here to meet with the group?"

So at 6:45 Senator Humphrey goes down to the Bush holding room, they let him in, and he asks Bush. Bush replied, "I'm not meeting with anybody. I'll be on the stage, and you better have Reagan there." He then kicked him out of the room.

Humphrey came back with that report at 6:50 p.m. Reagan looks at us and says, "By God, I am not going through with this if Bush is going to screw with these guys."

As usual, Sears was a step ahead of everybody else. He said, "Let's ask these guys, Governor. If you don't show up, there is no debate because you are trying to defend the others."

Reagan was still saying, "Well, I don't want to do it. It's not fair."

Sears replied, "One of the things you can do then is take them up there on the stage with you. We'll get somebody to bring chairs up. How can Bush prevent them from participating then?"

Reagan answered, "Okay, I'll do it."

It is now five minutes before 7 p.m. We head out, Lake leading the way for the pack of five, Sears and Reagan bringing up the rear. It is now about two minutes before seven. Bush is already seated at the podium with his microphone. Reagan comes in and sits down behind his microphone, with the other four standing behind him.

George Bush just sort of freezes and won't even look up at them. We have people out getting chairs to bring up for the other participants. Reagan tries to take the microphone and moderator Jon Breen, the editor of the *Nashua Telegraph*, explains, "We cannot begin until the other candidates leave the stage; we've all agreed to a debate between Governor Reagan and Mr. Bush, and that's the way it's going to be. Therefore, we can't start."

Reagan grabs his microphone and says, "I just want to tell you I insist that these candidates be allowed to participate."

At this point, Breen says to the sound guy, "Would you turn off Governor Reagan's microphone?"

Reagan wheels around and says, "Mr. Green, I paid for this microphone."

Of course the sound guy turns out to be a Reagan guy, so he blinks and does not turn it off.

Bush still had not looked up at Reagan or said anything else.

At that point, Dole, Baker, Crane and Anderson said they were leaving. "Go to it, Ron!" They patted Reagan on the back on their way out.

Lake had to go up and whisper to Reagan, "You have to stay," as we still weren't sure Reagan would not get up and leave, being the kind of guy he was.

He stayed and had a good debate; however, the whole debate was over before it started.　　　　　　　　　　*—Charlie Black*

No Debate Without the Frontrunner

Factoid: Massachusetts Governor Michael Dukakis led in the 1988 New Hampshire Democratic presidential primary with 36%. Congressman Dick Gephardt was second with 20%.

In the 1988 presidential campaign, I worked for Congressman Dick Gephardt and was working against Al Gore at that point in my career. We were at the New Hampshire League of Women Voters debate, which up until 1988 had been the premier debate. It wasn't like now where there are something like 36 debates every month. So it was a very big deal. All the networks were carrying it.

I was the lead advance and I had conducted the negotiations on the debate. One of the big bones of contention in our negotiations was paper on the podiums. The League preferred that there be no pen and paper up there. The Paul Simon folks really wanted a piece of paper because their man was a little older and might want some notes to remind him. Gephardt didn't need any paper.

The final agreement was that each candidate had the option to bring a single three-by-five card of notes for their closing points.

Keep in mind that Gephardt had just won the Iowa caucuses, so all guns were aimed at him right now.

On the night of the debate, I was in the holding room with Gephardt.

The deal was that once your candidate was taken backstage and turned over to the production staff, all the campaign staff had to remain in the holding rooms. We couldn't be out walking around.

I briefed Dick about the event and told him he had the option of having the three-by-five card if he wanted to make some notes before he went on. He said he didn't need it. When the time came, I escorted him backstage and turned him over to the producer.

As I walked back to the room, I glanced up at the live monitor, which showed what was going on on the stage. It wasn't on the air yet, but it was live on the monitor. I watched as Gary Hart walked onto the stage with an full sheet of paper in his hands. Then Paul Simon walked on, and he had a file folder with a sheet of paper.

I look at my bosses and say, "These are the rules, and they're breaking them. Do you want me to do something about it?" They decide it's not a big enough deal to do anything at this late point.

Then Al Gore walked onto the stage. He was carrying a briefing book that was four inches thick. It was easily the biggest briefing book I'd ever seen, and I'm sure it was all aimed at Dick Gephardt. I turned and looked at campaign manager Bill Carrick and pollster Ed Riley. They looked at me. Finally someone said, "Do you think you can stop it?" I said, "I'm on my way."

I took off literally running all the way around the auditorium to get to the back stage. Secret Service and staff are yelling at me because they'd already done the lock down, and I was not allowed back there. I get behind the stage with about a minute and a half to go before we go on the air. The producers are screaming at me, asking me what I think I am doing there.

I quickly explain that Senator Gore's staff has broken the debate rules because he is onstage with a briefing book. They say, "Kiki, you can't possibly expect us to do anything about it now. We're about to go on the air, so we have to go with it." I firmly refused to go along.

In the meantime, Fred Martin, who was Gore's campaign manager at that time, comes out and he's furious with me. He's pointing out that Al Gore was a U.S. senator, and I couldn't do these things. I told him that my beef wasn't with Al Gore but with his staff, who were in the room when we'd made the commitment that there would be no briefing materials at the debate. I insisted on the book being taken off the stage.

Keep in mind that I was only 24 years old when I was doing this.

There's a lot of mayhem, and people don't know quite what to do. Finally I look up and say, "Listen. If I go to the edge of the stage and gesture to Dick Gephardt, he'll know I'm there for a reason. He'll get up and walk off the stage if I ask him to. He is that disciplined a candidate."

They all look at me like I'm crazy. By now there are only thirty seconds until airtime, and the clock is ticking. Then I say, "If the briefing book is not removed from the stage, then Dick Gephardt will be removed from the stage. You'll have a nationally televised debate without the frontrunner candidate."

The producers finally send a woman who's working for them up on the stage to retrieve the book. They keep telling me after she leaves, "You can go back to your holding room now." And I say, "I'm not going anywhere until I see that the briefing book is off the stage, and we're on the air." I watch this poor woman tremble as she comes down off the stage. She has this huge black three-ring binder in her hands, and she says, "He is very, very, very angry."

My task completed, I returned to the holding room. My bosses were very happy with me. Media consultant Bob Shrum, during his candidates' debates, is so loyal that he can't stand to stay in the holding room. He has to go out and pace. So it was my job to go out and walk in the foyer of this theater with him. In the middle of the debate, one of the very first gay activists on AIDS jumped up on the stage and disrupted the debate.

Of course, since we were out in the foyer, we couldn't see what the problem was, we just could hear all the commotion as the Secret Service wrestled this guy to the floor and removed him. Bob and I hurried back to the holding room to see what had happened.

Someone looked up and said, "It was Al Gore trying to find Kiki Moore for getting his briefing book."

The best part of this story is that today I'm the vice president's spokesperson. He didn't know who I was back then. I was just a 24-year-old kid on my first presidential campaign. But somewhere along the line he's probably heard the story.

Al Gore did fine that night without his book.   *—Kiki McLean*

CHAPTER 20

Presidential Campaigns in the Homestretch

☆ ☆ ☆

William Jennings Bryan, in 1896, set off on what many believe was the first national campaign.

Bryan went town to town on a train, stopping often to give a speech from the back of the last car. And, boy, could he give a speech. This is the same 36-year-old Illinois congressman who won his party's nomination after delivering the famous "Cross of Gold" speech on the floor of the Democratic convention in Chicago. People came from miles around just to hear Bryan's orations.

Bryan was challenging Ohio Governor William McKinley, who preferred to campaign the traditional way. He sat on his porch in Canton, Ohio, and seldom left town. In fact, during the campaign he never ventured outside of Ohio. McKinley won by a 271-176 margin in the Electoral College.

Four years later Bryan tried again, but the Republicans put New York Governor Teddy Roosevelt on the Republican ticket with McKinley – probably the first time the vice presidential nominee really mattered – and while McKinley never campaigned, Roosevelt campaigned coast to coast and was easily Bryan's match on the stump. In the election of 1900, McKinley won a 292-155 victory in the Electoral College.

But modern campaigns, seeing the voters, going town to town, was now the way it was done. Fast forward all the way to 1948, when President Harry Truman, framed in the press as practically dead and buried, took to the rails and campaigned furiously across the country. No pollster, no expert, no newspaper predicted a Truman victory over Republican nominee Thomas Dewey. But Truman covered more than 30,000 miles by train and, by his own count, saw nearly 15 million people. "Give 'em hell, Harry," they said, and that's exactly what he did. On Election Day Truman surprised just about everyone with a 50-45 win over Dewey, completing one of the greatest turnarounds in campaign history.

But in 1952, more voters saw the candidates on television than in person, though TV sets were still scarce. General Dwight Eisenhower's campaign produced the first political commercial – an animated spot designed by Walt Disney with dancing elephants saying "I like Ike" – and campaigns via the airwaves were here to stay.

The 2000 showdown between Governor George W. Bush and Vice President Al Gore wasn't the only squeaker in the past half century. Political pollsters say Vice President Hubert Humphrey, with just another day or two to campaign in 1968, would have caught Richard Nixon. Though the popular vote was close that year, Nixon with 43.6 and Humphrey with 42.9 percent, Nixon blew it out in the Electoral College, winning 301 to 191. That was the year Alabama Governor George Wallace was running, and he got 13.6 percent and 46 electoral votes.

Here are some stories about the homestretch run from managers and consultants who were there at the time.

Reagan Opens Campaign at the Neshoba County Fair

Factoid: Ronald Reagan beat President Jimmy Carter in Mississippi in 1980 by less than 2 percentage points, to take the state's seven electoral votes.

Philadelphia, the county seat of Neshoba County, Mississippi, is of some renown in civil rights history in the South. Three young civil rights workers were killed there in June 1964 for registering blacks to vote. Their deaths were the substance of the movie

"Mississippi Burning," released in 1988.

After the 1980 convention in Detroit, the Reagans went back to California to the ranch for a week because the Democrats were having their convention. The first movement from them out of the ranch, out into the campaign, was to be August 4, a Monday.

Congressman Trent Lott, Reagan's Mississippi chairman, comes to me and says it's was imperative that we do this Neshoba County Fair. He says it is a big political thing and all the politicians come and everybody stands in the piney woods and shakes hands. I said, "I don't think they will, because they are not supposed to leave the coast until the day after the fair."

Lott was asking me to get the Reagans to come off the ranch a day early. Let me tell you, in the Reagan campaign, there is a rule. When they are on the ranch, you leave them alone. If you mess around with their time, the threat is not from him, but Nancy will definitely get you.

Bill Timmons was the political director of the campaign, and I went to him and said, "We have a great opportunity here. The opportunity is to show the South that we are part of them by going to this county fair."

In the end the Reagans were told they were coming off the ranch on Saturday, instead of Sunday, and they were going to overnight in Los Angeles and fly out first thing in the morning to Meridian, Mississippi. They arrived about noon in Meridian, which is 40 miles from Philadelphia, and we had buses and cars because we had to take the traveling party and the press. This was the first event of the fall campaign.

The political guy was required to either be on the plane or to stand at the bottom of the steps when they came in, for any last-minute briefing. I was standing there and Lyn Nofziger came running off first and said, "You had better get out of here because if she sees you, you are fired." So I snuck off and got behind a bus where Nancy couldn't see me. We loaded up the party. There were about 20 cars and 10 buses. We took off up the road. I was sitting on the last bus with a producer from NBC.

At every gravel crossroad there would be two or three cars with people waving at the motorcade. Then you would see a house up on a hill, and there would be people sitting on the front lawn, waving at the motorcade. The TV producer turns to me and says, "What are you doing? Are you trying to play games with this?" I told him we only got the go-ahead for this event three days earlier.

The Neshoba fair crowd on a Sunday is usually about 5,000 people. There were at least 30,000 people out there. Both Lott and I knew that if you took Reagan to rural Mississippi, they would come.

The stage was a flatbed truck with a sound system. Reagan made the infamous speech about states rights, one of the high points of the campaign. At the end of his speech, the Rotary Club, which runs this thing, gave him a rocking chair. By that time Reagan is in his short sleeves. He sits in the rocking chair and pulls Mrs. Reagan down on his lap, and that picture was on the front page of every newspaper in the South the next morning.

They finally left, and all the way back to Meridian they had whole church congregations waving to Ronald Reagan. These were black churches and white churches. Hundreds of people were now standing at the little crossroads waving signs that said "God Bless Reagan."

This was the opening shot across the bow of President Carter. The signal from Reagan was, "We're coming after you in your home country." And we did.   —*Kenny Klinge*

'You Ought to Be in Charge' in Dallas

Factoid: Ross Perot took 19% of the popular vote nationwide in the 1992 presidential election. His high-water mark was 30.6% in Maine.

Ed Rollins, who was very close to the Reagan operation and a true believer in the Reagan revolution, called me one day in 1992 after he'd become convinced the Bush campaign was destined to fail. I didn't need any convincing because, frankly, I agreed with him.

The Bush campaign had lost terrific opportunities. The economy was faltering; people were concerned. The typical symbol of the campaign was a golf cart and a cigarette boat. And there was just no sensitivity to what people were concerned about. George

Bush was not going to win re-election.

And I could just see that, with the Bush collapse in 1992, we would find ourselves in a very deep hole in the Congress as well.

After a lot of soul searching, Rollins had agreed to go to work for Ross Perot as his co-campaign manager with Hamilton Jordan. Rollins asked me to come down and serve as media consultant for the campaign.

It was an amazing experience for a lot of different reasons. The first senior staff meeting in which I participated with Ross Perot was memorable. He walked into the room, and he was about five foot six inches tall, so when you stood up to shake his hand, you towered over him. He would look right into your eyes, and because he was shorter, you had to look down. He would demand of each of us, "What do you do? Who are you?"

He sat down at the table and proceeded to outline a problem. Then he went around the table, pointing at each person and saying in his rapid-fire way, "What do you think?" "What do you think?" Finally he found an answer he liked, and he said, "You're smart. You're brilliant. You know what you're talking about. Everyone else here is stupid. You ought to be in charge." Then he got up and walked out of the room.

About the third time this happened, it occurred to me that he already knew what he thought the answer should be. He would go around the table until he found someone who agreed with him. Then he would tell them they were smart. Everyone else was a moron. Of course, it alternated pretty much on a daily basis who was the moron and who was the brilliant person. Genius was not consistent in this campaign.

After two or three weeks, it was apparent to me that we were working for a psychopath. And I don't mean that in the clinical term; I mean we were working for someone who had no business running for president of the United States, someone who certainly didn't have the temperament to be president of the United States.

I went in to see Ed Rollins and said, "I've got to leave this campaign. This is not working." And Ed looked back at me and said, "I've been thinking exactly the same thing." So about four o'clock that afternoon, we had a press conference to announce we were leaving the campaign. Ed was the show at the press conference.

We walked back up to our offices, and within 15 minutes there was pandemonium. About 40 or 50 people worked for the Perot campaign as field organization. Most of them were former cadets from West Point, because Perot loved the military academies, having been a graduate of the Naval Academy. Our offices were swarmed by people going through our computers to see what we had or didn't have. Pretty much everything we had in our desks went into a box, and the box went out on the front porch. We were ushered out of the building.

The next morning, Perot announced he was dropping out of the campaign. *Time* magazine and *Newsweek* and everybody else had "quitter" printed on the front page, which galled him to no end, I'm sure. Of course, two months later he got back into the campaign. It was an interesting time. 				*—Tony Marsh*

Bush Speaks Spanish Like They Speak in the Bars

Factoid: In the state with the largest share of Hispanics, New Mexico, Vice President Al Gore is listed as having won in 2000 by 365 votes. Some observers point out that there were so many irregularities it's impossible to know who won; 42.1% of the population is Hispanic.

W e were hired during the 2000 presidential campaign to test Hispanic voters, to learn their reaction to Vice President Al Gore speaking Spanish and Governor George Bush speaking Spanish. At the time, the Gore people were very self-confident that their Spanish was much stronger than Bush's, that Bush didn't speak good Spanish and that his Spanish often had errors in it much like his English.

We went in and saw the Hispanic voters and tested both Gore and Bush speaking Spanish. The Hispanic voters said Gore's Spanish sounded like he had just come out of a high school Spanish class. Bush's Spanish sounded like he had picked it up in a neighborhood bar.

We said to them, Bush's Spanish has errors and he is not really that fluent. They said, yes, but he makes errors just like we do.

It was a very interesting example of an endemic problem to the Gore campaign, thinking that being smarter and more educated and more foreign policy oriented would develop rapport with the voters, when in fact it got in the way of developing rapport with the voters.

—*Celinda Lake*

'I Love Ronald Reagan...but'

Factoid: In the 1980 presidential election, Ronald Reagan carried Colorado over President Jimmy Carter by a 57-42 margin, winning the state's eight electoral votes.

In 1980, I was with Decision Making Information in Santa Ana, California, doing Ronald Reagan's survey work throughout the nation.

One of our interviewers called up a woman in Colorado and started going through the survey. In the surveys, you start off with general questions and work your way down to the specifics, putting the vote intention question in after doing some issue and image work.

One of the questions was on the name identification for Reagan and Carter. This woman happened to like Reagan and disliked Carter. They went through all the different issues and on every single position she would say, "Well, I'm just like Reagan. I believe this..."

They got all the way through the interview and down to the questions that said, If the election were held today, would you vote for Ronald Reagan, Republican, or Jimmy Carter, Democrat? Of course, the interviewer thought he knew how she would respond. But the lady replied that she would vote for Jimmy Carter.

The interviewer continued to go right through the script, and it is just bugging him how all the way through she had disliked Carter and loved Reagan. She also referenced Reagan several times and said his image was strong.

At the end of the interview, the interviewer simply could not take it any longer. He told her he had just one more question. He reminded her that she obviously loved Reagan. She replied, "Oh, yes, I do. He is just wonderful."

He reminded her that she had agreed with Reagan on every issue. However, when it came to the vote, she said she was voting for Carter. He said she just had to tell him why. She answered, "Well, it's quite simple. Every person who has been elected in the year that ends with zero has died in office, and I love Reagan too much to subject him to that."   *—Gary Lawrence*

BOOK FIVE

When Campaigns Go South

☆ ☆ ☆

One of the glories of the political campaign business is that there is always a judgment day looming out there soon. Unlike some lines of work that seem endless, political campaigns have a start, a middle and, thankfully, an end. Somebody is going to win and somebody is going to lose.

For the record, in a democracy it takes two to tango. If we didn't have losers, it wouldn't be a democracy. Remember how, in the old USSR, the Ruskies would claim they had democratic elections. But they had only winners on the ballot, no losers. Voters were required to show up at the polls and vote for the only candidate on the ballot, the Communist candidate.

Not everybody can be a winner. Republican Governor Harold Stassen of Minnesota probably set the record for futility. Stassen was elected governor in 1938 at the age of 31 and was re-elected to two additional two-year terms before resigning in 1943 to join the Navy. His most serious campaign for president was launched in 1948 when he won several primaries before stumbling in the Oregon primary. He and Senator Robert Taft of Ohio took New York Governor Tom Dewey to the third ballot at the 1948 GOP convention in Philadelphia. Stassen was a player at the 1952 convention before throwing his support and the Minnesota delegation to General Dwight Eisenhower to ensure a first-ballot victory over Taft. Stassen ran for president seven more times, but never with success.

The list of lovable losers is long. David Treen ran three times for Congress in Louisiana in 1962, 1964 and 1968, before winning in 1972. He was re-elected three times. He also ran once for governor in 1971, before winning in 1979. Voters dumped him four years later. Treen tried for a comeback in 1999, trying to win the first district congressional seat in a special election, but failed.

Reasons why candidates lose abound. The fact that 90 percent of incumbents seeking re-election are successful also makes clear that 90 percent of the challengers lose. Thus, bucking the entrenched incumbent, while perhaps a noble cause, is the biggest reason for defeat in our political system. The second biggest factor that determines winning and losing is the partisan make-up of the jurisdiction. For years and years, no Republican was elected to anything in the Southern states – the Solid South – because the vast majority of voters considered themselves Democrats and acted like Democrats when they got into the voting booth.

A third prominent factor that leads to losing elections is the high political tide that seems to rise up every decade or so and sweep out one party or the other. The Democrats in 1994 lost 54 seats in the U.S. House of Representatives, giving the Republicans control for the first time since 1954. In 1974, Republicans suffered the throes of Watergate and the Nixon resignation and lost 48 seats in the House. The tide ran high for the Democrats.

In 1964, Democrats won 36 new seats in the House, swept in on President Lyndon Johnson's landslide victory over Arizona Senator Barry Goldwater. Interestingly, in Alabama in 1964, the Republicans actually picked up five seats. The Crimson Tide was apparently running the other way, but only in Alabama.

Factor out incumbency, heavy partisanship and a partisan tide running one way or the other, and you finally get down to the campaigns that are truly competitive, perhaps only a fifth of the races or less. A competitive race suggests that either side has a legitimate shot at winning, and now the best candidate, or the smartest campaign plan, or the quickest counter-punch comes into play. In 2000, seven of 34 U.S. Senate races were competitive enough that the winning margin was less than 5 percent. Of the 11 gubernatorial races in 2000, three were settled inside a five-point margin. And of the 435 House seats in 2000, only 19 were settled by less than a five-point margin.

CHAPTER 21

The Art of the Dirty Trick

☆ ☆ ☆

D irty tricks in political campaigns are as old as elections. Though some dirty tricks are just an annoyance, or even seen as clever, some get very close to the ethical line between fair and foul play. What campaign staff hasn't, while working late at the headquarters, telephoned the nearest pizza delivery store and ordered up six pizzas with green peppers and anchovies delivered to the headquarters of the opponent, where the staff is also working late?

The dirty trickster with the most repute is the old Richard Nixon nemesis, Dick Tuck. Tuck is in the dirty tricks hall of fame mostly because many of his tricks – though not all — were downright clever. Nixon was running for president in 1968 under the slogan "Nixon's the one." Who else but Tuck would hire three or four very pregnant women to appear at Nixon rallies carrying large signs on sticks saying "Nixon's the one"?

Nixon's own trickster, Donald Segretti, was not nearly as clever, but perhaps more effective. It's said he organized the theft of a ream of letterheads from the Ed Muskie presidential campaign in 1972 and sent out letters discussing Muskie's opponent's sexual misconduct. While the sexual misconduct Segretti's letter suggested was pretty racy in 1972, it would probably be very tame by today's standards.

In the 2000 U.S. Senate campaign in Minnesota, Christine Ganhus sent out a number of e-mail messages, using an alias, disparaging one of the candidates in the Democratic primary, Michael Ciresi. It turns out, with modern technology, that e-mail messages are pretty easy to trace, and the disparaging messages were traced back to Ganhus, who happened to be the campaign manager and soon to be wife of the incumbent Republican senator, Rod Grams. Ciresi lost the primary to Mark Dayton, 41-22, and the dirty e-mail probably didn't affect the outcome in the least. Dayton, though, dumped Grams in the general election, 49-43. Disparaging e-mail, along with Grams' other legal problems, probably did affect the outcome of that election.

In the mayor's race in Broomfield, Colorado, in 1999, incumbent Mayor Bill Berens was caught on videotape at a Kinko's store faxing an anonymous statement charging that the local police were investigating his opponent, City Councilman Larry Cooper. The news release claimed police had Cooper under scrutiny as a suspect for attempting to steal Berens' yard signs. Berens, despite his dirty trick, was elected to a fourth term as mayor of Broomfield, a Denver suburb.

Knowing that all is fair in love and war, here are some tales of political dirty tricks, some on the clever side, some downright mean, some probably over the line.

Sundlun in Diprete's Future

Factoid: Democrat Bruce Sundlun defeated three-term Rhode Island Governor Edward Diprete in 1990, 74 to 26.

In the fall election of 1990, Bruce Sundlun, having won the three-way Democratic primary, was facing incumbent Republican Governor Ed Diprete, who had had another big scandal. The Rhode Island economy was in the tank, unemployment was rising, and the fresh reform candidate, Sundlun, was attractive and growing stronger every day. We were going to win the race.

Late in the campaign, we learned the governor's office ordered Chinese food every Friday from the same restaurant and had it brought in.

We found a baker who would put custom sayings inside the fortune cookies. We printed those up about two weeks before the general election.

The staff paid the restaurant to substitute our fortune cookies for their own. When the governor and his senior staff had their afternoon lunch on Friday, two weeks from election, we gave them a little bit of indigestion. When they opened their fortune cookies their fortunes said, "Governor Sundlun is in your future."

—George Burger

The Superglue Trick

Factoid: Idaho Republican Congressman Steve Symms defeated four-term U.S. Senator Frank Church in 1980 by less than one percentage point.

In 1980, Congressman Steve Symms was running against U.S. Senator Frank Church. It was an understatement to say that the electorate was engaged and passionate about the race. Even though Symms was well known in the first district, he wasn't known statewide. But people were coming out of the woodwork to try and elect Symms over Church.

A man named Gary Loyd was kind of our unpaid consultant in that race. Weekly, he visited just about every coffee shop in the valley, so he was our eyes and ears to the grassroots. He did a lot of things on his own.

One of the best dirty tricks I ever saw happened on Election Day in 1980. Most of Loyd's family were union folks from Bannock County. So in his mind, Election Day fraud and monkey business was business as usual.

He said, "I know these guys are going to try to pull something off on Election Day, and I want to throw them off stride." So before the sun came up, Loyd went to the Church campaign headquarters. He had something like superglue in a syringe. He proceeded to fill with glue the locks to all the doors at their campaign offices. When Senator Church's staff showed up on Election Day to finish turning out the vote, they found they weren't able to get into their offices.

Of course, Loyd was sitting in his pickup truck across the street watching the whole thing. It delayed them a couple of hours before they finally got into their own offices. *—Phil Reberger*

Locking Up the Opponent in New Jersey

Factoid: Senator Bill Bradley won re-election in New Jersey in 1984, beating Republican Mary Mochary by a 64-35 margin.

The presumed Republican nominee for U.S. Senate in 1984 to challenge Senator Bill Bradley was a woman named Mary Mochary, who was the mayor of Montclaire and a successful, wealthy lawyer. An old judge named Robert Morris challenged her in the primary. He was never a serious candidate, and his campaign was totally unorganized. He just wanted to run for office.

President Ronald Reagan was flying into New York for an event. Roger Stone, Mochary's consultant, had made arrangements for her to be one of the official greeters on the tarmac when Reagan came in on Air Force One. This primary opponent immediately began objecting, saying that in the interest of fairness, he needed to be included.

So Stone called the Secret Service anonymously from a phone booth and said there would be this lunatic at the event trying to get in to greet the president. He went on to give them Morris's name and physical description. Two hours before the president showed, Morris was picked up and rushed off by the Secret Service. He was detained for about four hours. He never knew what hit him.

—Rick Reed

The Legendary Trickster Dick Tuck

Factoid: Congressman Richard M. Nixon, from California's 12th district, was elected to the U.S. Senate in 1950 when he defeated 14th district Congresswoman Helen Gahagan Douglas by a 59-41 margin.

Dick Tuck, a legendary trickster, worked in California for many years and was the nemesis of many Republicans and Richard Nixon specifically. He was an operative, a clever guy possessing a great sense of humor. Stu Spencer told me this story, as have others.

Nixon was on a whistlestop train tour through Southern California while running for the Senate in 1950. They had a stop in Orange County with a few hundred people in attendance.

The band was playing and Nixon was introduced. People started to cheer and Nixon began to give his speech. Tuck, dressed up as a train conductor, stood on the track in front of the engineer and signaled the engineer to start moving. Nixon was still in the middle of his speech as the train pulled off into the distance.

—Don Ringe

The Rolls Royce With the du Pont Bumper Stickers

Factoid: Pierre du Pont of Delaware ran fourth in the 1988 New Hampshire presidential primary election with 10%. Vice President George Bush won with 38%, followed by Senator Bob Dole at 29% and Congressman Jack Kemp at 13%.

The New Hampshire presidential debate in 1988 contained a big Republican field that included George Bush Sr., Pete du Pont and Jack Kemp. I was working on the du Pont campaign at the time as the national political director.

Du Pont was easily the wealthiest candidate in the field and an heir to the du Pont fortune.

We gave Roger Stone, who was working for Jack Kemp, credit for this deed, though he never owned up to it and we couldn't prove it.

Right in front of the convention center where the debate was being held was a lineup of handicapped parking spaces that everybody had to walk past to get into the building. One very big Rolls Royce parked sideways with du Pont's bumper stickers on it took up two of those spaces. The car was locked with nobody around.

—Tim Hyde

Getting Even With Pierre the Fourth in New Hampshire

Factoid: Vice President George Bush won the 1988 Republican primary in New Hampshire with 37.8% of the vote. Senator Bob Dole was second, followed by Congressman Jack Kemp. Former

Delaware Governor Pierre "Pete" du Pont was fourth with 10.7%.

In 1984, I was running Bush's re-election campaign. During the last couple weeks of the campaign, it was clear Reagan-Bush were going to win re-election. The vice president was running around the country helping candidates for Congress. He was only going in for candidates who were on the bubble, either incumbents who could lose or challengers who could win.

Delaware Governor Pierre du Pont called me and said, "Listen, my wife's running for Congress. It's not going real well, to say the least. Could the vice president come up and help?" (In 1984, Elise R. W. du Pont lost to Tom Carper by a 59-41 margin.) The vice president agreed that we should do this because du Pont had done a lot for the party. We actually changed the schedule around for her and had the only good event of the campaign with Mrs. du Pont and the vice president. I remember standing on the tarmac and Pierre du Pont looking me right in the eye and saying, "We'll never forget this. We really appreciate this."

Four years later, I ran the New Hampshire Bush campaign in the primary of 1988. We were all disappointed in Delaware Governor Pierre du Pont. I loved him at the time, but now I was a jilted lover because he was the most negative of all the candidates toward Vice President Bush. He was almost nasty. There is nothing worse than a jilted lover, so I had a standing rule that if anyone in the campaign referred to du Pont by anything other than Pierre the Fourth, he or she would be dismissed from the campaign.

The state of New Hampshire had one fundraiser for the GOP party. It was the event before Governor John Sununu formally endorsed Vice President George Bush. He didn't want to hurt Governor du Pont, because they had a relationship.

When du Pont walked in and started shaking hands at the table I was sitting at, I stood up, pretending to leave the table.

"Oh, let me introduce you," I said. "Tony, this is Pierre du Pont the Fourth. Mary, this is Pierre du Pont the Fourth. Frank, this is Pierre du Pont the Fourth."

He went to another table. I followed him and started introducing him again. "Oh, Governor. Let me introduce you. Frank, Pierre du Pont the Fourth. Joe, Pierre du Pont the Fourth."

After about three times of doing this, he left. He was really steamed.

I'm the type of person who never forgives a slight to my boss. I flash back to the day on the tarmac when he gave me his word that he would always remember. Some guys are just good "forgetters."

—*Ron Kaufman*

CHAPTER 22

Exposing Real Mischief

☆ ☆ ☆

Though some folks see politicians as just a bunch of crooks trying to get rich at the public trough, most are as honest and hard-working as the next guy. Every once in a while, someone in the campaign business steps over the line and finds themselves not just in hot water, but facing jail time.

The most publicized case in 2000 occurred in Austin, Texas. Juanita Yvette Lozano, an employee of one of the media consultants for the George Bush presidential campaign, mailed a videotape to the Gore campaign showing Bush practicing for a debate with Al Gore. She also sent a 120-page Bush memo about debate preparation. The Gore campaign management had the good sense to immediately put the material into the hands of the FBI. Lozano is facing up to 15 years in prison.

An earlier edition of Debategate took place in the 1980 presidential campaign between President Jimmy Carter and Ronald Reagan. A copy of President Carter's debate briefing book ended up in the hands of the Reagan campaign team. Unlike the Gore campaign in 2000, the Reagan team read through the book and was apparently better schooled in their preparation for the one debate Reagan would have with Carter, on October 28, 1980, in Cleveland. The Debategate caper didn't become public until 1983, when *Time* magazine correspondent Laurence I. Barrett mentioned it in a two-paragraph item in a book.

There are a number of theories about how the briefing book got from the Carter camp into the hands of the Reagan debate preparation team. One of the most intriguing theories is that a disgruntled campaign worker in the Carter operation, who had worked for Senator Ted Kennedy during the primary and was still smarting from Kennedy's loss, basically slipped the book "over the transom" at the Reagan headquarters. Stories still abound as to what really happened, but no guilty party was ever named.

The story broke in March 1980 in the *Philadelphia Inquirer* about a U.S. senator, five congressmen and the mayor of Camden, New Jersey, being filmed by the FBI accepting bribes from what they thought were Arab businessmen. The FBI got a lot of heat for "entrapping" the elected officials in Abdul Scam, or better known in the press as Abscam, because there really were not any Arab businessmen and the officials were not actually being bribed. But they were indicted, tried, convicted and jailed. Hosed were New Jersey Senator Harrison Williams, New York Congressman John Murphy, Florida Congressman Richard Kelly, the lone Republican, New Jersey Congressman Frank Thompson, South Carolina Congressman John Jenrette and Pennsylvania Congressman Michael Murphy, who coined the phrase "Money talks, bullshit walks." On FBI videotape, no less.

Here are some tales of real mischief, told by political pros who were there at the time.

A Plain Brown Envelope for Flood

Factoid: Daniel Flood was first elected to Congress in 1944 and with two breaks served until resigning in 1980. All told, he was elected to 15 terms.

One of the major political movers in Wilkes-Barre, Pennsylvania, is a guy by the name of Andy Sardoni, a longtime Republican who owned a construction company. He grew up in the valley there and his dad was also very involved in politics.

Once every two years when it became time, his dad would give him a brown envelope full of money to take over to Congressman Dan Flood's home with very specific instructions. "You don't talk to anyone or anything, you just go over there, put it into the mailbox and come back."

Fourteen-year-old Andy got over to Flood's place. The mailbox was so full of brown envelopes he couldn't get one more in. He wondered what to do. Finally, he knocked at the door and handed Mrs. Flood the envelope.

He got home and got whipped bad.

It was no wonder Flood got indicted.

—Dick Minard

Clements Starts Cleaning Up Supreme Court

The Chief Justice of the Texas Supreme Court, John Hill, had run against Clements for governor in 1978, a race that Clements won by less than a point.

Hill went to Clements and said, "Bill, if you and I can bury the hatchet and agree on somebody to appoint as my successor, I will resign as chief justice. We need to clean up this court here. I've been part of the mess; I admit that. But we have got a horrible situation here; it's just a sinkhole. The trial lawyers are poring money into these judgeships. We're getting unqualified guys from the legislature. It's now become like a farm team for the court. They serve their time in the legislature and we reward them with an appointment to the court. The trial lawyers come in and pour this money into these races. I've been a judge for a long time, and these are terrible lawyers. Our cases are drifting more and more in the wrong direction."

Consequently, he and Clements found a young guy, Tom Phillips, who had been a brilliant student at Baylor, then had gone to Harvard Law School. Clements had appointed him to a district court in Houston in 1981. They agreed that he would be the ideal appointment to help clean up the court.

Hill resigned, Clements appoints Phillips, but his appointment was only a recess appointment. He has to run for election in 1988 to fill out the un-expired term, which ends in 1990. The first time Phillips ran, the Democrats raised $3 million, while we raised $2.4 million and won.

The trial lawyers in Texas, such as Joseph Jamail, who is one of the richest trial lawyers in America, had won the Pennzoil case and his fee was in the millions. Jamail was one of the lawyers putting in money for the Democrats.

In 1988, *60 Minutes* did a piece on the Texas Supreme Court, a documentary in which they interviewed Jamail and one of the judges. They had Jamail on tape with Mike Wallace saying to him, "Mr. Jamail, you don't think there's anything wrong with you giving these large sums of money to these judges?"

Jamail, on camera with a drink in his hand, says, "Hell, man, if those of us who benefit from their decisions don't support them, who the hell do you think would?" This is filmed at a Democratic fundraiser for the candidates. In the show, they cut to a judge, who is one of the beneficiaries. Mike Wallace says, "Judge, don't you feel anything about taking money from a guy like that, who says he's doing it because your verdicts benefit him?" The judge said, "Mr. Wallace, how dare you suggest that I would exchange my vote for a few dollars from this man?" While he's saying that, they flash on the screen $375,000.

We used that over and over. We used the *60 Minutes* piece in about four elections.   *—John Deardourff*

CHAPTER 23

A Classic Case of Shooting Yourself in the Foot

☆ ☆ ☆

Every election season, more than a few candidates for high public office – even some opposed to private ownership of firearms – get out the trusty revolver, insert six cartridges into the cylinder, aim the gun directly at their feet and begin pulling the trigger. Some are good enough shots to hit their foot all six times.

Maine Senator Edmund Muskie was the favorite to win the Democratic presidential nomination in 1972. He was the clear front-runner coming into the New Hampshire primary. But in February 1972, on the back of a flatbed truck, Muskie saw fit to take on William Loeb, the publisher of the *Manchester Union Leader*, who'd written several scathing editorials, one even going after Muskie's wife. With the snow falling around him, Muskie said, "By attacking me, by attacking my wife, he has proved himself to be a gutless coward." Muskie was photographed by both TV cameras and still photographers with tears in his eyes. First, he violated the fundamental rule against going after people who buy ink by the barrel. Second, "real men" didn't cry in public in those days. A political firestorm ensued, and his campaign was on the way out.

President Gerald Ford, debating Jimmy Carter on Oct. 6, 1976, in San Francisco, said, "There is no Soviet domination of Eastern Europe and there never will be under a Ford administration." A firestorm followed and American voters, already believing Ford was somewhat of a klutz, were now convinced he wasn't too bright either. But President Carter returned the favor in his only debate with Ronald Reagan, on Oct. 28, 1980, in Cleveland. Carter said, "I had a discussion with my daughter, Amy, the other day, before I came here, to ask her what the most important issue was. She said she thought nuclear weaponry and control of nuclear arms." Amy Carter was 12 years old at the time. American voters, who didn't think Carter was the sharpest knife in the drawer, were now convinced he was in over his head.

Political campaigns at all levels are filled with missteps and mistakes. A truism applies that the campaign that makes the fewest mistakes is most often the winner. Here are some stories from political pros who were there when candidates and campaigns aimed the pistol at their foot and were right on target.

Not Following the Schedule

Factoid: Democratic Congressman Charles Whitley was re-elected in 1982 to a fourth term in the U.S. House, defeating former POW Red McDaniel by a 64-36 margin in the 3rd district of North Carolina.

Red McDaniel was a POW and had actually shared a cell with John McCain during the Vietnam War. He was a wonderful man. He never walked outside in the morning without thanking God for a beautiful day. He told me that he had spent over a year without seeing the sunshine from his prison cell.

This former Navy captain was determined to run for Congress. He was a conservative and a solid Christian. This was right after Ronald Reagan was elected president, so a strong feeling ran among Republicans that it was possible to take out one of the old hard-line Democrats. McDaniel was running against Congressman Charlie Whitley in the 3rd district in North Carolina.

We go in and assess the situation to figure out the campaign strategy. We had determined after looking over the district that it was very rural. It was a fairly condensed district, and there was a little country store about every five miles. We believed that one of the easiest ways that McDaniel, who was not well financed, could put together his grassroots organization would be for him and an aide to get in his RV and go from country store to country store.

We figured he had to make this pass around the district three times. The first time he would introduce himself saying he was running. The second time he would go back and talk a little on the issues. Then on the third time he would try to move votes in October of the election year.

They struggled and didn't raise as much money as they'd hoped, but they were going along. Ronald Reagan called him an American hero in the televised endorsement he did.

For some reason, the campaign just wasn't moving and we couldn't figure out why. Every week, they'd send us these extensive campaign schedules showing us all the little towns they were covering, driving hundreds of miles in the district.

We'd go down every couple of weeks and get into the van with them. We'd do meetings in the morning then ride around the district. McDaniel was doing well, so we couldn't figure out what the problem was.

About two weeks before the election, I was in the district and drove with his wife, Dorothy, to a campaign appearance she was making on his behalf. As we get about an hour down the road, she turns to me and says, "You know, I really believe we would have won if we had followed your campaign plan."

I look at her, and I said, "What do you mean?" As far as I knew, they were doing exactly what we had laid out for them.

Dorothy said, "You know those schedules you get every week? They just type them up for you. The only time they go do them is when you come to town."

So it was the grand admission from the candidate's wife that told the truth. McDaniel was soundly trounced. All the thought we had put into it was all for naught, because he just would not get out and do the campaigning.

Great strategy, but it was never implemented, so it was not a winning campaign.

—*Ladonna Lee*

Boschwitz's Biggest Mistake

Factoid: Rudy Boschwitz served two terms in the U.S. Senate, winning election in 1978 and 1984 before losing in 1990 to college professor Paul Wellstone by a 50-48 margin.

In the 1990 campaign cycle, Rudy Boschwitz, the incumbent Republican senator, was in an even race with his opponent, Democrat Paul Wellstone. Boschwitz had dropped about 23 points in three weeks.

We were at a loss as to why it had happened in concert with the Grunseth incident. The best political minds around us couldn't figure out how to get traction against that. Rudy, to his credit, was trying to do constructive things. He wrote a letter to rally the Jewish community. The letter described his philosophy and talked about all the many things he'd done on behalf of Israel. It was a very moving, quite lengthy, single-spaced letter.

Rudy's letter had one line that addressed Wellstone. He informed the reader – and it was going to just a small group of Jewish supporters — that Wellstone had chosen not to raise his children in the Jewish faith.

The significance of the line flew below the radar of everyone who read the letter, including me. And I believe to this day that it absolutely ended his race.

Wellstone came back with an ad, a very smartly designed counter-punch, with the theme that Boschwitz thinks there is something wrong with being a Christian in Minnesota. We sank like a rock after that. I think it was the most definitive campaign mistake I've ever observed, and certainly the bigger mistake I've ever been associated with.

—Tom Mason

Losing With Dignity in Texas

Factoid: In a rematch in 1970, Democrat Preston Smith won a second term as governor of Texas, beating Paul Eggers 54-46. Smith defeated Eggers in 1968, 57-43.

Paul Eggers was running for governor of Texas in 1970 against the incumbent, Preston Smith. Smith was not very strong and did not have strong numbers. The Republicans thought we had a real opportunity for a win.

Eggers had run in 1968 and was under-financed, but he had run a good campaign in terms of the results. Senator John Tower urged Eggers to run again then recruited me to manage the race.

Eggers was having trouble getting support in the party, particularly from the conservatives. The Republican candidate for lieutenant governor, Byron Fullerton, was on the faculty at the University of Texas Law School. He was articulate, conservative, philosophically consistent and had a real following in the party. Our problem was that he had not endorsed Eggers. This was October, and it was starting to become an issue that our lieutenant governor candidate had not endorsed the candidate for governor.

Several of us, including John Knags and myself, had a number of conversations with Fullerton. He finally agreed that if Eggers would ask him, he would endorse him.

Eggers agreed to come to Austin on a Sunday. He normally did nothing on weekends. We sent the plane up to get him and he grudgingly came to Austin for the meeting at the old Sheraton Hotel on the river. We went up to Fullerton's suite. We were there for almost three hours. Everybody knew why we were there. Eggers knew well what his mission was, but he just would not ask Fullerton for his endorsement, and Fullerton was not going to cave in.

We left the meeting and were out on the street walking down the sidewalk. The question arose as to why Eggers did not ask for Fullerton's endorsement.

He replied, "You all have the wrong goal. You don't share my goal. Your goal is to win. Mine is to lose with dignity, and I will not ask him to endorse me because that is not dignified."

That can put a damper on the campaign team, to put it mildly.

—*Eddie Mahe*

O'Keefe Self-destructs in Montana

Factoid: Republican Lieutenant Governor Judy Martz became the first woman elected governor of Montana in 2000 when she defeated State Auditor Mark O'Keefe 51-47.

A group of Montana businesspeople had gotten together and

formed an organization they called "People For Montana." They decided they wanted to discuss some of the issues taking place in the 2000 race for governor. In a two-week period in late August, the organization ran a television ad attacking the record of Mark O'Keefe, a millionaire candidate who had been the state auditor for eight years.

O'Keefe, in an unusual campaign strategy, decided he had to go on a three-city tour of the state to combat this group of businessmen. He decided to go to the businesses of three of the main players in this group of Montanans, and with big banners that said "corporate giveaways" or some kind of anti-corporate message, give a speech about how these big, bad companies were out to destroy him.

In those planned events, O'Keefe proudly proclaimed that he was going to be business' "worst nightmare." Those two words led to his demise.

You learn many things on a campaign late at night or early in the morning. I received a call on my cell phone in late August about 6 a.m. from one of our biggest supporters in Billings who asked, "Have you read the paper yet?"

I had been up until two in the morning, as we often were, so of course I had not gotten up to read the papers yet. He immediately read me the whole article and said, "Worst nightmare. Let's get on this thing."

By the time I got into the office at eight people all around the state were already working on this issue. When I talk about how their strategy was the momentum turner for our campaign, that was it. When people read that comment in the paper that morning, they knew this was what we needed.

The Martz campaign capitalized on it at every opportunity. It turned the entire campaign around. From the moment he said those two words, it was almost as if the tides changed.

We went on the offense against those two words, saying that while we had been talking about job creation and economic growth for the past year, O'Keefe himself said why it was Montana shouldn't elect him—it was going to be the worst nightmare of the people who were creating the jobs.

Not only that, it rallied people from every corner of the state. It rallied the grassroots, it rallied the businessmen, organizations and associations. Pretty soon, you had this whole groundswell of people whose sole objective was to talk about Mark O'Keefe being Montana's worst nightmare.

Authors Note: *A well-known Montana Democratic insider, active in statewide campaigns in the 2000 election cycle, said the O'Keefe campaign, with a large cadre of consultants, pollsters and advisers, held weekly (and sometimes more often than that) conference calls with the full team of advisers participating. In late August, when the Montana business group began running their TV ads "attacking" O'Keefe, the team was faced with decisions on how to react.*

Democratic pollster Celinda Lake, a key operative on the O'Keefe strategy team and, incidentally, a Montana native, is said to have led the team to the decision that O'Keefe needed to make a statement about being tough on Montana business. Lake is given credit, by the Montana Democratic insider, for suggesting the "worst nightmare" line.

The day before O'Keefe launched a three-city tour to combat the business group TV attack, he was asked for a response to the attack by Chuck Johnson, the state bureau chief for the Lee Newspapers in Helena. O'Keefe read Johnson a statement that included the line that he would be business's worst nightmare if he was elected governor. Johnson, not believing what he'd heard, asked O'Keefe to repeat the statement, not once, but twice. O'Keefe read the statement again, and then again, each time including the phrase "worst nightmare." Johnson's story ran on the front page of Montana's daily newspapers the next day. O'Keefe had successfully inflicted on his own campaign a fatal blow.

—Shane Hedges

CHAPTER 24

Just a Bad Day at the Office

☆ ☆ ☆

In political campaigns Murphy's Law applies frequently: If anything can go wrong, it will go wrong. The presses have just finished printing 100,000 campaign brochures when the huge typographical error is discovered. The candidate, usually fast on his feet, chooses the editorial board meeting at the largest newspaper in the state to make the biggest gaff of the campaign.

Ed Bethune was running for Congress in the 2nd district in Arkansas in 1978. Late in the campaign, 25,000 fundraising letters, already stuffed and sealed into the envelopes, arrived at the campaign headquarters ready to go to the post office. There was just one problem—a misspelled word. Not just any word, but the candidate's own name. Bethune was spelled "Bethue" throughout the letter, including the letterhead and the pre-printed signature. To the campaign's credit, they quickly ordered a dozen rubber stamps that said, "There's a big mistake in this letter. See if you can find it." They stamped the 25,000 envelopes across the front in red ink and hauled them to the post office. They reported that the financial return from the letter was the best of the campaign, and dozens of checks came back with a note attached asking what the mistake was. Bethune, by the way, became the first Republican elected in that congressional district since Reconstruction.

The tradition in Montana is for the Republican "team" to fly around the state to the seven TV markets on Saturday before the November election, trying to gin up a last round of news stories and build momentum for the election. The trip is always well-planned and all the TV cameras show up, along with a bunch of cheering volunteers. On the third stop of the day on the 1994 fly-around, Senator Conrad Burns—accompanied by Governor Marc Racicot and the congressional candidate, Cy Jamison, plus a few others—flew into Kalispell for the press conference and rally. Their airplane taxied up and was met with . . . a resounding silence. Nobody was there. No press, no volunteers, no nothing. As it turns out, Kalispell is probably the only town in the state with two airports, and the multitudes were, of course, at the other airport. Burns was re-elected handily and even got 60+ percent in Flathead County.

Here are some stories from campaign managers and consultants about their bad day at the office.

That Wasn't Shalala on the Phone

Bruce Sundlun had been elected the "ethics governor" of Rhode Island in 1990. In order to avoid impropriety, we had a private telephone line put into the governor's office that Sundlun could raise money through on his own time and the taxpayers would not be billed for it. This is when they had two-year terms for governor in Rhode Island. It was very much like being a House member where you had to raise money all the time.

In 1992 Bill Clinton was elected president and Donna Shalala became Secretary of Health and Human Services. Rhode Island was the first state in the nation to receive this Medicare waiver. They had done a great job at getting all the necessary paperwork and documentation together, and they really wanted this waiver. In late winter of 1993, this was a very big deal.

There had been some preliminary discussions with Shalala about how the announcement of the waiver would work. She said she would only do a telephone announcement and press conference, in an open format, if she could pick up the phone, dial the governor and Sundlun would answer. No intermediary, no switchboard, no nothing. We only have one line that doesn't go through the state switchboard, the governor's private line.

One of the guys in the press office, Mike Cabral, ran the wire from the governor's office into the big state conference room,

which is right next to his office, where they do the formal ceremonies. Shalala is to call and inform Sundlun at the stroke of 11
that the president has approved the waiver .

A little background about Governor Sundlun. He is now on wife
number five. Sundlun is a wonderful man and full of a zest for life.
At that time, in his first term, his wife, Marjorie, had been injured in
a jogging accident and was severely mentally impaired. After the
accident, and following an appropriate amount of time, the governor started associating with other women.

All of the television stations in Boston, as well as the television
stations in Providence, were there to film this big event, and we had
the *Boston Herald* represented. For Sundlun, this was an unusually
large press conference.

Shalala was to call at the stroke of 11, and the media was
assembled. Everything was miked up for live television in
Providence and Boston, as well as live radio. Right at the stroke of
11 o'clock the phone rings. The governor picks up the phone, a big
grin on his face, ready to receive the approval from the president of
the United States for the first Medicare waiver in the country.

The first words that come across are "Hello, Bruce." It was his
girlfriend, and it was captured on live television. Sundlun turned
beet red and said, "Now is not a good time."

The nightly news and the promos for the nightly news featured
life's most embarrassing moment. They had promoted it so hard
that the stations went live on this. Shalala's call came five minutes
later. It was anticlimactic.   —*George Burger*

The Wrong Logo in Cowboy Country

*Factoid: Senator David Karnes, who had been appointed to fill a
vacancy in Nebraska, defeated Congressman Hal Daub in the 1988
Republican U.S. Senate primary election, 55-45.*

Congressman Hal Daub was running for U.S. Senate in the
Nebraska Republican primary in 1988. He was working hard in the
western part of the state, where the Republican base is.

He does a fairly typical campaign ad where with a rancher

working his cattle in the lot, and Daub is out there working with him, apparently understanding the cattle business. At the very end, they are walking away, talking, and you can read the logo on the back of Daub's jeans: Jordache.

Everybody in cowboy country had a fun time with that.

—Scott Cottington

Despite Bad Luck, Bauman Beats Malkus in Maryland Special

Factoid: Maryland State Senator Bob Bauman was elected to Congress in August 1973 when he defeated Democrat Fred Malkus 51-49 in a special election in the 1st district.

Maryland's first district went through two special elections in two years. Republican Bill Mills was elected in a special election in 1971, replacing Rogers C.B. Morton. Then a second special election was called in 1973 after Mills took his own life. Republican State Senator Bob Bauman was running for Congress in the second special election.

Everything seemed to go wrong for the Bauman campaign. The Republican incumbent, Bill Mills, had committed suicide under the guise of overwhelming guilt about Watergate. He had apparently taken some money from the RNC out of the White House that he thought was illegal.

Then, while we were trying to put the campaign together, Bob Halderman and John Erlichman went on the radio with their Watergate testimony. About that time, the tapes story leaked out.

We finally got Vice President Spiro Agnew's endorsement and announced that he would appear as keynote speaker at the Bauman Round-up, a wind-up campaign gala. That came out one day and the next day the Baltimore newspapers were running headlines that read, "Agnew to Be Indicted."

The big campaign gala was supposed to be a beef barbecue. This was a time when beef was in short supply. It was known as the Nixon Beef Shortage. Who was our master of ceremonies to introduce "Indicted Agnew"? None other than Earl Butz, the Nixon secretary of agriculture.

But, with intensive telephone banks and a very good turnout effort, Bauman won the campaign.   *—Buddy Bishop*

Moving to Florida, Win or Lose

Factoid: Ruth Ann Minner was elected governor of Delaware in 2000 when she defeated Republican John Burris, 59-40.

In the 2000 election John Burris, a Republican candidate for governor of Delaware, hired me as an adviser. His heart, in many ways, was not in the campaign. It was not a very pretty campaign from top to bottom.

When a lot of my friends worked on his Senate race back in 1984, he had spouse problems at the time. He now had a new wife and even more spouse problems. She was not the most popular person in the campaign. She's in the campaign headquarters along with about 20 volunteers, which was all the campaign had left.

She said, "Everybody wants me to be in two places at the same time. I'm sick and tired of this campaign. We just bought a house in Florida, and win or lose we're moving there the day after the election." That put an end to the interest the few remaining volunteers had in Burris's campaign.   *—Tim Hyde*

Baucus Gives It All in 5K Race

Factoid: Max Baucus won a third term in the U.S. Senate in 1990 when he defeated Montana Lieutenant Governor Alan Kolstad, 69-29.

Nike sponsored a five-kilometer race in Washington, D.C., and they pushed hard to get members of Congress and the administration to participate. They had this thing about who's the fastest man in the Senate, who's the fastest man in the House, etc.

Since Max Baucus is a runner and in fairly good shape, Max participated for a number of years. Baucus was pretty proud of being the fastest man in the Senate for 10 years. Senators and members of Congress would have five people on their team, and at least one of the team members had to be a woman.

Max was trying to put together a team of his staff or even former staff, but he was having a tough time. It didn't quite make sense to me. Nobody wanted to run with Max.

I was going to work on Baucus's campaign in 1989 and wasn't doing anything on a Sunday morning, so I went out to watch the race. Baucus ran so hard that at the end of the race he was down on the grass vomiting.

Here's the United States senator who, in front of national TV cameras and his colleagues in the Senate, has run so hard that he's on the grass vomiting. When his staff people come across the finish line, Max was berating them because they weren't vomiting. Obviously, they hadn't tried hard enough to win this race.

It just goes to show how competitive Max Baucus really is. One of the reasons Baucus has continued to win is because he is so competitive. He is a difficult person to work for because nothing you ever do is good enough. However, it is easier to work for Baucus if you understand that he holds himself to the same standard. He works 18 hours a day and at the end of the day he's pissed about the things he didn't do, rather than about the things he did. It's what makes him an effective candidate. But you almost had to see him vomiting on the grass to recognize how competitive Baucus really is.

—Dave Hunter

CHAPTER 25

When TV Goes Bad

☆ ☆ ☆

There's a truism in the political campaign business that more campaigns are lost than are won. It's not a play on words, you can be sure. Some campaigns are, of course, coming down the stretch and are able to pull a rabbit out of the hat and produce a victory. But more often, one of the campaigns in a competitive race stumbles in the final days and victory falls away from their grasp. More times than not, it's because they put a television commercial on the air attacking the opponent, and it boomerangs. The attack is either so lame that voters easily see it's a last-gasp effort to win, or the commercial is factually wrong and the other side is able to refute the charge and gain the upper hand. Counter-punching in October is indeed a true art, but it's also the time when the simplest mistake becomes overwhelming.

Senator Jack Schmitt, running for re-election in New Mexico in 1982, should have been cruising to an easy win over Attorney General Jeff Bingaman. Schmitt was an astronaut who had walked on the moon, he was as honest as the day is long and he had a decent record in his only term in the Senate. Two years earlier, the New Mexico prison had erupted in one of the bloodiest riots in American history. Thirty-three prisoners died and eight guards were brutalized, though all survived. As attorney general, Bingaman conducted the initial investigation in the riot. Late in the campaign, the Schmitt campaign aired a commercial charging Bingaman with doing a poor and incomplete job in the investigation. Bingaman was able to counter-punch with credible evidence that he, in fact, had done a very good job. Schmitt's campaign went into the toilet and he lost, 54-46.

Here are some stories by political TV producers about the time their TV spot went bad.

Vilsack Upsets Lightfoot in Iowa

Factoid: State Senator Tom Vilsack beat former Congressman Jim Ross Lightfoot to capture Iowa's governor's office in 1998, by a 52-47 margin.

Anytime I hear someone say, "There's no way we can lose this race," I know there's a way. Jim Ross Lightfoot should have been the next governor of Iowa in 1998. But a combination of things went wrong, including a bad use of an issue.

John Maxwell was a good general consultant. He left the campaign about a month before the general election, which upset the whole apple cart. The campaign brought in Tom Synhorst, who is a good political operative. But Tom had more on his plate than anyone in politics. Nancy Lightfoot, the candidate's wife and campaign manager, ended up as the chief decision maker.

Lightfoot wanted to be governor about 80 percent of the time, but he didn't have the fire in his belly 100 percent of time. He had a campaign organization that was well set up, but the campaign was emotionally so distressing all the time that it was just terrible. The switch in consultants at the last minute compounded that stress.

On the other side, State Senator Tom Vilsack was running an excellent race with some excellent media. Lightfoot was so far ahead in the polls when we went into the general that we had an ad cut before the primary thanking people for electing Jim. We reserved the time to run that on the air, and we bought the time three weeks out. We were that sure of winning.

The closest thing to a slogan we had was "Governor Jim Ross Lightfoot." After the fact, we realized that we never tested it. The ads were very low-key and elegant with slow-moving waving flags, cornfields in Iowa. They moved numbers in the right way, and everything was going fine. Except that, we discovered later, people thought it was presumptuous to be calling him governor before he was elected.

The biggest mistake, and where the numbers started to turn on us and we never regained our footing, was an issue that was pushed hardest by Nancy Lightfoot.

She picked as a big issue the problem of nude dancing. Tom Vilsack had voted to allow nude dancing in local neighborhoods. This bill had come up in the state legislature, and he'd been a key person against the measure that would have banned nude dancing in neighborhoods, therefore, supposedly being for nude dancing.

Not only did she want a nude dancing TV spot, but she wanted a devastating spot that showed nude dancers. It was one of those instances that come in every campaign cycle where you bite your lip and hold your tongue.

So we cut this spot in the seedy part of Hollywood. It had the flashing lights, the dark alleys. They got researcher after researcher to confirm it. We had bill numbers. We had votes. We had it all listed on the screen. We hit this spot like a ton of bricks. It was artistically good, but there was just one horrible flaw. Vilsack had never voted that way.

Vilsack let it run a day or two, so we could dig our hole deep, then he came back very calmly and said, "You know, that's just simply not true. Here's the real vote. And I'm sorry they have gone so far off the deep end." That set the tone for the remainder of the race, as we went grasping for straws from a 30-point advantage to a loss by five points. We appeared to be desperate.

After the election, I went to Iowa and met with the Lightfoots, then took a day off and stayed at this little bed and breakfast in the town of Perry. An older man was taking me to my room, and he asked me what I did. I told him. He proudly told me that Tom Vilsack had stayed in that very room before. So I said, "I hate to tell you this, but I represented Jim Lightfoot."

He said, "Oh, tell me you didn't. I always thought that man was so great. Then he went out there and started calling himself governor before we even had an election. I figured he wasn't the man I thought he was." Talk about adding insult to injury.

—*Fred Davis*

The Competent Consultant's Nightmare

Factoid: Martha Wilkinson, wife of Kentucky Governor Wallace Wilkinson, attempted to succeed her husband in 1991 but pulled out of the Democratic primary at the last minute. Lieutenant Governor Brereton Jones won the nomination with 38% and was elected governor in the fall when he defeated Congressman Larry Hopkins, 65-35.

A lot of people thought Governor Wallace Wilkinson wanted his wife to succeed him as governor of Kentucky in 1991. Wilkinson had become governor out of the blue in 1987, winning an upset in the Democratic primary with just 35 percent of the vote. Wilkinson implemented a state lottery, with the money going to improve schools. Education is a huge issue in Kentucky. They are very aware of their image as a state that doesn't educate its kids effectively.

Martha Wilkinson had been a quiet, dutiful wife without any public profile at all. She hadn't really been involved too much. People didn't know much about her, except that her rich husband Wallace didn't want to give up his governorship and wanted to put her in there so he could, in effect, still be governor.

We were battling the perception of Martha Wilkinson on a lot of different fronts. She had been a former schoolteacher. With education being a key issue in Kentucky, we saw a great opportunity. The centerpiece of her education plan was going to be competency testing for teachers. Martha, as a former schoolteacher, would have some credibility on the subject. It was going to give us an opportunity to define her and give her a profile that was independent of her husband.

I was in the studio one night, at Modern Video in Philadelphia, making a television advertisement about competency testing for teachers. We put up the text to accompany the narration, and I didn't notice it at the time, but *competency* was spelled wrong. The ad was made, the dubs were sent to the stations and the spot went on the air.

There it was, Martha Wilkinson on camera talking about how teachers ought to know the subject, ought to be able to pass the test, ought to be able to spell and do math if they wanted to teach our kids. If they couldn't pass the competency test, they didn't belong in the classroom.

You can imagine the editorials. It was absolutely my fault for being careless and not dotting all the I's and crossing all the T's. It was not Martha's fault, she had nothing to do with it, but she was the butt of jokes and the butt of columns and the butt of editorials and the butt of everything you can imagine. It fed everything that people instinctively wanted to believe about her. That is the consultant's nightmare, spelling competency C-O-M-P-T-E-N-C-Y.

—Steve McMahon

Attack Spot Backfires in Illinois

Factoid: Charles Percy served three terms in the U.S. Senate from Illinois, from 1967 to 1985. He lost a bid for a fourth term to Congressman Paul Simon in 1984, 50-48.

Chuck Percy, incumbent Republican senator, was running against Paul Simon, a Democrat congressman, in the 1984 Illinois Senate race. Percy was never terribly popular and had only barely won his race in 1978. He was deeply in trouble in 1984, even though it was a big Reagan year. We had fallen behind.

At some point – I believe it was during the Iranian hostage crisis — Paul Simon had been very pandering toward the Ayatollah Khomeini. In the end, we thought this might be the nuclear bomb we could use to blow up Simon with his "sucking up to Khomeini" comment. We produced what I thought was a terrific ad, and I thought it would really blow him away.

However, Percy was uncomfortable with bringing up the Ayatollah and using the inflammatory footage of the embassy being burned and whatnot. Percy kept delaying and delaying.

We wanted to use the commercial during the first week in October, and we kept saying there was a limited window in which this ad could run. We believed it couldn't run too close to the election because it would look desperate. We keep telling Percy that we've got to do this sooner instead of later.

Percy kept delaying, so we didn't get to run it until late

October, and it absolutely backfired. It looked so out of left field
for this milquetoast, moderate Republican U.S. senator to suddenly
accuse Simon of being what amounts to an Arab sympathizer. It
completely backfired.

Percy went south; Simon went north. We were dead. That may
have been the biggest backfire commercial I've ever worked on.

—*Larry McCarthy*

Paving Commercial Offends Rural Voters

*Factoid: Montana Lieutenant Governor Ted Schwinden defeated his
1976 running mate, Governor Tom Judge, in the Democratic
primary in 1980, then defeated Republican House Minority Leader
Jack Ramirez in the general election, 55-45*

Ted Schwinden beat Jack Ramirez for governor in 1980 when
Ronald Reagan swept the country and swept the West. There were
very few Democratic victories in governors' races that year.

One of the reasons Ramirez didn't win came at the end of that
campaign. The Ramirez campaign ran a TV ad attacking Schwinden
for paving a portion of a highway between Wolf Point and Scobey.
The highway department had taken a road that was previously gravel
and paved part of it. The pavement literally stopped at the road to
Schwinden's house.

The truth was that Schwinden didn't have anything to do with it.
The decision had been made earlier. In politics, however, that
doesn't count for anything. Particularly when they can run the TV
footage of the pavement stopping at Schwinden's mailbox 11 miles
north of Wolf Point.

The critical mistake they made was they opened the ad with a
line that said, "Most people think that Highway 30 from Wolf Point
to Scobey goes from nowhere to nowhere." Then they go on to
explain about paving the road.

When they put that ad out we in the Schwinden campaign got
thousands of phone calls from people in eastern Montana, saying,
"That bastard. What does he think he's talking about? He's accusing
us out here in eastern Montana of living from nowhere to nowhere?"

This was 1980, and it was much easier to go over the edge with negative campaigning than it is today. Ramirez lost a whole bunch of rural eastern Montana counties that Reagan probably carried by 40 points. I think that putting out this negative ad in the last 10 days of the campaign cost him many rural votes that should have been Republican votes because he offended the sensibility of people in eastern Montana.   —*Dave Hunter*

Backlash From Black Radio

Factoid: In the off-year elections in Mississippi in 1979, Bill Allain was narrowly elected attorney general, defeating Republican Charlie Pickering, 52-48.

In the 1979 campaign for attorney general in Mississippi, the Republicans had a great candidate named Charles Pickering. I was involved in the campaign trying to work black voter issues. At the time the Republicans hadn't yet won a statewide election in Mississippi, but Pickering was thought to have a chance to break through.

We cut some radio ads targeted to the black community that were released prematurely. The radio ads started running on Thursday, before the Tuesday election. The ads charged Pickering's opponent, Bill Allain, with being a member of "the White Citizens' Council." That gave Allain the opportunity to react and put our candidate clearly on the spot. I think it was a backlash as a result.

Although I was not directly involved in the design of the ads and how they were released, I felt that they got by me, and I felt bad about it. I left Mississippi with my tail between my legs.

One of the great calls I got was from Kenny Klinge who said, "Stuff happens. Sometimes we control it, sometimes we can't. We need to pick ourselves up and move on." Kenny and I are great friends to this day. I remind him that when I was at my lowest level, he was there to pick me up. That was one of those things you're always going to feel bad about. Although I couldn't control it, it impacted the area I had responsibility for.   —*Bob Wright*

'Goober' Wins Oklahoma Primary

*Factoid: In the Oklahoma 2ⁿᵈ district, Democrat Brad Carson beat
Andy Ewing in the 2000 general election, 55% to 42%.*

$\mathbf{D}$r. Tom Coburn had been the congressman in the 2ⁿᵈ district in
Oklahoma for the past three terms and had joined the conservative
fad of term-limiting himself to just six years.

My candidate in the 2000 primary was a guy named Jack Ross.
When you looked at all the candidates, he was the obvious choice
for winning. He was the good-looking businessman. However,
several things were working against him.

Number one, he contacted me only a month before the primary
election, so he was way late in getting started. Second, he hadn't
raised sufficient money to run a competitive campaign. And third,
but most important, he was not Congressman Coburn's personal
choice for the nomination.

Coburn had about an 85 percent approval rating in the district.
He was a longtime pediatrician who had delivered most of the kids
born in this rural area outside Muskogee, Oklahoma. He was
devoutly religious and known to be a very honest man. He had done
as much in Washington as probably anyone can in only six years in
Congress. He had gone into the job with this term-limits pledge. A
man of his word, everyone knew he'd keep his pledge, but that
limited the things he could accomplish.

And this was the big flaw. Jack Ross would not sign the term-
limits pledge. Coburn really wanted to stay in the seat and probably
wrestled long and hard about whether to live up to his term-limits
pledge. Jack Ross said he thought the term-limits pledge was a
limiting factor and the district deserved someone who would be
there longer. As a result, Coburn decided to recruit another candidate, a guy named Andy Ewing.

I grew up in an adjacent congressional district, knowing Andy
Ewing from seeing his many automobile TV commercials. I think
every television market probably has one of these guys. Andy was
the corn-pone hick. He was a good guy, and no one would ever say a
bad thing about him, but he made his money by being corny on TV.
His slogan, which I remember from childhood, was, "Annnnndy

Ewwwwing. In Muskogee."

Now there are about four weeks left in the campaign. Ross has enough money for two ads, and that was stretching it. We had to accomplish two things. Number one, we had to show that Ross was a viable alternative to this sort of puppet character. That was not hard to do because Jack really was a class act.

The second thing we had to do – without saying a bad word about Ewing because we knew that would backfire – was make voters think twice about voting for Ewing. We had to help voters come to the conclusion that this was that goofball from TV who you just couldn't vote for.

So two weeks from the mid-August election, we did this ad that showed Ross as the Marlboro man. He was a cutting-horse champion, and we got him on his horse with a cowboy hat and a beautiful western shirt, and he basically just rode through all these pretty fields.

It was very successful, and everyone loved it.

Then came the second commercial. We sat around at the office and worked and worked to try to get this ad down. We tried every concept of the anti-car-dealer idea we could think of. At some point, I said the problem was that while Ewing was really a good guy, he was just sort of a "goober."

One thing led to another and we ended up with our second ad. We got a number of people from the local district including the superintendent of schools, a church leader and a political activist to appear in the spot. I don't think one person in that commercial was a day under 60.

We shot it in a very old log cabin that utilized several different parts of the cabin so it had the same feel without looking like everyone was lined up to talk at once. They all said either nice things about Ross or nice things about Ewing. Then they'd say that they just couldn't see Andy as a congressman.

The whole trick to the ad is right at the end, when somebody says, "Yeah, Andy's a good man." Then it cuts to this little old lady who's sitting at the window. She looks up at the camera and says, "Andy Ewing is a nice man, but he's kind of a goober." And that was the end of the spot.

You'd think hell had melted the ices of the damned. I've never in my life had so much press generated from a TV ad for a candidate.

Our Marlboro ad had moved our numbers dramatically, but it was obviously not going to move our numbers enough to win. I think we were down about 35 points at two weeks out. Ross probably wasn't going to win, but we wanted to do the best we could for him. The "goober" ad started running on Thursday morning. It was the lead news story on two of the network broadcast stations for that area. It was the lead story on the third station the next day. These were long news stories – between five and eight minutes long. Reporters would go into the district and ask people if they knew what a goober was.

Andy Ewing took the bait. He had an "I'm not a goober" press conference. As fate would have it, hardly anyone attended his press conference, and he held it in this great big room in the press club. The reporters showed these wide shots of Andy speaking to an empty room. All their questions for him were about "what is a goober?"

One of the stations went back to their old files and pulled a clip of Goober from *The Andy Griffith Show* and compared the two on their telecasts.

Ross spent the last week of the campaign handing out little bags of Goobers candy everywhere he went. We lost by about eight points, but we made up 25 points in three weeks. Everyone was pretty happy except for Ross, of course, because he'd wanted to win.

Unfortunately, Ewing was damaged goods and eventually lost the general election to Democrat Brad Carson.   —*Fred Davis*

BOOK SIX

Good War Stories Well Told

Every endeavor has its favorite war stories. In the news business, reporters tell about stumbling onto that great story they hope will lead to a Pulitzer Prize. Traveling salesmen have stories about sales made and sales missed, and a few damsels met along the way. Lawyers tell about loony clients and obstinate juries. Most stories from farmers have to do with the weather. Political campaigners are certainly no different and have their own brand of war stories.

There's a certain camaraderie that develops in a political campaign, not unlike foxhole buddies in a war, or a sports team playing through a season. Your comrades become your best friends, if only for the duration of the campaign. Men and women have come together to work long, hard hours often under a great deal of pressure.

One of the fundamental reasons campaign junkies become addicted to the political wars is that they see it as a mission, a cause. They see themselves on the side of right against wrong. And in blinding moments, maybe they even see themselves as good against evil.

Campaign warriors are very competitive—they thrive on the hyper atmosphere of a campaign war room. How many places are there to work where you can write ad copy for TV, radio or mail and call a normally decent human being a sleazy, tax-raising, baby-killing polluter. Well, there aren't many, that's for sure.

The best managers in the campaign business are those who can stand in the headquarters with the walls caving in, the opponent attacking their candidate on statewide TV, the press calling to ask about the stupid joke the candidate told at the last rally and still say, "God, I love this job."

In fact, if you're a campaign dropout, it's often because the competition is too fierce and the blood pressure gets too high. Soon you're counting the days, then the hours, until it's over. Please, God, let it end soon. The other chief cause of campaign dropout is when corporate America realizes how good you are, how much pressure you can take, and offers you a real job with a big salary and benefits. Beats the seasonal nature of campaigns every time.

Political war stories, traditionally, are told in proximity to a bar. As a consequence, the stories are known to improve over time. Like the old country song says, "The girls all look prettier at closing time." That kind of atmosphere, that kind of competition, that kind of life is ready-made for some good storytelling.

CHAPTER 26

Good Stories Live on in Campaign Lore

☆ ☆ ☆

S ome stories from the political trenches are just good stories, well told. They may or may not have had any impact on the outcome of an election, but they're just plain good tales. Think about a gathering of political pros, from either side of the partisan fence, at a family reunion. The same old stories get told over and over, but the relatives never seem to tire of hearing them.

In the 1988 Conrad Burns Senate campaign in Montana, money was very tight until near the end, but when donors saw that Burns was gaining rapidly in the polls on Senator John Melcher, contributions came pouring in. On the Friday before the election, the Burns campaign found themselves with several thousand dollars of unspent funds, and they understood that the single biggest mistake in campaign politics is to end up on Election Day with money in the bank and a narrow loss at the ballot box. They set out to spend the money however they could. One Burns campaign consultant, Ladonna Lee, was calling TV stations asking if any additional spots could be bought for the last three days of the campaign. She called out to the TV station in Glendive – the smallest TV market in the United States – and asked for availabilities, or "avails," as it's known in the trade. The owner of the station asked how much money she might like to spend. Lee said she could spend as much as $2,100. "Honey," the station owner replied, "for $2,100 you can buy the station."

That story has been told around every bar in the West where campaigners gather to share stories and consume drink. Here are some well-told stories from all over the country.

'Maggie, They're Trying to Screw One of Your Old Friends'

When Hubert Humphrey went back to the Senate after the 1970 election, a man who has a business in Moorhead, Minnesota, comes in to see Humphrey one day. He had these little chopped-off trucks that pulled prefabricated homes and delivered them. Over the years, he had built himself a pretty good business to the point where he now could apply to the ICC for an interstate permit.

The man pulls out this old tattered newspaper clipping from 1953. There had been a little story about a letter from Humphrey congratulating him on this new business he had started. Humphrey had written to let him know if he could ever be of any help to just let him know. The man had been holding on to it all these years.

Humphrey said, "Tell me what I can do."

The man starts to tell how he built this business and applied for this permit and the hearing officer said he was going to get it, yet they had called the day before to notify him that, instead, they were going to give the permit to a friend of Congressman Wilbur Mills, in Pine Bluff, Arkansas. He said, "I just remembered this letter and wanted to see if there was anything you could do."

Humphrey said, "Well, let's check with the senior senator," at which time he wheels around and dials the phone. The women always knew it was him because he would say, "Is the senior senator in? Tell him the junior senator is on the phone."

He said, "Fritz, an old friend of ours here has a little problem. Can we come up to see you?" Walter Mondale agreed.

He goes up and when they get inside, Humphrey says, "My friend, I want you to tell Senator Mondale here this little problem you have."

So he tells him. Mondale starts to say, "You know, as a U.S. senator, we really can't interfere."

Humphrey jumps in and says, "What Senator Mondale means to say is that this may take a little time. Where are you staying?"

The man replied that he was staying at the Quality Inn on Capitol Hill.

"You go back to your room and we'll call you," Humphrey told him.

After the businessman left, Mondale says, "Don't you think you got his hopes up a little bit?"

Humphrey replied, "Get Maggie on the phone."

Warren Magnuson was the chairman of the Senate Commerce Committee. This was old politics at its best. As Mondale hands the phone to Humphrey, Humphrey says, "Everybody has forgotten that Warren Magnuson was born in Moorhead, Minnesota. It's a pile of sand."

"Maggie, Maggie, listen," Humphrey says. "They're trying to screw one of your old friends up there in Moorhead." The guy had his permit before the sun went down that afternoon.

—D. J. Leary

Bringing Peace to the Middle East

Factoid: Golda Meir was the fourth prime minister of Israel, holding the post from 1969 to 1974. Jacob Javits served four terms in the U.S. Senate from New York, from 1956 to 1980.

While I was still in school in 1972, one of the jobs I had for Senator Jacob Javits was to drive him around. Frequently, this entailed trips to the airport. One day I was in the file room filing away, and I got the quick summons that I had to go pick up the senator, whose plane was going to land at 12:45 p.m. at Dulles Airport, which was quite a trip in those days. He'd just come back from the Middle East and needed to be at the Capitol to vote before 1:15 p.m., so I knew I had to rush him back.

I was very young, and I'm sure I was dressed in jeans and a sloppy sweater because I was expecting to file that day. Senator Javits came running out of the airport with just one big carry-on bag, so I put it in the back of his Ford Mustang, a hot car with a huge engine.

When you drove with Senator Javits, you drove fast because he wanted you to go as fast as you could. So we're roaring down the Dulles Access Road toward the Beltway. All the while, he's regaling me with stories about him and Israel Prime Minister Golda Meir, who had been meeting every day and every night trying to bring peace to the Middle East. I was completely stupefied at these great tales of war and peace and life and death.

So we roar up to the Capitol steps and get there with only thirty seconds to spare. As he raced up the stairs, he yelled at me to take his bag back to his apartment at the Watergate Hotel.

I hopped back in the car and drove over to the Watergate, parked right in front as I usually did when I went to his condo, opened the trunk and pulled his big carry-on out. As I jerked it, I noticed that it was partially unzipped. In fact, it was so unzipped that as I grabbed the handle, some of its contents dropped out onto Virginia Avenue. Right on top was the biggest box of condoms I'd ever seen in my life.

All I could think of was "Golda Meir?"

I still remember this like it was yesterday. I don't think I'd ever seen such a huge box of condoms. He clearly bought them by the gross. It was not your little box of 12 condoms, this was 144.

So whenever I hear the phrase "bringing peace to the Middle East," I think back fondly of Senator Javits, who was known as quite a ladies' man.
                                                            —*Larry McCarthy*

Playing Atlantic City With John Y. Brown

Factoid: John Y. Brown was elected governor of Kentucky in 1979, defeating former Republican Governor Louis Nunn, 59-41.

John Y. Brown was particularly close to DNC chair Chuck Manatt and Manatt had made Brown head of the committee to elect Democratic governors, which later became the Democratic Governors Association.

This was the mid-term convention in 1982, in Philadelphia. Brown was bored to tears. He didn't have much of a role at this convention. About six o'clock, John Brown's lead supporter, a guy by the name of Larry Townsend, a prominent businessman in Louisville who had been for Brown forever, came to me and said, "Go get Matt Reese, would you? John wants to go to Atlantic City. We are only 60 miles away; we might just as well go down and have some fun."

The people invited were Manatt, Brian Lunde, Pat Caddell, Reese, Townsend and me. Manatt and Lunde had to stay at the convention, because they were party officials and actually had work there. The next day they were trotting out the field for 1984. Senator John Glenn would speak, as would Senator Ted Kennedy and former Vice President Walter Mondale.

Brown charters a limo and we're off on this 60-mile trip. I am sitting next to Caddell watching Reese and Brown in the back playing gin for $10 a point. Halfway there, Reese is several thousand dollars ahead, which to Brown was like so many nickels and dimes. Brown had called his good friend Steve Wynn, and when we arrived we were ushered into the Golden Nugget as if we were the kings of Persia. We went up to Wynn's private suite for a big dinner.

While we are eating, Wynn and Brown go away for about half an hour to talk. When Brown returns we go down to the casino where Brown informs us he has the "power of the pen," which in the casino means he can simply sign for whatever he needs to gamble and he is considered good for it.

We get to the tables and three people decided to play, Brown, Caddell and Reese. The rest of us decide to watch. Reese understands a little bit about the dice, Caddell is an absolute novice and Brown is an acknowledged grand master of the dice.

Reese is quickly run out of the game and prefers to play blackjack anyway. Brown stands at the table less than ten minutes, has already signed for a $10,000 marker and has no chips in front of him. He calls for another marker of $10,000, for which he signs and goes through this too in less than five minutes. After half an hour, Brown had gone through $40,000 and was asking for another marker.

Brown started into his fifth $10,000 marker and the dice turned. All this time Caddell has been playing along steadily and has won virtually no money, but he hasn't lost much either. Brown is playing in increments, probably a thousand times higher than Caddell, but Caddell was learning. Caddell is the master of numbers and there are no number games he cannot figure out. Caddell is trying to emulate Brown's every move as the dice warm up, except that

Brown has a way of casting chips in the air while the dice are on the way, which Caddell can't follow.

When they closed the tables at 4 a.m., Brown was ahead by $182,000. On those very same dice, Caddell lost $10. He could not follow the intuitive nature of Brown's play while the dice were in the air.

Brown was nice enough to let me carry the chips over to the cashier. Wynn came down to the cashier and Brown walked out of Golden Nugget at five minutes after four to hop on Wynn's private jet to fly back to Lexington with $182,000 in cash in a grocery bag! The rest of us took the limo back to Philadelphia.

—*George Burger*

Watergate Wasn't Nixon's Only Problem

Factoid: Angelo Roncallo was elected to the U.S. House of Representatives in 1972 and served one term from the 3rd district of New York.

Years later, people know President Richard Nixon was in deep trouble. Often forgotten are his problems with the milk fund. The milk fund people, those nice people who have giant dairies, had contributed something like $250,000 in cash. The White House had so much cash rolling around in the 1972 election they didn't know what to do with it.

Mr. Nixon — or somebody — took the $250,000 in cash and gave it to Bebe Rebozo, down in Florida. The press is going at the president pretty good about this money. They want to know who has this money. Was it a payoff? What was it for?

So the president calls up to Capitol Hill and says, "I want all you men to come down here. We'll do breakfast at the White House." He said he was going to tell us the truth about the milk money.

Well, those in power made sure they were there Monday morning even if their name started with "W." People jockeyed around to make sure they were in the first group. We knew he was going to repeat to each group the same thing each morning all week long. So on Monday there were 50 or 60 guys there, and then the attendance dropped off after that. By Thursday afternoon, everyone is splitting. Congress is out for the weekend, and they're on the plane to go home.

The last bunch of us, mostly freshmen, decided we might as well go on Friday. The service was great. The food was good.

There's a little holding room as you go in, where you stand around and drink juice and coffee while you wait. And as you can imagine, things are tense at the White House those days. You could feel it. The Marine guards and the Secret Service are all tense. There are only about fourteen of us, so it's going to be an intimate little breakfast with the president.

An aide comes in to inform us that we can come into the next room, and that the president will be right with us, so we file into the next room and sit down. The table is set with just the right amount of settings. It's a big square where we're all sitting on the outside of the table. It's all very formal.

Angelo Roncallo from Long Island sits on my right. Now, Angie was quite a character. He's a huge man and weighed a good 400 pounds.

It's all very quiet, and we're barely whispering while we wait for the president to come in. Angie is talking to the guy on the other side of him. He was so big he couldn't turn his neck without shifting his whole body to look the other way. By the way, I think Angie was under some sort of cloud for past indiscretions up on Long Island.

The congressman sitting to my left, Bill Ketchum from California, had a great sense of humor. We're sitting there quietly waiting for everything to begin.

Then the president comes in. He's very formal when he addresses us as he sits down. Everything is still very quiet. A priest comes in to bless everything.

There's silence in the room. Bill, on my left, whispers, "David?" He hands me a dirty, crumpled up dollar bill and says, "Take this bill and stick it under Angie's second plate there." There were two plates stacked in front of each of us. When I questioned him, he said, "Just do it." So I take this dirty one-dollar bill, and with Angie turned the other way, I slip the bill under his plate.

So we're sitting there, when Bill says, "Lean back, I'm going to talk to Angie a minute." He goes "Psst, Angie." And the poor guy has to move his whole 400- pound body around in the chair in order to face us. He slowly moves around and says, "What is it, Bill?"

"We've got a hun," Bill whispers.

Angie frowns and says, "What do you mean?"

"It's a hundred-dollar bill. Just like in the old days. There's a hundred-dollar bill under the plate."

Angie says, "No, that's not going to happen in the White House."

Bill says, "David and I got a hundred-dollar bill, Angie. It's under that second plate there."

Angie slowly lifts his plate, slips his pudgy hand in there and pulls out this filthy one-dollar bill and looks at it. He turns his whole weight and almost lunges past me. He snarls, "You son of a bitch, Bill."

That got the president's attention. He turned and said, "What's the problem, Mr. Roncallo? Is there a problem?"

Angie quickly says, "Nothing, Mr. President. I just slipped in my chair." One of his knees had slipped, and he was having a hell of a time getting his weight back up into the chair.

Bill had told several of the other congressmen what he was going to do, so the guys were just fighting to keep their composure as Angie got himself back under control. It was the best practical joke I've ever seen in all my life.   *—David Towell*

Ground Zero in the Anti-war Movement

We elect our delegates by a caucus system, which requires people in precincts to show up at a location and vote. The former governor's chief of staff, Irv Nemerov, was against us; he favored the Vietnam War. I was leading a bunch of student activists who were against the war and for Gene McCarthy. In precinct 17 of the old sixth ward in Minneapolis, 1,700 people turned out for the caucus in 1968.

The supporters of Hubert Humphrey and Lyndon Johnson, our opponents, said it was sensible to be involved in the war in Vietnam. At one point, they copied DFL letterhead and put out false addresses for the precincts in hopes that all the students would show up at the wrong place. Unfortunately, it didn't work out too well because, students being students, they can actually read, and most of the people who were stupid enough to support the war were older and probably had failing eyesight, which caused many of those people to show up at the wrong place instead. I think it backfired.

At the precinct caucus, which I chaired, the war forces and the Humphrey forces had about 500 people. We had about 1,200 people. Both sides had enough, however, that there was a considerable amount of floor fighting.

Nemerov, who was heading up this effort for Vice President Humphrey, accused us of stacking the meeting with people who weren't really residents. They brought in some private detectives with badges to swear people under oath and take statements that they were, in fact, residents. This was a way to scare students away, primarily because many of the students were cohabitating with students of the opposite gender and the University of Minnesota had a rule against that.

The tactic didn't work very well. We were accused of an unfair voting process. I volunteered to go first and said I would name my five people who would be our official vote counters. I read off the list, starting with Mother Rosemary Innocent. I named five Catholic nuns, all of whom were there in habit, including Mother Superior of St. Mary's Hospital, which happened to be in this precinct. They were all residents from the convent attached to the hospital. They were McCarthy supporters. As you might expect, they were against the war.

I named my five and had them all come up. Mother Superior and all her little bunnies came up in their habits. I looked down at Nemerov and asked for his five people, and he had the good sense to say, "Oh, no, no, no. Your five are fine with me."

I'm sure they counted the votes accurately. We won about 12 to 5. I mean, what do you expect?   —*Vance Opperman*

Vice President Pulls Boulter Over the Line in Texas

Factoid: Republican Beau Boulter beat five-term incumbent Jack Hightower in 1984 in the 13th district of Texas by a 53-47 margin.

In 1984, Vice President George Bush was campaigning for close races for Congress. I received a call from Greg Graves, the NRCC field guy for Texas. He said, "Listen, Ron, I'm down here in Amarillo, Texas. We have a guy running in 13th district, Beau Boulter. He can win this race, but the establishment is not with him. In fact, they hate him. He just can't get the base together. The only way we're going to do that is if the vice president comes in for the campaign." He added, "T. Boone Pickens is a big force down here. He's adamant that no one should be helping this guy."

Sure enough, within 10 minutes four phone calls came in from the vice president's best friends in Amarillo, who were saying, "Kaufman, I understand you guys have considered doing this event for Boulter. I would personally kill you if you do."

I presented all this information to the vice president. He said, "I'll be quite honest with you. I think we can make a difference, and this looks like one of those places." We put it on the books and went through a difficult time with a lot of good friends.

When you're flying with Air Force Two, the press plane always lands first. I went in the press plane for this leg of the flight because we were going to have an airport rally when we landed. Sure enough, when we landed Boone Pickens very graciously met the plane. The entire establishment was there along with a huge crowd.

The vice president landed, met everybody and gave a great speech. The way it works at the end of the rally is that Air Force Two takes off and then the press plane leaves. I'm down on the ground, waving good-bye to Air Force Two, standing with Boulter. He actually had tears in his eyes while he said, "This is the happiest day, Ron. I appreciate this."

I told him this was part of my job.

In 1986, Boulter called the White House and said, "Do me a favor. Could you come down to Amarillo and spend a couple days here telling everybody how important I am to President Reagan and Vice President Bush?"

I talked to Vice President Bush, and then I went down to Amarillo for two days doing the Chamber of Commerce dinner and some press events. I told them I was honored to be there and what an integral part of the Reagan/Bush administration Boulter was.

Afterwards, I received a very nice letter from Boulter saying, "Ron, you made it so much easier. I'll always remember it."

Boulter won re-election easily that year. On election night, I was in Houston with Vice President Bush. I had everyone's phone numbers of where they were going to be that night. As the results came in, the vice president would call them. I tracked down Boulter and give the phone to the vice president.

After the vice president congratulated Boulter I got back on the phone and Beau said, "Ron, I'll never forget this. This is a terrific effort; I appreciate it."

"Well, it's my job," I replied.

In 1987, Lee Atwater and I were sitting down talking about the upcoming presidential campaign. We were discussing who was going to help with the campaign in Texas.

I said, "Ideally, we want Senator Phil Gramm helping us. The perfect person for the vice president would be Beau Boulter because of where he is from. He would be terrific."

Atwater says, "No, no, no, he's not going to be with us. He's not on the list."

I said, "Boulter owes us because we've helped him every time. He is a good Christian whom I know would never lie."

Atwater said, "Ron, I hate to tell you this, but he'll break your bubble, you silly Yankee. Charlie Black has already told me he's got Boulter lined up for Kemp."

I went nuts! I picked up the phone, called Boulter's office and got his chief of staff on the phone. I said, "You tell the congressman I'm going to be over there in 25 minutes and I'm not leaving until I talk to him."

I have huge respect for members of Congress. They run for office. We don't. They take the risks. We don't.

I went storming up to Capitol Hill and walked into Boulter's office. Three staff members were there. I walked up to his desk and said, "Congressman, I understand there's a crazy rumor out there that you're not going to support the vice president for the presidency. You'd rather have Jack Kemp."

He replied, "Well, Ron, Jack, Joanne and I pray together."

"You know, that's funny, Beau. I didn't see Kemp out there on the tarmac fighting for your life. George Bush took his best friends to help make it happen for you because you were in trouble getting elected. You gave me your word. Let me tell you something, you little son-of-a-gun. If you are doing this because you're running for

Senate someday, and you think this will help you run statewide, I'll give you one freaking promise. You will never get a damned dime from anyone who can spell Bush without a C. Take it to the bank, you little weasel."

The next day there was a big story: "Bush hitman threatens congressman."

I immediately got a call from the vice president's office asking me to come see him. I told myself I was going to die.

I entered the vice president's office and said, "Mr. Vice President, I just want you to know that I'm sorry."

He said, "All I want to do is to tell you one thing. I didn't know you had the guts!"
                                                        —*Ron Kaufman*

'Turn Off the Popcorn Popper, Mayor'

Factoid: Democrat Bill Purcell was elected as the 68th mayor of Nashville in September 1999, getting 47% in a 10-candidate field that included former Mayor Richard Fulton.

Bill Purcell had only been mayor of Nashville for a very short time. We were out in the city one day driving along the edge of the downtown area. He asked if I'd ever been to the city's thermal plant.

This is a facility where they truck in all the garbage to downtown Nashville. They dump it and then burn it, which produces energy for heating and cooling a number of downtown buildings. It was a wonderful innovation in 1970. It's now a worn-out machine that they are in the process of replacing.

I told him that I had not seen the plant, so he suggested we go look at it. We pull in and there are garbage trucks lined up, which is very pleasant just before lunch. We walk inside this big bay area. A truck would back in and dump its garbage into a big pit. Then you'd see this big shovel-like thing come down, scoop up the garbage and take it to another area where it was burned.

Over to the side was a truck that had dumped its garbage in the middle of the floor. There was a small fire burning. We asked what it was. The guy in the public works truck said that something caught fire inside his truck. When that happened and they were close enough to the plant, they would come up there and dump it out. Then they waited for the fire department to come and put the fire out. We asked how long that took and he explained that it didn't take long since the firehouse was only two or three blocks away.

The mayor and I were new to the job, so we thought we'd wait around and see how the process worked. We stand there and the fire is getting bigger and bigger. People are beginning to get nervous. Suddenly a tire catches fire and thick black smoke starts billowing out.

The mayor decided we should step outside, along with the other people there. We asked how long they thought it would be before the fire truck got there. The man patiently explained that they were usually there by that time. It was getting a little awkward, so the mayor decided we would get in our car and go see if a fire truck was on the way. Actually, we were just trying to think of a way to get out of there gracefully.

We start heading down the street, and both of us are hoping we'll see the fire truck roaring up the street at any moment. No truck. So we stop at the fire hall and go in. There's a fireman with his feet comfortably up on a desk talking on the phone. He recognizes the mayor and the firemen are all glad to see him.

The mayor finally says, "Captain, we were just up at the thermal plant, and they have a fire." The captain looks at him with a smile on his face and says, "Oh, mayor, there's always a fire in the thermal plant." So we try to explain that the fire is not where they burn the garbage but on the floor. He assures us that he really doesn't think it's a problem. So we ask him to humor us and call up there to see if they need help. About that time, the bells go off and a loud speaker booms, "Station five, station five, fire in the thermal plant!"

As they rush off to their fire trucks, the captain turns and yells, "Mayor, will you turn off the popcorn popper?"   —*Bill Phillips*

Showdown in Virginia City, Montana

Factoid: Conrad Burns was the only Republican challenger to defeat an incumbent senator in 1988. He beat John Melcher in Montana, 52-48.

In the beginning of September 1988, I was the driver for County Commissioner Conrad Burns and his wife, Phyllis, in his rundown old Chevy van. The seat was broken, so he had a two-by-four jammed under the back of the headrest, which held up the driver's seat. Burns was running for the U.S. Senate against John Melcher.

We arrived in Virginia City at 2 p.m. on a hot late summer day. Virginia City is so small you could probably throw a football from one end of the town to the other.

I said, "All right, Conrad, you get out here and start down that side of the street and, Phyllis, you go down across the street, and I'll meet you at the other end. I'll start doing cars and any of the businesses while I'm waiting for you. We'll meet at the end."

Burns didn't say anything and just sat there looking straight ahead. Phyllis is filling up her hands with flyers. I said, "Here, Conrad," as I handed him some flyers.

He said, "No, I think I'm just going to let you and Phyllis get this town."

I said, "Conrad, listen. If they see you on one side of the street, everybody is going to know you're here. Just walk in a few doors and they'll think you were here all day long. Go in there and pass a few of these out. People are going to catch you, so Phyllis and I will get most of it anyway. By the time you finish visiting, we'll be back down here and we'll be out of here in about 20 minutes at the most."

"Nope, I'm tired," Burns said. "You guys go."

I said, "Conrad, we're not going to get back to Virginia City again. You need to do this."

Burns said, "I told you I'm too damn tired."

Phyllis looked over at me and said, "Well, I'll let you guys figure this out. I'll be on the other side of the street." She got out of the van and slammed the door.

Burns looked at me and said, "You go. I told you I'm tired, and I'm not getting out of the van. You guys are making me go to too many places."

I could tell he was not going to converse on this issue anymore. The van was still running because I was ready to drive to the other end. I reached over and turned on the heater and turned the radio off. As soon as I turned the heater on, he gave me with a sharp look.

"What the hell are you doing?" he said.

I said, "Well, if you're not going to get out and hand out those flyers, you might as well just sit in here."

He reached over and slammed the heater switch off.

I said, "Now, Conrad, get out there. We'll be done."

"No, I told you, damn it. I'm the candidate and I ain't doing this. I'm tired."

I said, "Fine."

I reached over and turned the heater back on again. This time I locked the windows because he was fiddling with the window, trying to roll it down. I told him, "If you touch that heater, I'll break your damn arm."

I'll bet we sat there for about 10 minutes. The first part of September is pretty hot. It was just like sitting in a pot of soup. The next thing I know, Conrad said, "Unlock my damn door, you crazy son-of-a-bitch."

He got out of the van and started walking the street. I went to the other end of Main Street and started handing out flyers. Neither Phyllis nor Conrad ever said a word about it.   —*Leo Giacometto*

Hiding Under the Bed From the Governor

Factoid: Minnesota Governor Wendell Anderson won a second term in 1974, defeating Republican John Johnson, 63-30.

Governor Wendell Anderson had brought me in to work on some of the communications in the press office in 1973. I did a number of things, some of which didn't work out.

One of the things I worked on for the governor was his weekly radio program that ran statewide on the public radio stations. He recorded with a freelance radio guy, then we would take the tape down to the network's number one station. In one instance, things were very tense in the legislature, and the governor did a rather gratuitous radio attack on a particularly difficult Republican senator, Charlie Berg from Chokio. When we listened to the tape, the governor's press secretary, Ted Smebakken, and I put our heads down. This was going to cause nothing but trouble.

After we sent the tape down to the station I said, "You know, I could edit that thing out of there."

He said, "Maybe that's what we ought to do." I edited the tape to take out the attack on Senator Berg. I hand-delivered the edited tape to the radio station, which was going to send it around to the other stations.

The radio station played the wrong tape, and it was such a spectacular attack on this senator that it drew press attention. After the press started getting into it, the radio station pointed out that they had played the wrong tape. There was a subsequent tape with the attack edited out. Now this was really getting interesting.

I had done the editing without telling Governor Anderson. Now he found out somebody was fooling with what he was putting out. Things were getting a little tense, and it was very clear that the less he saw of me, the better.

The governor was going to an event in northern Minnesota, and the guys doing the event up there were having problems with some media arrangements, so they called and asked if I could come help them.

I went and helped them put the pieces together, and suddenly we looked out the window off the motel and up came the governor's car being driven by a state patrol officer. They pull right up to the door outside the room we're in. The governor gets out of the car and starts heading to the door. I said, "He'll die if he sees me, or he'll kill me, one or the other. Don't let on that I'm here. I'll be under the bed." I dove under the bed and listened to the conversation, and there was no indication that I was around.

I still see Anderson occasionally, but I've never yet had the nerve to tell him about hiding under the bed. It might bring up all the other reasons why he didn't want to see me at the time.

—D. J. Leary

Richard Bryan's Worst Day

Factoid: In 1988, Nevada Governor Richard Bryan beat incumbent Senator Chic Hecht by a 50% to 46% margin.

I was a senior in high school in October 1988 at Wooster High

School in Reno, Nevada. My school principal and government teacher coordinated a speaking engagement by then Governor Richard Bryan, who was in one of the nation's most competitive U.S. Senate races that year against incumbent Senator Chic Hecht.

The principal and the government teacher, like many in public education, were to the left of center and were big fans of Governor Bryan. As educators, they couldn't necessarily endorse anybody, but there was always a clear sense of who they were supporting. They arranged this big rally in the theater to do a question-and-answer session with Governor Bryan. I was president of the Young Republicans and was convinced this was set up and the principal and teacher were proud that they were going to deliver hundreds of their students to Bryan.

The day of the rally, we wore our "Hecht, Yes" shirts. The campaign's original slogan was "Stick with Chic," but the Democrats discovered that if you whited-out the W and the H on "with" you came up with "Stick it Chic," so they abandoned that slogan and went with "Hecht, Yes."

The school billed this rally as non-political. Of course it was political. It was, after all, one month before the most competitive election in the country. So we came into the rally with our T-shirts underneath our sweaters, sat down, heard Governor Bryan's pitch for 15 minutes, and then he asked for questions.

There were a lot of competitive issues in that campaign, but one issue in particular the Hecht campaign had really seized upon and turned into a key strategy. They had been down 20 or 30 points at one time, and they'd brought it back to what was essentially an even race. One of these issues was the political use of the state-owned airplane.

So I stood up and started questioning the governor on the airplane for five minutes. Then somebody else stood up and started berating him. The Hecht campaign was handing out literature that you could fold into an airplane and throw. Let's just say that no one got out of line, but we were certainly not on our best behavior.

After a half-hour of this, Bryan began to lose his cool. You can't rattle him usually. But he started to get so upset that he answered one of the students who was peppering him with questions in a terse tone. He was booed because of it.

You can see the government teacher and the principal trying to stop this—but what do you do? It was a tough crowd, and the governor finally left. This was supposed to be an easy appearance for him.

Governor Bryan went on to win a very narrow victory that year.

In 1994, I was working in the Jim Gibbons for Governor campaign. Dick Bryan was running for re-election to the Senate. I saw him at a function in Fallon where we were chatting. I had not seen him since the incident at Wooster High School, so I introduced myself.

"I don't know if you remember or not, but I was the student at Wooster High School in 1988 who led the conflict in that school rally." You could see his face change as I described it, and he said, "Oh, yes, I remember that."

Then he went on to tell me—and it was one of my proudest moments in politics—"Josh, I've been in this business for 30 years, and that was by far the toughest hour I've ever spent politically in my entire life." *—Josh Griffin*

'I'm Not Even Listening,' Clements Said

Factoid: Bill Clements was elected the first Republican governor of Texas in 108 years when he beat John Hill in 1978, 50 to 49.2. Four years later Clements lost to Mark White, 53-46, but then in 1986 he defeated White, 53-46.

Bill Clements has the largest collection of books on Texicana in the world. He's not an intellectual, but he is a well-read, thoughtful, bright man who made a huge amount of money as a businessperson. He was trying to recapture the governor's office in 1986, after winning in 1978 but losing in 1982.

It was a long campaign because he had to win a primary against two much younger Republican congressmen, Tom Loeffler and Kent Hance.

Then, in the middle of the summer, they called a special session of the legislature, which we decided opened an opportunity for a lot of advertising against Governor Mark White. Of course, there was also the general election after Labor Day.

During the course of that campaign, we produced a ton of commercials, more than we'd ever done before. We did 45 or 50 commercials. We ran a set of them during the primary, we ran another whole wave of them during the summer, during the special session of the legislature, and we ran another set toward the end.

As the campaign progressed, each time the campaign committee met there seemed to be more people showing up. Clements's and Karl Rove's view, and the view of others, was that once we won the primary we ought to bring the leaders from the other two campaigns into the Clements campaign. Once we began to look as though we were doing all right, some Democrats began to defect, and by the time we got to the fall the meetings were huge. There would be as many as 30 or 40 people around a very large table.

Clements would say, "Let's show them the TV spots, John."

I would put these spots up on a big projector screen. There would immediately be this long-winded discussion of almost every frame of every commercial, with everybody in the room having some view—none of them informed by actual experience with television advertising.

Some of the views were so inane they would have been embarrassing. Clearly this was not the way to reach any kind of agreement about which commercials to put on the air.

The problem was that you had guys on the Democratic left of center who had one view about what issues were important and people on the far right who wanted to do something else. Some people were prepared to say anything, however incorrect or libelous, about Mark White, and other people didn't think we should say anything at all about Mark White. When you get that many people in a room, you get this situation in which everybody feels like they're going to be insignificant if they don't have something to say. Consequently, it just escalates.

One woman in particular was an old Republican warhorse in Dallas. She was a very hard-working, loyal member of the party and a good friend of the Clementses, personally. She really knew nothing about advertising; however, her tactic was that she had discussed these ads with all her friends and political associates and none of them liked them. She would have numbers, such as "I have talked to 82 people who said that's a bad commercial. We ought to get that off the air."

These meetings went on hour after hour. I got increasingly irritated and short with some people.

When this woman was going on I always tried to position myself as far away from her as I could. She was at the other end of the table, going on and on, and Clements could see I was getting irritated. He leaned over to me and said, "John, this is the price we pay for having these people on our campaign. Don't worry about anything they say. I'm not even listening. You and I will decide when the meeting is over what commercials are going on the air. Just hear them out; that's all we have to do. Just sit here a while longer and hear them out, then we'll go off and decide about this."

That was the end of it. He taught me a lesson I should have learned long before that this is the price you pay for having people willing to work so hard for your campaign, and that whatever they know or don't know, just sit there and listen. We did.

—*John Deardourff*

Ventura Almost Blows Bank Loan With Drugs, Prostitution Position

Minnesota has a strange campaign finance system for statewide candidates. You get what is called check-off money, and it depends on how many people in your party check-off on the income tax. The Ventura campaign had about $350,000 earmarked for it. In Minnesota, you get $350,000 after you raise a bunch of $50 contributions.

The second part is that you don't get the $350,000 until December, after the election. So you have to get an unsecured bank loan—but you can't guarantee it, you can't pledge the collateral. You basically can't do anything to get that money.

You also have to have 10 percent of the vote to qualify for the state funding. Jesse Ventura was sitting around the 15 percent mark in the polls at that time.

We went to nearly 25 banks. Some of the banks initially said okay, but then the next day something happened. Bill Cooper, the chairman of the Republican Party, is also a big shot in the banking community. I knew somebody was sabotaging us. We went for a month trying to figure out how we were going to get that bank loan.

Steve Minn, a city councilman from Minneapolis and activist in the Independent Party, has a neighbor who was vice president of the Franklin National Bank. Finally, Minn said, "I think we may have a shot here."

We went to the Franklin National Bank and negotiated some hefty points, as a high-risk loan. We worked on it for three or four days. We were now only a week out from the election and we hadn't gotten our money yet. We had a date of the Thursday before the election to close on the loan.

The day before the loan closing, Ventura was at a forum in Forest Lake. He was asked about his positions on legalizing prostitution, marijuana and drug use. Ventura, being his natural self, said he thought we should consider legalizing prostitution and that the drug war was foolish, so he thought we should legalize marijuana.

The headlines in the paper the next day declared, "Candidate Ventura in Favor of Prostitution and Drugs." His wife looked at him in the morning and said, "You idiot! You just blew the bank loan!"

I met Ventura at noon to go into the bank to close the loan. "What bank is going to give you a loan now?" I asked him.

The timing of his blooper with the newspapers had a lot of people believing he had just committed political suicide.

But the bank overlooked that little stunt and we closed on the loan.   —*Dean Barkley*

Bishops Suggest Stevens for Supreme Court

Factoid: John Paul Stevens of Chicago was appointed by President Nixon to the 7th District Court of Appeals in 1970. President Ford nominated him to the Supreme Court on December 1, 1975, and he was confirmed 16 days later.

I was working for Cardinal Francis McIntyre in Los Angeles, and he was a very strong anti-abortion guy. I was his outside public relations counsel, and State Senator Anthony Beilensen introduced a bill that Governor Reagan signed, the most liberal abortion bill in America at the time. So we started the Right to Life League. We put the Catholic moms together and it spread all across the country. I have never talked much about this, to this day.

If I ever wrote an article for *Reader's Digest* about the most unforgettable character I ever met, it would be McIntyre. He was a character. He had 55 schools in the Los Angeles archdiocese that were all paid for. He was on Wall Street before he went into the priesthood. He was a businessman.

After McIntyre, Timothy Manning became the archbishop. Manning didn't know how to use me, so I went to him and told him I thought we should part ways.

Then in 1975, I was running the Gerald Ford presidential campaign and the bishops were all meeting in Washington, D.C. Now this is like a Mafia meeting of all the bishops. Manning – he's a cardinal now — calls me up and says the bishops would like to talk to me. All the power of the Catholic Church in America was there.

We sit down and have lunch, and Bishop Bernardin of Cincinnati says, "Can I call you Stu? Okay, Stu, we're interested in the United States Supreme Court."

I said that I assumed they were. Ford had an opening. We talked about it, and I told him I just didn't know. We talked some more and the lawyers talked. Finally I asked if they had any suggestions. Out of the briefcase came four names.

I told them I'd meet with the president at the White House every night at six o'clock while I was in town, and I would tell Ford I had met with them and that they had an interest in this appointment.

That evening I went over to the White House, and at the end of the meeting I told Ford I'd met with all the bishops of the Church and said they were interested in his Supreme Court appointment. He said, "Yeah, I bet they are." I told him they had some suggestions, pulled out the piece of paper with the four names on it, and he took it, looked at it, opened the drawer, put the paper in the drawer and that was the end of the conversation.

Several weeks later, Ford nominated John Paul Stevens to the Supreme Court. His name had been on the list. From that moment on, the bishops thought I had delivered. All I delivered was the names. Maybe Ford in his own head said, well, this isn't going to hurt. But I didn't push it. After that I was always getting calls from the bishops.   —*Stu Spencer*

Action America Supports Huckabee Travel

Factoid: In a special election in Arkansas on July 27, 1993, Republican Mike Huckabee was elected lieutenant governor defeating Nate Coulter, 51-49. The special election was called when Jim Guy Tucker vacated the seat to become governor, following the resignation of Governor Bill Clinton.

After Mike Huckabee won the race for lieutenant govenor, he was a very popular and entertaining speaker. And, because he was a Republican, elected in Bill Clinton's Arkansas, he was really in demand. He didn't want to turn down anybody, but the lieutenant governor's position only paid about $18,000 a year, not enough to live on. He could have another job, but because he was speaking so much on behalf of Republican groups he hardly had time to hold another job. We had to figure out a way to at least pay his expenses and give him an honorarium.

He also had an opportunity to go out and speak against the Clinton health care plan. He took it on himself to read the Clinton plan and understand it, and as an Arkansan he could be a spokesman against the big government health care plan.

We formed a group called Action America, activating citizens to influence our nation, to be the vehicle. We formed this entity, got it filed as a 501(c)4, and I started raising money to pay for Huckabee's travel.

We received a few big personal contributions of $1,000 or $1,500, and a couple of associations in Washington gave to us because Huckabee was out speaking on the conservative cause. When we announced Action America, we had a press conference and gave out the list of donors who had funded us.

We raised a total of $100,000 over a two-year period. Huckabee was now governor. The media wanted to know about Action America. When Huckabee was asked about it, he just said, talk to Greg Graves.

Huckabee didn't call and tell me, so the *Arkansas Democrat* reporter called me and said he wanted to talk about Governor Huckabee. He asked about Action America. Although I had helped finance it and fund it and was one of the founders of Action

America, I pretty much stepped away from the daily operation.

The reporter asked me for the list of donors. I told him I didn't remember who they were to begin with and secondly I didn't have to tell because one of the things we promised our donors was that we wouldn't give out their names. It became a press firestorm.

I was asked why I didn't just give the press the names. I said I was not going to go back and look them up. Well, could you just call them and ask if you could tell us their names? I said why would I waste my time doing that? What if Governor Huckabee tells you to give us the names? I said he didn't give his word, I gave mine. I used the line "You can't gain public trust by breaking a private confidence." The governor picked it up and liked it, and that was his answer from then on.

Every time I would go to Arkansas it was the first question: Who were the donors to Action America? I had worked in the state for a number of years and had never had my picture taken by the press. Because of that story, people realized I was close to the governor. Every corporate operative in the state wanted to meet me because they didn't know who I was. I wasn't trying to hide. I just don't operate where I am going to get my picture in the paper and talk to news guys.

Later, I was going to an Arkansas Highway Commission meeting to meet the players on the commission. The highway commission in Arkansas is a very big deal, as it is in most states. Reporters were there. I went with Bill Vickery, who had been Tim Hutchinson's campaign manager. There was a reporter from Fort Smith there and these radio reporters. The reporters are talking to Vickery and ask him who was with him. He told them I was Greg Graves. They said, "Oh, that's Greg Graves. Let's go see if we can't talk to him."

They wanted to know what I was doing there. Are you moving to the state? What kind of business are you and Vickery doing? What do you plan on doing? I was going to give a nice little public relations answer about what we were doing. So they ask if I'm ready. I said yes. They turn on the tape recorder and the first question was, Tell us who the donors are of Action America. I didn't say anything. The tape was running and I was silent. I wait 30 seconds and then one minute. They are beginning to cough a little and I still don't say anything. Finally I said, "You can't gain a public trust by breaking private confidence," turned around and sat down.

Then I see this newspaper reporter grab a photographer. This guy makes a beeline out of the building. I look out the door and he is going to his car and pulling out his cameras. I told Vickery, let's get out of here. There was a back door to the room we were in.

He walked in with his camera as I am headed out the back door. We walked to the other side of this building, to the parking lot, and as I am getting into the car, here is the cameraman running out, snapping pictures as I am standing over the car and covering my face. It was the first time I have ever run from a camera.

—*Greg Graves*

CHAPTER 27

Only in Louisiana

☆ ☆ ☆

It has happened countless times. The political pro shows up to start talking through the campaign with the candidate and their team, and the first thing he hears is how they do things differently here. Whether it's in Dubuque or Paducah; Albany, New York, or Albany, Oregon; Jackson, Michigan, or Jackson, Mississippi—it's always the same. We do things differently in this neck of the woods, the locals always say. But, as it turns out, that's not true. Things are alike just about everywhere.

Except in Louisiana. When the locals tell you they do it differently in New Orleans or Shreveport, they know what they're talking about. Any place that spawned Huey Long and Edwin Edwards can, without hesitation, be viewed as a different brand of politics. For the politicians and the voters, there's a higher level of intensity in Louisiana campaigns that just isn't seen in places like Georgia and New York, where politics is also a blood sport.

Several points are worth remembering. Among the 50 states, Louisiana has, constitutionally, the strongest state executive, vested with more patronage and able to direct more funds than any other state executive in the land. And patronage doesn't exist only with the governor. In the larger parishes, the sheriff is endowed with a great many patronage positions.

When Henson Moore found himself in a re-run election in 1975, he quickly discovered that in many of the rural parishes in the 6th congressional district he had a ready-made campaign organization. Moore was a Republican, and that part of Louisiana hadn't elected one of those to Congress since Reconstruction. The dozens of workers that came out of the woods in those rural parishes made it clear they really were not that interested in whether Moore won or lost, but they needed a good warm-up campaign to get ready for the sheriff's race later that year. Moore's campaign – which he won – was just spring training for the workers, who were already choosing up sides for the upcoming sheriff's campaign.

Here are a few stories told by some old Louisiana hands, who know when and where crawfish come from and how to eat them.

Writing a 30-minute TV Show for Edwards

Factoid: In the open gubernatorial primary in Louisiana in 1991, Edwin Edwards led the field with 34% and David Duke made the general election run-off with 32%. Incumbent Governor Buddy Roemer missed the cut with 27%.

Edwin Edwards was renowned for speaking extemporaneously. He insisted that anything he was given, any document, be no longer than one page. No meeting we had could last more than 30 minutes. If you had something you wanted to talk to him about, you had to schedule an appointment well in advance. It was not a situation where he was hanging out at the campaign headquarters.

Principally, we would meet him at Ruth's Chris Steakhouse. Early on in the campaign there was a rolling party at the steakhouse at nine o'clock.

Most people who work in this business know that political campaigns are usually eighteen hours a day, seven days a week, with people eating cold pizza off their desk at odd hours. Louisiana was totally different. About five o'clock every day, the conversation turned to where we're going to dinner, where we're going dancing.

Once Edwards took my partner Bill Morgan and me aside and told us he wanted us to keep an open tab at the restaurant and submit those invoices to the campaign. His friends and his fundraising people were to drink and be fed at the campaign's expense.

We wanted to do a 30-minute program, and we ended up doing two for him during the course of the campaign. Mark Mellman did some polling for us through the Democratic Party. Edwards didn't really believe in polling, so we needed to get it done through the party. The polling showed that the campaign had become "event driven." There was a large body of voters who, when an event happened, would blow over to Duke. Another event would happen, and they'd blow over to Roemer.

We felt that a 30-minute program bought on every station in the state, and timed properly, would blow people toward Edwards. We envisioned this as a full-blown production done in a studio.

Edwards's concept was entirely different. He thought we would just turn the camera on, and then he would hold forth. He was absolutely insistent. He did not need to see a script. He did not need any preparation whatsoever. All he needed to know was when to be at the studio.

My partner and I really agonized over this because we knew it needed organization. I undertook the project of writing the program soup to nuts. The whole thing was scripted out. Then we asked for a meeting. Edwards didn't want to have a meeting, but he finally agreed to meet at his home in east Baton Rouge.

He was a little irritated right from the start that we even wanted to have this meeting. Then when I pulled out this long script and indicated that was what we wanted to talk about, he was very unhappy. He said he wasn't going to read it. He thought he had made it clear that he didn't need a script and didn't want a script.

But as we started talking and discussing the program, he flipped the pages, and halfway through the 30-minute meeting, he began to read the script. So we just sat there silently while he read. Then he started to laugh because we had included his jokes and sayings that he used on the campaign trail. We had pulled all this stuff together in an organized way.

Finally he looked up at me and said, "I can't memorize all of this."

I assured him that he didn't have to. The point was that we'd just organized it. I told him I could have a teleprompter there for his speech. He wasn't familiar with the machine, but we put it on a teleprompter, and he worked off that script the whole time. People who had been with him a long time were pretty amazed because they'd never seen him work off any sort of script before.

—Bill Fletcher

The Old Trick of Attacking Yourself

Factoid: In the 1994 New Orleans mayoral primary election, attorney Donald Mintz got 37% and Marc Morial got 32% in a 10-candidate field to make the March 5 general election. Morial was elected in the general election, defeating Mintz 54-46.

In Marc Morial's first campaign for mayor of New Orleans in 1994, his chief opponent was a white guy named Donald Mintz. Mintz was an attorney with a burning ambition to be mayor and a colossal opinion of himself. He had run and lost in the previous election against the incumbent mayor, Sidney Barthelemy, in 1990.

Mintz has a black guy on his staff from the University of Mississippi. He put out flyers attacking himself so that he could claim we were racists. We caught on to the trick and put charges against him, but nothing ever happened. However, it gave us an issue we could pound the hell out of him with.   —*Jim Carvin*

Moore Wins Congressional Re-run in Louisiana

Factoid: Republican Henson Moore was elected to Congress on January 13, 1975, in what was a re-run of the November 1974 general election in the 6th district of Louisiana. He beat Jeff LaCaze by a 54-46 margin.

Henson Moore, a young lawyer in Baton Rouge, had never run for office before. In 1974, Moore ran for Congress in the 6th congressional district of Louisiana, where a Republican had not won in a century.

President Richard Nixon resigned from office in August, six weeks before the first primary, and Moore had no chance of winning. Moore had announced in April and raised a total of $30,000 by September; the campaign budget was $90,000. We were not doing very well, with Moore only having 30 percent name recognition.

Then we got our break. In the Democratic primary, the incumbent, John Rarick, who was a right-wing reactionary, got beat. The election was held on Saturday, and many conservative Democrats who voted for him had all driven over to Houston to watch the LSU-Rice football game.

Rarick lost in the primary to Jeff LaCaze, a local TV sportscaster. All LaCaze had was name recognition, but he also had the backing of the black community and the labor union groups. When LaCaze won the Democratic primary, everybody assumed it was all over.

It just so happened that the primary was on a Saturday and we had booked California Governor Ronald Reagan to come in on Monday for a fundraising lunch for Moore. That was the only day we could get him, but it just happened to be the Monday after the upset primary.

The tickets were $100 each, which was a lot of money in those days. We wound up selling 300 tickets. Suddenly, we had $30,000— as much as we had raised in the whole campaign up to that time.

We also got a lot of news coverage out of Reagan's visit. Everybody knew who he was, and he just knocked the crowd off its feet. All of a sudden Moore had conservative credentials. We gave him a script and he said exactly what we wanted him to say; he was just wonderful. He made a TV ad that really gave us a spurt.

On general election night, with one precinct out yet, we were about two hundred votes behind. We didn't know which precinct that was. Right at the last minute, somebody called and told us the precinct that was out was Magnolia Woods, which was Henson Moore's home precinct. We carried it by about three hundred votes, which put us about one hundred votes ahead.

In Louisiana, a Republican winning an election by one hundred votes is not going to cut it because you tend to have problems with folks in the middle of the night.

We launched into a big voter security deal. In Louisiana, after the polls are closed they open the seal on the back of the electronic voting machines and look at the counters, similar to an odometer of a car. Under Louisiana law, that is the official number for the vote. But this is where you get all the discrepancies because people misread the numbers, they transpose figures, they add them up wrong. All kinds of things happen.

They open them up, record the results on sheets of paper and then call them into the secretary of state's office. Folks know when they re-open those machines on Friday is when you really learn what is on there because you get to go back over it.

On Thursday, before they opened the machines up, we were scared to death that the bad guys were going to change the counts on those machines because they were being serviced by the same people who service pinball machines.

The chairman of the Moore campaign was Jimmy Boyce, a Caterpillar dealer. I went over to Boyce's house and said, "Jimmy, I'm afraid when they open those machines tomorrow, we are going to be in bad trouble because somebody could get in there and change those machines. I don't know what to do about it."

We thought about it for a while and I finally came up with an idea that I've not revealed until this moment. I decided to call a press conference because this was the number one thing on the news media for three days in a row. I called a press conference, got the entire press corps over to the Moore headquarters and sent Henson off to campaign somewhere.

I announced that I had gotten a phone call in the middle of the night from somebody in one of the country parishes who had seen people breaking into the voting machine warehouse. They wanted to let us know it was going on. That was as much information as I had, but I had turned it over to the authorities, and we were calling the FBI. Anybody caught doing that would be put in jail. I made it as strong as I could, but it was totally fabricated.

Sure enough, when they opened the machines up that Friday, they counted all the votes and we won by 144 votes. However, when they opened up one of the machines, they found that one of the counters had broken. It had counted zero votes for LaCaze. There were around 300 votes in the machine, we had gotten maybe 100 of them, and he got zero. Obviously, about 200 people had tried to vote for him, but his counter just didn't work.

As soon as that was discovered, it became headline news. LaCaze immediately claimed he was the winner because those people obviously voted for him. Unfortunately for LaCaze, the Louisiana law says that what is on the counter is the final arbiter. There is no other recourse.

LaCaze sued to have the Secretary of State not declare the election results official. He got an injunction for a while and everything was up in the air.

In the meantime, LaCaze went to see Edwin Edwards, the Democratic governor, to seek his advice. Edwards advised him not to sue; that was a big mistake. Instead, he said, "Just accept the loss, go up to the U.S. House of Representatives, which is controlled by the Democrats, show them what happened and they will declare you the winner."

LaCaze didn't take Edwards's advice and, consequently, we fought it out in court. We went to the state Supreme Court a couple times to work out all the details and finally had to have a trial . During the entire two weeks while we were waiting to go to trial, Moore was off campaigning. I sent him out of town; he couldn't talk to lawyers or anything.

Our story was, we won the election, you saw it yourself on election night, and now the Democrats are trying to steal it from us. They want the judges to give what the voters wouldn't give them. That was all he said, over and over again.

There was no case law in the country on something like this. At the end of November, State District Court Judge Melvin Shorress did the only thing he could do—he threw the election out and said we had to run the whole election over again.

The judge set the new election date for January 13, so we had to campaign over Christmastime. On Election Day it rained four inches, yet 17,000 more people voted than had voted in the November election. In the final outcome, Moore won big.

—*Jay Stone*

Whorehouse Owner Gets Lucky, Gives 50 Gs to Lambert

Factoid: In 1979, Republican David Treen and Democrat Louis Lambert were involved in one of the closest gubernatorial races in Louisiana history. Treen won by just half a percent.

In Louisiana, they have a process where all of the big-money guys have to talk to the "the man." They want to see the candidate face to face. I'm in this hotel by the airport in New Orleans, and this guy had an appointment to see David Treen at eight o'clock at night at the hotel. Treen got hung up in Baton Rouge and could not get back.

So I brought the guy up to the room and said, "Dave is very sorry that he could not be here, but can I help you?" He says, "Yeah, I got the best whorehouses out on Highway 90. They're the cleanest whorehouses in New Orleans." I'm sitting there, going "What?" So he gives me this whole speech about these great whorehouses he runs.

I asked what that had to do with the governor's race, and then I asked him if he wasn't worried about the sheriff. "No, I'm worried about the state police, we have the sheriff taken care of," he said. So I listened to this crap for a while and finally told him he was lucky Dave Treen wasn't there because Treen probably would have thrown him out on his butt. I politely told him that I was not going to take his 50 grand.

He looked at me and said, "If you don't want my money, then I'm going to go across the street to see Louis Lambert." I told him to go right ahead and see Lambert, who was the Democratic nominee.

I called Lambert's consultant, Matt Reese, the next day and said, "Matt, after this is over we have to talk." I just wanted to know. Matt agreed to talk. So after the campaign was over, Matt called me one day and said, "Yep, Louis took it!"

I said, "I can't believe this crap."   *—Stu Spencer*

Women Wore White Gloves to Fundraisers

Mary Evelyn Parker, the Democratic candidate for state treasurer in Louisiana in 1968, was going to a fundraiser at a restored plantation in central Louisiana. In the 1960s in the South, women still wore white gloves and funny little hats to fundraisers. We pulled into the plantation, and all these ladies were waiting on the front porch. The whole place was decorated with red, white and blue signs and banners saying "Elect Mary Evelyn Parker for Treasurer" that I had designed.

I pulled the car into the shade of a tree, rolled down the windows and lit a cigar while Mary Evelyn was up talking with the ladies. The ladies would always say, "No, I don't drink, but I will have a little sherry," and then they would drink quarts of it. So the ladies were buzzing inside.

This was a time when all the windows in a Buick rolled down; they called them hardtop convertibles. Somebody grabbed me by the shoulder. I looked and it was a short little man wearing two revolvers strapped to his legs like Matt Dillon, a big cowboy hat and a star that said sheriff.

He said, "Son, are you Mary Evelyn's driver?" I said, "No, I am her political consultant." He said, "Well, aren't you driving?" I said, "Yes, sir." He said, "Then you are her driver right?" I said, "Yes, sir." He said, "Well, how do you protect her?" I said, "Sheriff, I don't know, what do you mean? We don't have any trouble." He said, "You don't know what is going to happen. How do you protect her, do you have a pistol?" I said, "No, sir. I don't have a pistol." He said, "You don't have a gun of any kind?" I said no.

He told me that we had to take care of this. He turned to his deputy and said, "Go back to the squad car and get that pistol out of the back." He brought me a big snub-nose, shiny revolver and told me he took this off of a woman who killed her husband. "I kept the pistol and let her go, he deserved killing," he said. He asked me if I could shoot. I said, "I'm a Texan, I can shoot. I spent my life with guns, sheriff." He said, "That's bullshit. Get out of the car and shoot that stump." He was pointing to a stump about 20 yards away. So I shot and hit it several times, and then he asked if I could reload, so I reloaded. He nodded with approval. He liked the fact that I was comfortable with a pistol. I kept shooting at the stump and he kept emptying this box of shells.

Pretty soon all the ladies were out on the veranda looking down on our little scene and applauding every time I hit the stump and dust would come belching from the stump. I was a major hit. The sheriff's name was Pat Doucet. He told me to keep the pistol in my pants. I told him I didn't want to carry a pistol in my pants. I was afraid I would shoot off something inappropriate.

I put the pistol under the front seat of the car, which is where it stayed until the car dealer who furnished cars for politicians (there was always a dealer there who would furnish statewide candidates free transportation) cleaned the car up. After he got the car back, he found himself a nice pistol that had all the serial numbers rubbed off.

—*Ray Strother*

Johnston Loses Gubernatorial Race, Wins Senate Race

Factoid: Bennett Johnston narrowly lost the gubernatorial nomination to Edwin Edwards in 1971, but ran for U.S. senator in 1972. He got 55% in the general election, with John McKiethen getting 23% running as an independent, while Republican Ben Toledano got 19%.

The 1971 gubernatorial election in Louisiana included a strong group of candidates such as Congressman Edwin Edwards and State Senator Bennett Johnston, but the strongest guy in the race was former Congressman Gillis Long.

Long was a tremendous intellect and a social liberal. He had the ability to raise money that was unfathomable to anybody else. Long would come into town and raise $100,000 in an evening, which in those days was huge money.

Frank Friedler, a New Orleans city councilman, was the finance director for Johnston, who at the time was a little known state senator from Shreveport. Sam LaBlanc, my brother, was Johnston's campaign manager. Nobody knew Bennett so it was difficult to raise money for him.

Friedler decided he was going to raise the money they needed to finish out the race. He threw a dinner party for 20 key people. After the dinner, he closed the door and locked it. He said, very simply, "In front of you is the note. Nobody leaves until everybody signs up."

He had three or four shills ready to go for $25,000 apiece, so they kicked in right away. Then the rest of them were intimidated into contributing until they were down to the last guy. Everyone pressured him into doing it. That was how they managed to complete the election, financially.

Johnston lost to Edwards by 4,000 votes out of something like a 1.5 million cast statewide.

Johnston turned right around and decided to run for U.S. Senate in 1972 against six-term incumbent Allan J. Ellender. My uncle, George Reese, was then running Johnston's race. Everyone said it was doomed from the start because he was running against an institution like Ellender. On the other hand, Johnston had spent all this money running for governor and he had nothing else to do.

Johnston's campaign got poll results back that said he had no chance — and Johnston denies it, but this is true — unless Allan Ellender dropped dead. Three weeks before the primary election, when no one else could get into the race, Ellender died.

Shocking everyone, Johnston won the race in a walkaway, proving once again that luck and timing are the most important things in politics. *—Rob Couhig*

Making B/W Television for Mary Evelyn Parker

In 1968, consultants and candidates were all of a sudden worried about television, the new medium. They had never had to contend with television before, but John F. Kennedy had beaten Richard Nixon, people said, because of his television appearances. So candidates were in tune with this new medium. In Louisiana it was still black-and-white television. I was hired to produce television ads and be the political consultant for Mary Evelyn Parker, the state treasurer candidate, which sent me running to the library to find out what the hell political consultants did. I wrote her speeches, scheduled her speaking engagements, wrote the news stories and later produced her television spots.

Paul Yacich was just out of the military where he had been an electronics man, but he was now chief engineer at the first station in the South, WDSU in New Orleans. I'd heard of Paul and so I went to him and said, look, I have a client coming in here tomorrow to make a live television show.

We were still doing live 30-minute shows. Videotape was still fairly primitive. It was two-inch tape, which you would have to edit with razor blades. Mary Evelyn was a dazzling speaker and was going to do the show. But I had never been in a television studio.

I bluffed Yacich. I said, "Here are two $100 bills. Walk me around and teach me the names of all these machines and what they do, and I will take some notes." He spent about three hours with me, teaching me what a television station does. He let me watch a couple of local television spots being produced in the studio. Everyone produced them in the studio then. Videotape took an 18-wheeler to carry the equipment around, because it was monstrously heavy stuff and the cameras weighted 500 or 600 pounds.

I took Mary Evelyn in the next day and started talking to her about quad-video and the rest. I asked him for a couple of boards to absorb the sound on the side of her, and I asked for lower lights. I sounded pretty good.

We began our live broadcast. She was wearing a charm bracelet. I asked her to take it off, but she said no, because her dead husband had given it to her and it was good luck. Unfortunately every time it hit the desk it sounded like a freight train wrecking, and we were on live television. This kept going on. I was signaling her to take the bracelet off, but she kept refusing to take it off. She finally ran out of coffee and things to say. She said, "Raymond, what do I say now?" For the rest of the show I had to give her lines. She would look into the camera, but people were hearing both my lines and hers.

—*Ray Strother*

Working to Get the Alien Center in Oakdale

My job in the Dave Treen administration was governmental affairs, which means I was supposed to deal with Congress and local governments. Congressman Jerry Huckaby's office called one day and wanted to know who in the world was trying to build an illegal alien center in his district in northeast Louisiana.

I checked around and found out the federal government was trying to build an illegal alien center. It wasn't a jail; it was a detention center for the Cubans or whoever tried to cross the border. The intention was for them to stay there a while, and then they would be sent out of the country. Treen had just put me on his task force to create jobs.

I called the congressman back and explained that if he didn't want the center in his area, the governor would stop it. "I don't want it," Huckaby replied.

I called the head of the Chamber of Commerce in Oakdale and said, "This is one of those things you have to ask for. It would create around 800 great federal jobs; however, you have to call me back and tell me you want this." He waited about five minutes. Central Louisiana had 35 percent unemployment at the time, so he called me back and said, "Hey! We want it. What do we have to do?"

"You just started the process," I replied.

We had been working for a year and a half to get this thing done when I got a call from the governor demanding, "Who in the hell is trying to build an illegal alien center?"

"I'm telling you, Governor, they want it," I answered.

"How in the world could they want that?" he asked.

"Sir, they've been praying at night," I said. They really were holding all-night vigils for this. "They were hoping you would call them."

He said, "Get the mayor on the phone."

Mayor George Mowad had been waiting for him to call for two years. When the governor actually called, the mayor stated, "I can't believe you called. We really want this illegal alien center."

They got it built, and the unemployment in Oakdale is down to almost nothing. Everybody works at the detention center.

—*Bob DeViney*

The World Watched Louisiana

Factoid: Edwin Edwards won a fourth term as governor of Louisiana in 1991, defeating David Duke by a margin of 61-39.

One thing I will never forget about the 1991 Edwin Edwards campaign was that when we needed television crews, we had to compete with Japanese and European TV stations. The world was in Baton Rouge, Louisiana, for that campaign because it was so noteworthy. When I needed satellite time, it was a problem. The whole world watched that campaign.

We hired a woman to go to Florida to raise money from the Jewish community there. After a week, she returned and said, "I'm wasting my time and your money. Everyone I talked to had already sent money before we even asked them."

The policies and statements of David Duke were so based in racism and division it became a crusade for those of us who were working in the Edwards campaign. It became less about Edwin Edwards and much, much more about beating David Duke.

On Election Day an African American radio station in

Louisiana, with no encouragement from the campaign whatsoever, substituted their regular highway traffic reports for reports from the polling places. "Over at Buena Vista School, the lines are short right now, so go vote." That was something that happened completely spontaneously. It was that kind of campaign.

—*Bill Fletcher*

Traveling With the Band Across Louisiana

Factoid: Singin' Jimmie Davis, running again for governor of Louisiana in 1971, traveled with a band and closed every campaign appearance singing his all-time hit song, "You Are My Sunshine."

The Spear family had a lovely woman in the band, and some of the younger band members, like Eddie Raven, who was 19, would circle that bus like a wolf looking for a way to get into the flock.

Jimmy Davis came up to me, because I was the protector of the band, and told me I had better keep Eddie Raven away from his wife and that little girl in the Spear family. So that was one of my jobs.

One night, traveling with the band, we ended up in Opelousas, Louisiana, at a good Cajun seafood restaurant.

We were drinking beer and eating crawfish, and in comes two-gun Pat Doucet. He sees me, and he is so drunk he's bouncing off things. Sheriff Doucet owned two brothels, one called Maggies and the other called The Gate. Later, he and some other guys owned a place called The Spot, which was a trailer off in the woods.

He walks up to the table, hugs me and says, "Raymond, I am so glad to see you. You are doing such a wonderful thing for our state, electing that wonderful man, Jimmie Davis (which means we are going to open up gambling and the whorehouses again). I love you boys like you were all my sons. All of you band members, if I could adopt you, I would." He just kept hugging me. I was embarrassed. In the South, men don't hug.

He says, "I got to do something for you boys," so he pulled out some business cards from his pocket, took a pencil and starting writing on the backs of the card. He finished the cards and said, "Give one of these cards to all the boys."

243

Eddie Raven asked me, "What you got there?" I said, "What I think I got here is a free pass to the whorehouse." It was a business card for The Gate, with a picture of a naked woman holding her breast saying "Bet you didn't know we had these." On the back Pat had written, "Give these boys anything they want for free. Pat."

So Eddie says, "Where is this whorehouse?" I told him it was about half a mile from there. Eddie said let's go. I told him the governor would get mad at us because I was supposed to get the boys on the road that night for an eight o'clock performance. Well, I was outvoted.

A corrugated iron fence surrounded The Gate, with a 10-foot-tall gate that was open. In the parking lot were about six other cars. A deputy sheriff sat outside at a desk by the front door.

As you went in, he took your gun and your driver's license. I didn't have a gun, but two of the band members did. He told them they would be returned as they left, but it was a way to keep down trouble. So we went in and sat in the living room and a parade of working girls came by, some of them quite pretty. I had gone to high school with one of them in Texas. I was embarrassed, but she wasn't. The boys went upstairs and I waited, sat there and talked to this girl and drank some beers. I finally rounded them all up later and made it to north Louisiana by amphetamines and liberal doses of alcohol. Every night, no matter where we were, they would start running toward the station wagon because we were going to The Gate.

I spent the rest of that campaign shuttling between a whorehouse and the campaign. Davis, of course, lost.

—Ray Strother

'Gillis Would Never Tell a Lie...'

Factoid: Gillis W. Long was elected to Congress in 1962, representing Louisiana's 8th district, when he defeated Republican John Lewis, 64-36. He was out of Congress for eight years but was elected again in 1972 and served six consecutive terms.

Avoiding a direct question is a tough assignment for a politician. Of course, it's always better to tell the truth. Sam Rayburn used to say, "Tell the truth the first time and you'll never have to remember what you said."

Congressman Gillis Long of Louisiana used to tell about how his cousin, Senator Russell Long, his campaign manager, would introduce him to crowds. "Gillis is brilliant, articulate, honest and would never tell a lie unless it was absolutely necessary." Gillis asked him to drop the last part.   —*Gary Hymel*

Winning and Losing With Buddy Roemer

Factoid: Congressman Buddy Roemer led the primary election field in 1987 with 33%. Former Governor Edwin Edwards qualified for the run-off with 28% but chose not to compete, giving Roemer the statehouse.

Buddy Roemer was a colorful character elected governor of Louisiana in 1987. He ran for re-election in 1991 against Edwin Edwards and David Duke.

One night I was sitting in my library on Capitol Hill, in D.C., watching the crack addicts who walk down the street, trying to break into cars, when all of a sudden a commercial came to me with clarity. I sat there and wrote it. I called Roemer, and he said, "Okay, you got it, let's film it." I went down and filmed the commercial, and it ended up on everybody's reel. Roemer's last line on the commercial was, "I don't like Louisiana politics, but I love Louisiana." People really liked it, and it had some truth to it.

The 1987 race was a huge upset. He was running fifth, three weeks from the election, and won in the first primary. By the time the commercial had run a second week, Roemer was in first place.

I didn't hear from Roemer for four years. I was in Louisiana when I got a call to come up to the office at the Capitol in Baton Rouge. I went up and he was sitting at his empty desk with a sheet of paper. He said he wanted me to help him write a letter to his wife. I asked him why and he said they were separated. He wanted to write a letter and ask her to come back. I asked him, "How long have you been working on this?" He said, "I've been thinking about this for hours." I told him I couldn't help him with it, so he pushed the letter aside and said, "I really mistreated you."

"No, I don't think so," I said. "I am a political consultant. I don't want anything, and I have never wanted anything. My obligation to you ended the day you were elected."

He said, "Yes, I know, but I don't think you got enough credit for that election. I want to hire you again. I want you to do my re-election."

I had a house in Washington, but it didn't have much furniture in it. So I moved into the Governor's Mansion. It was quite good. You have 24-hour-a-day service, cooks and laundry downstairs, and your every whim catered to. It was a terrific life. Roemer, being Roemer, would close himself in his bedroom with Lyle Lovett records and sit there and listen to music and wouldn't campaign. Late at night he would ask me to come listen to music with him. I started badgering him about how he had to get out there and get his campaign going. He said, "Oh, David Duke can't beat me, and Edwin Edwards can't beat me." So, he wouldn't campaign.

At the time I was using my old plane, a Mooney 252, to fly around to see Clinton (who I represented) and then Mark White in Texas. One day I realized I didn't have any suits or shirts, so I landed in Baton Rouge, called the squad car and the police took me to the mansion.

A guy named Harris Diamond from New York ran out and said, "Raymond, what are you doing here?" I said, "I came to pick up some shirts." He said, "You can't be here." I said, "I live here, I live upstairs." He told me to come back later. I said, "No, what the hell is going on?" Right about that time, somebody came out of the dining room. I looked in, and sitting there were James Baker, Mary Matalin and a host of Republicans. I said, "What is going on?" So Buddy comes out of the dining room and says, "Raymond, now look, the president of the United States wanted to send these people down to talk to me, and I am going to talk to them. You don't have a thing to worry about. I am a Democrat today and I will be a Democrat tomorrow. Go on up to bed."

I said, "No, I am leaving. I just came to get some shirts."

I got my shirts and suits, went out the back door, got in the squad car and went back to my airplane. The next morning in Austin, across the bottom of the front page of the newspaper, is the headline: "Roemer changes parties."

Finally, Buddy calls me one day. He says, "Raymond, we have to reach some conclusion on this. Are you going to come back or not?" I said, "I don't think so." He says, "Let me ask you some questions. Before you left who was I running against?" I said, "David Duke." And he says, "What do you think about him?" I said, "He is the Ku Klux Klan, he is evil." Buddy said, "Who else was I running against?" I said, "Edwin Edwards, the most corrupt man in the history of Louisiana politics." He said, "Right! You know who I am running against now?" I said that I didn't. He said, "Edwin Edwards and David Duke. What's changed? Do you want to see one of those guys elected?" I said no. He said, "Let me put it to you this way, if I went to prison, you would bring me cigarettes (he was a chain smoker)?" I said, "Yes, I would bring you cigarettes." He said, "If we were the same blood type, I suspect you would donate blood?" I said, "Yes, I would." He said, "But if I change parties, you would run? I just want to test the boundaries of your friendship." I said, "Okay, I will finish the race."

Dick Wirthlin was doing the polling, and we got a poll back that showed a three-way tie. I said to Roemer, we are in big trouble, and we are going to lose this race. Buddy said, no way. He never campaigned, so we lost the race.

The next morning, his mother was there. She had a little desk in the hall. She was kind of the social secretary. She said, "Raymond, we had everything, we had television, we had money. All we didn't have was a candidate." I said, "You are right."

—*Ray Strother*

Election Night in Louisiana

Factoid: Before being elected governor of Louisiana in 1979, David Treen was elected to Congress four times from the 3rd district, from 1972 to 1978.

Election night in Louisiana was a very tense night, as it was not clear who would win. When things are tense and depressing, David Treen flourishes. I was sitting on the bed talking on the phone getting the returns from different places in Louisiana. When we got those returns, we added them up and it was clear Treen had won.

Treen walked into the bedroom of the suite and I stood up and said, "Congratulations, Governor. You're going to take office."

Instead of jumping up and down, Treen said, "What do you mean?" I replied that he had just been elected governor of Louisiana. He said, "That's impossible. Let me see those numbers." Instead of being happy, he was angry.

Treen had run because his wife Doty wanted to come back to New Orleans. Treen liked being in Congress, where he had served four terms, so he had to do two things. He had to satisfy Doty and within the party there was a huge rivalry between Treen and Henson Moore, the congressman from Baton Rouge. John Cade got Treen to run for governor to keep Moore from running for governor. They had to pay Treen a salary to run for governor.

Treen had anticipated that he would run, fight the good fight, have a good time, then his friend Jimmy Fitzmorris, the lieutenant governor, would become governor, and he would just go back to Washington. The last thing that crossed Treen's mind was that he would become governor.

I thought it was interesting that, not only was he not grateful to us for electing him, but he resented it. I saw Treen only a few times after he became governor and a common statement about Treen among his supporters was that once he became governor, he unplugged the phone.   —*James Farwell*

CHAPTER 28

More Good Stories, Told Shortly

☆ ☆ ☆

Say what you want about politicians and political campaign workers, but it's undeniable that many of them are among the best and the brightest. To make certain elements of the campaign process work, and work successfully, those in the business have to be as creative as anyone on Madison Avenue. A well-turned campaign slogan or a great punch line in a political TV commercial is a thing to behold. So is the implementation of a well-thought-through campaign strategy, or an effective counter-punch.

Democratic vice presidential nominee Lloyd Bentsen, in his debate with Senator Dan Quayle in Omaha in 1988, was in the weeds awaiting just the right moment to put the hurt on the Republican vice presidential candidate. Quayle was asked by NBC anchor Tom Brokaw to detail what qualified him to be president, should the case ever arise. At the end of a detailed answer, Quayle also noted that he had been in Congress as long as Jack Kennedy when he sought the presidency. Bentsen's rejoinder: "Senator, I served with Jack Kennedy, I knew Jack Kennedy, Jack Kennedy was a friend of mine. Senator, you are no Jack Kennedy." Bentsen had the upper hand in the debate, but Quayle was the vice president for the next four years.

There's real beauty in a well-told short story with a punch line. Here are a few short stories that make the cut.

Inter-party Squabble Goes Back 65 Years

Factoid: Democrat Woodrow Wilson was elected president in 1912 with 42% of the popular vote when former Republican President Theodore Roosevelt ran as a third-party candidate, on the National Progressive ticket (Bullmoose), leaving incumbent Republican President William Howard Taft in third place.

In 1978 I was working for Pete Domenici on his first re-election campaign for the U.S. Senate. My task was to go to every county and talk to active Republicans to get them on board for Domenici as campaign county coordinators or something. In Socorro County, New Mexico, I went to see Holm Burson, the main Republican in the county. Burson was a banker who raised a lot of money and gave a lot of money. Domenici had asked me to go and see him.

I got in late in the evening and called Burson, then went by and saw him and stayed the night in town. The next morning I got up and called Anastasio Torres. Torres was a longtime Republican, but over the evening he had heard I had visited with Burson. I went to see Torres and he was very distant and cold. He said, why are you here? I said, Pete Domenici is the first Republican senator we have had since Reconstruction, and it is really important that we re-elect him. We need your help. I just came by to see if we could count on you.

He said, Pete is a very good friend of mine, but who else are you working with in the county? I said, last night I went to see Holm Burson. He says, I don't work with Holm Burson. Oh, you don't? I asked. Torres said, we split over the presidential fight, and I just am not going to work with him.

I said, you mean Ford and Reagan in 1976? He said, no, Taft and Roosevelt in 1912. Torres at the time was 88 years old. New Mexico became a state in January 1912. Old wounds are slow to heal in Socorro. —*Greg Graves*

Carter Has Bunny Story for 6-year-old

I am a well-known liberal Democrat. When Carter became president I was known as what we all call a Kennedy Democrat. I got a phone call at one point in 1989 from Congressman Tip O'Neill, who said I might get a call from the president. O'Neill said he talked to him that morning and he was going to organize a campaign for re-election. He wanted to expand his base and bring in some people who might be able to reach out to the liberal end of the Democratic Party. "You have a lot of experience in that world, so he will call you," O'Neill said. I said thank you and didn't think anything of it.

A day or two later I came home and my son Christopher, who is now in his 20s, said, "Daddy, the mayor called."

I had run the campaign for Boston Mayor Kevin White the previous couple of times. He ran four times and I ran the first two campaigns. White is kind of my mentor in politics. He is a generation older than I, but there is a long-standing friendship and history between us.

Christopher said, "I really like the mayor, Daddy." I said, "Really, why do you like him?" He said, "He told me a story about bunny rabbits." I am reading my newspaper and thinking, Mayor White has never told any kids' stories. He's a mayor, he's a tough guy, he has never told any kid who answered the phone anything except goodbye. He doesn't tell stories about bunny rabbits to anybody, including his own kids.

I turned to my son and said, "Christopher, how do you know it was the mayor?" He said, "Well, Daddy, he called from his house." I said, "What do you mean, his house?" Christopher replied, "He said the White House." I told my wife this all sounded strange and asked whether she had answered the phone. She said no, she was outside in the back, and the phone rang and Christopher talked for about 15 minutes. "I didn't know who he was talking to," she said. "I thought he was talking to you."

I picked up the phone, called the information number at the White House and said, "Hello, this is Jack Walsh, is the president there? Within 20 seconds this Southern voice comes on and says, 'Jack, thanks for calling me back.'" It was Jimmy Carter.

—*Jack Walsh*

Taken to the Woodshed on Social Security

As DNC chairman one of the things you did was get out and show the flag. You made the rounds through the states. On an early trip I was in California, and there was a guy by the name of Dan Blackburn who had been in radio and television and covered Washington for a while. He put together the Friday Group, which is not unlike the Sperling group, where every Friday they would have a lunch and reporters would come in and some visiting personage like me would speak and take questions.

At this luncheon there were a lot of issue questions. One of the things being debated at the time was the budget deficit. What is the Democratic Party going to do about the budget? I didn't have any magic answers, but I said to this group, when people examine and put together a budget, it is basically a plan based on priorities. So I think, in looking forward, if you have a deficit then you have to look at everything. Every card should be on the table, and then you can decide what you want to do. Someone said to me, well, let's talk about Social Security. Are you saying that in examining the budget they should take a look at means testing for Social Security? I said, I am not saying that it ought to be adopted; I am saying it needs to be looked at. I don't think anything should be off the table in this initial examination. Well, there was a lot of note-taking going on.

The meeting adjourns and one of the NBC affiliates says, can we get you to say that on camera about Social Security? I said sure.

Within 20 minutes I get a call from headquarters in Washington informing me that California Senator Alan Cranston has just condemned me on the floor of the United States Senate. "Who is this chairman in my state suggesting that means-tested Social Security should be looked at? We have a contract with the American people." I was taken to the woodshed big-time!

After that, Speaker Tip O'Neill invited me to weekly whip meetings so I could get a sense of what was going on. You know, he was probably saying, don't screw up again, sit with us and we will tell you what to say and what not to say.　　　　*—Paul Kirk*

Carolina Blue Is the Top Priority

Factoid: Democrat Norman Sisisky defeated five-term incumbent Robert Daniel in 1982, in the 4th district of Virginia, by a 54-46 margin.

In 1982 I was running Norman Sisisky's campaign in the 4th district of Virginia when he was challenging Bob Daniel. I was on the phone with Mike McLister about doing the media for the campaign. Right in the middle of cutting a deal, McLister puts me on hold and says, "I'll be right back." I was on hold for 15 minutes.

This is for $40,000 to $50,000, which in 1982 was a nice piece of business. I was getting pissed off.

Finally he gets back on the phone and tells me he's sorry, but his season tickets for the University of North Carolina basketball games were screwed up and he had to make sure he got them straightened out.

—Tom King

You're in North Dakota Right Now

In my 1986 campaign for the Montana House of Representatives, I was going door to door on the country roads near Wibeaux. The town is up on the North Dakota border and out in the middle of nowhere.

I had talked to one of the postmasters, and he told me nobody would complain if I stuck these little scratchpads in the mailboxes, so I did, because some of the houses were four miles back from the road. I would put a pad in each mailbox I went by. If the house was right by the road, I'd drive up and knock on the door instead. It was a form of going door to door, but you only saw a house about once every 30 mailboxes.

I saw this house out past Wibeaux and went up and knocked on the door. I handed out my scratchpad and introduced myself: "Hi, I'm Leo Giacometto. I'm running for state representative. I'm from Alzaeda, and I'd sure appreciate your support."

"Oh, Leo, it's good to see you." He whips out his checkbook and gives me a check for 10 dollars.

I gave him the scratchpad and told him I really appreciated it. "Make sure you vote on Election Day," I added.

He said, "Well, Leo, you know we support you. Here's our contribution for your campaign."

I said, "That's very nice, but I really need you to show up and vote."

"Well, this is about all I can do because we're not registered to vote in Montana. You're in North Dakota right now," he said.

I got a $10 check and felt pretty stupid.

—Leo Giacometto

Politicians Sure Can Talk

I was in the small town of Mabel, Minnesota, in 1980 and didn't know anything about state government at the time. I was addressing a group of senior citizens, telling them, "Isn't it amazing that you live longer in Minnesota than in any other state in the union, in spite of mosquitoes, rain, these unbelievable winters and icestorms?" I was really laying it on them.

An older gentleman in the back kept raising his hand. I could tell I was getting to him, so I wanted to repeat this. I went through the whole thing again, saying, "Isn't it amazing that you live longer in this state in spite of all these obstacles of cold and mosquitoes and all those other things?"

Finally, I acknowledged the man and said, "Yes, sir. What would you like to say?"

"You're damn right and it seems like it."   *—Duane Benson*

Boggs's Office Had a Great View

Congressman Hale Boggs of Louisiana was running for majority leader in the House of Representatives in 1968. Congressman Wayne Hayes of Ohio was also running. There were a total of five candidates in the race.

One day Boggs got a call from Hayes, whom we heard might withdraw from the race. Hayes told Boggs he wanted to talk to him.

Boggs said, "Absolutely, Wayne, let's talk." Boggs was majority whip at the time and had an office in the front section of the Capitol. Hayes came over and sat down to talk to Boggs. The entire time they talked, Hayes was gazing around the room and seeing what a great office it was. He walked out of that room not having resigned from the race.

Boggs said, "That's never going to happen to me again. If a guy wants to talk to me, I'm going to his office." —*Gary Hymel*

Denton's Contribution to Equality of the Sexes

Factoid: Jeremiah Denton, who had been a POW, was elected to the U.S. Senate in 1980 when he defeated James Folson Jr. 50-47.

The Senate was having hearings on spouse abuse and domestic violence in the early 1980s. Senator Jeremiah Denton, from Alabama, was kind of perplexed. While sitting in there listening to testimony, he couldn't understand what all the fuss was about.

He said, "When a guy gets married, he expects a little sex once in a while." He then added, "It seems to me that what a guy needs is to come home from work and be served a martini by a woman who's well rested." Those were his two contributions to the domestic violence legislation. —*Scott Cottington*

The Speaker Is Out Fencing

Factoid: Ned McWherter was elected to the Tennessee House of Representatives in 1968. Four years later, he was elected speaker and served for 14 years – longer than any speaker in the state's history.

Ned McWherter was Speaker of the House in Tennessee during the time Ronald Reagan was president of the United States. The president was going to come down to Nashville to speak.

McWherter was a big, heavyset man from rural west Tennessee. His looks are very deceiving. You'd think he was similar to "Boss Hogg." However, he was very astute, had been a Budweiser distributor, was enormously successful, was Speaker of the House and went on to become governor of Tennessee.

President Reagan had been asked to speak to a joint session of the House and Senate of Tennessee. The House chambers would be used because of its larger size. We were told we would need to notify McWherter since he was the speaker in that chamber.

McWherter had a large farm near Dresden that he was always going out to, and often he would wear blue jeans and cowboy boots. Someone from the president's office called McWherter's office in Nashville and said they needed to coordinate the plans. They were told, "You need to call his office at home because he's gone home."

They called McWherter's house and told the person answering the phone, "The president wants to speak to Speaker McWherter."

"Well, Speaker McWherter is not here; he's out fencing," came the reply.

The White House caller asked, "Is there a number at the club where we might reach him?"

It took a while to explain that McWherter is 6-foot-4, weighs 280 pounds and was out on the farm building fence.

—*Cathy Thomas*

Talking Turkey With the Turkeys

Factoid: Phil Batt of Wilder, Idaho, served in the Idaho State Senate, was elected to one term as lieutenant governor in 1978 and was elected to one term as governor in 1994.

When Phil Batt was first considering running for the Idaho state legislature in 1964, he was in the business of raising turkeys. One day he went out to feed the turkeys in the morning and decided to try out his speech-giving talents on the turkeys.

Batt has a high-pitched voice, and people always said he would never get elected to office because of his voice.

He gets out there and talks to the turkeys. He starts giving his prepared remarks and all of a sudden, in unison, the turkeys flip their heads and gobble. Batt counted that as total approval.

—*Sandy Patano*

The Day the Minnesota Legislature Was a Zoo

During my first year in the Minnesota House of Representatives, we were in session on April 1, 1979, and decided it would be fun to have somebody offer an amendment to make the Capitol and the grounds a branch of the state zoo.

Rules have changed since then, but in those days you weren't on record as having offered the amendment unless you actually made the motion. Now it's automatic. You could do the kind of joke amendments that really aren't possible anymore.

We had a representative, John Clausen, a former Lutheran minister, who was going to offer the amendment. Then somebody said they knew a disc jockey with a gorilla suit. We could hire him for 30 bucks to come in and run through the chamber in his gorilla suit when this amendment was being offered. We passed the hat and got the $30 for the gorilla.

Clausen is on his feet when the doors burst open and the gorilla comes running in.

The night before, my husband and I had been out and had a baby-sitter, who allowed our kids to pop an entire jar of popcorn. There was popcorn everywhere. Nick suggested I take it over and give it to the people at the state office building. We gave it to the gorilla instead.

The gorilla was running through the chamber, flinging popcorn. Ray Faricy, one of the senior members and a big man, was presiding up in the speaker's podium. There is a large picture of Lincoln that hangs up there. The gorilla was running around, and then he ran up and grabbed Faricy by the legs, which amazed us because this gorilla wasn't very big and Faricy is very tall.

Faricy's head hit the Lincoln portrait behind the chair, and it started to swing. I was thinking, Oh my! This painting is going to fall down, and we're going to be blamed!

Some of the members were quite appalled that we had done this, probably rightly so. We did not get a vote as Clausen withdrew the amendment.

—*Dee Long*

Working Casework in Poor Counties

Jim Sasser was the first United States senator who had gone out to the counties where the people could actually come to the courthouse to meet with you. People had noticed in the newspaper that I was going to be at the courthouse. People would come for all sorts of reasons, such as if they had a problem with Social Security or were a veteran.

In one poor, rural county in 1979, I was in a small room in the courthouse in Hohenwald when an older man came in, looking tired and worn out. I said, "Tell me what your problem is." I had a sheet of paper to take down his name and Social Security number, adding what he needed and what we could do to help. I told him, "I just need one more thing from you. If you will just sign this, it gives us the permission to go ahead and follow-up."

He looked at that piece of paper and just stared at it. I repeated the instructions for him to put his name down on the paper.

The big man looked up at me and had huge tears coming down his face. I said, "Are you okay?"

He replied, "Honey, I can't write and I can't read."

Of course, then I started crying and apologized. It shook me to the very bones of my body. Here was a man who possessed such nerve to come up to see me, and I'm sure I was all dolled up to look as nice as I could. Most of the people don't go for help because they're embarrassed. He was probably plenty smart and had worked all his life and educated all of his children. There were times when people would bring their children, and the children would sign their names for them. —*Cathy Thomas*

Reagan Endorses Assembly Candidate

There was a special election for a State Assembly seat in the spring of 1977, in Los Angeles. Wilshire Boulevard cut the district roughly in half. It included the University of Southern California and was a very Democratic district. Only about half a dozen Republicans were in the primary. A well-known Democrat was the odds-on favorite.

The Republican National Committee boldly decided to go with a guy named Dan Smith, an assistant vice president of the Bank of California who had been president of the USC student body a few years before. And he was black. They endorsed this guy in the primary, but they couldn't give him any money, so part of the endorsement was to send me out there to work in his campaign.

After I'd been out there for a couple of months, I came back to D.C. to a campaign management college. On my return, I was on the nonstop flight out of Dulles Airport to Los Angeles. I saw Ronald and Nancy Reagan sitting there waiting for the same plane. He had unsuccessfully run against Gerald Ford in the 1976 primaries, but it was very clear he was going to run again in 1980.

I thought, *Well, this is perfect.* He'd been governor of California, and I was working on this Assembly race. I'm sitting back in coach, and he's in first-class. So I write him this long impassioned note on RNC letterhead. I say what a boost it would be to the campaign if he could get involved in this race even though I know it's difficult for elected officials to get involved in primaries. But it would be an enormous help if he could do something for Dan Smith.

After the flight attendant delivers my letter, Reagan turns it over and writes a note on the back. It goes on to say something like, "Tom, I'm so excited to hear that the RNC is involved in this campaign. Dan is a friend of mine and someone I've known for quite some time since he was in college at USC. By the way, I had a news conference in L.A. a couple of days ago endorsing him for this race."

Here I am, writing this letter to the guy who would be president in a few years, and I'd demonstrated absolute ignorance in a campaign I was supposed to be involved in up to my eyebrows. For some reason, they had neglected to call me from L.A. to inform me that not only had they won Reagan's endorsement but they'd had a news conference to announce it.   —*Tom Gildemeister*

Chop It Off in Troublesome Gulch

Factoid: Former Colorado Senator Gary Hart, widely seen as the early frontrunner in the Iowa caucus in 1988, quit the Democrat presidential race on May 8, 1987, five days after the Miami Herald *revealed actress Donna Rice had stayed at Hart's Capitol Hill town-house. The* National Enquirer *ran a picture of Rice on Hart's lap, taken while on a Caribbean sail on a boat named* Monkey Business.

The day after Donna Rice got caught with Gary Hart, in 1988, they made me Lee Hart's chief of staff. I wake up on Sunday morning like everybody else, and there is David Brinkley on the news, saying, since you went to bed last night here's what's new. The phone rings three seconds after the show starts and it is Paul Tully, the manager, wanting all hands on deck fast. I get there and hear I'm the new chief of staff to the candidate's wife, Lee Hart. Oh great, what is her attitude now? We don't know.

I go to Denver and drive to their house in Troublesome Gulch. I didn't know that Lee had a bunch of women friends all congregated there in a support group, and they were all cracking jokes. I knock on the door, walk in and there is a woman with a butcher knife. "We should have cut his thing off. We should cut all of their things off."

Now, I am the only guy walking in there going, hi, I am Joe Trippi. I am here to help you through this. Lee wasn't going to take any of that. I thought they were going to chop it off right there.

—*Joe Trippi*

Caught With His Pants Down

As a young boy growing up, I was a big fan of Richard Nixon's. I was probably the only young boy of my generation who was a fan of Nixon's, but I always was, even after he left office and through his later years.

After I got out of college, I had the opportunity to go to New York City to work on a television project about Nixon in April of 1983. It was about 38 hours of videotaped interviews with Nixon, basically telling the story of his life, his administration and his whole political career.

There was a studio on 42nd Street in New York called National Video. It was a big old warehouse that had huge rooms where they put together sets for video shoots. The first day we had this tear-down set that you could take down and put back together.

Before Nixon came, we had to put the set together, so I was there early in the morning in my work clothes. We built the set and then got notice that the president was on the way.

About the time someone told me the president was going to be there in 10 minutes, we went to change our clothes from work clothes to coats and ties to look professional when we greeted him. I asked where I should change, and someone pointed me toward his dressing room.

I said, "I can't use his dressing room." But they assured me that he was still 10 minutes away and that it would be fine. I went into the dressing room, took my shirt off and had my pants down around my ankles when the door opens. My first meeting with Richard Nixon was in a state of undress.

He looked up at me and said, "Well, I'm sorry. I guess I caught you with your pants down."

I apologized profusely and shuffled out of the room. I was better dressed the next time I met him. I'll always remember how gracious he was and that he wasn't upset at all that I was in his dressing room. He actually laughed a lot. I spent my whole life wishing to meet him, and that was how it was.   —*Hans Kaiser*

Politics Is Just Like Show Business

In 1965, Ronald Reagan was still in the process of considering running for governor of California, although Bill Roberts and I were convinced he was running. We were about five months into it with this exploratory committee, and Reagan and I had traveled around the state that week.

We were in Modesto, and he had given his speech at the end of the day. I took him back to his small hotel room. In those days it was just Ron and Stu. It wasn't "Governor."

I started walking back to my room and he said, "Stu, come here a minute, I want to talk to you."

So I go into his room, and he says, "You know, I got this politics thing all figured out." I looked at him and said, "What do you mean?" He smiled and said, "It's just like show business." I said, "What?" He says, "Yes, you have a great opening, you coast for a while and then you have a great closing."

I said, "You know, you're right, but I don't like it." He smiled that smile of his, and I shut the door and went on, but I have never forgotten that night. He really pissed me off.   —*Stu Spencer*

CHAPTER 29

Comedians in the Political Business

☆ ☆ ☆

Comedians in the entertainment field are famous for the art of the well-timed one-liner. They compile books of one-liners by Casey Stengel and Yogi Berra. Well, believe it or not, some politicians could have made it in show business. The hot and heavy of a good political campaign has produced some pretty memorable one-liners.

In 1984, former Vice President Walter Mondale had won the Iowa Caucus with nearly 50 percent of the attendees in his favor, but Colorado Senator Gary Hart had emerged from the pack as the number one challenger to the presumed favorite. Hart got "Big Mo" by winning the New Hampshire primary with 37 percent of the vote. For a few weeks, a heated race ensued between Mondale and Hart until Mondale borrowed a line from a Wendy's hamburger TV ad to challenge Hart's lack of substance on issues. On March 11, Mondale's line "Where's the beef?" reverberated across the political landscape, and he was soon back in the role of favorite.

Texas State Treasurer Ann Richards, later to become governor, got a lot of mileage out of her keynote address at the Democratic National Convention in Atlanta with her one-liner about then Vice President George Bush. "He can't help it if he was born with a silver foot in his mouth," Richards chided.

In 1840, the Whigs ran what was seen as the first modern campaign, with songs, slogans, advertising and organized rallies.

Their political campaign slogan was "Tippecanoe and Tyler too," which pushed the Whig ticket of William Henry Harrison and John Tyler to victory with 53 percent of the vote. Harrison had been the commanding general that defeated an Indian force in the Battle of Tippecanoe Creek in 1811, a precursor to the War of 1812. Tyler, who might have just been along for the ride, became president when Harrison died 32 days after his inauguration.

Here are some one-liners, some witty, some poignant, some important to campaign success.

'I'd Rather Eat Roadkill'

Factoid: Wyoming State Senator Barbara Cubin was elected to Congress in 1994 when she defeated Democrat Bob Schuster, 53-41.

W yoming State Senator Barbara Cubin was asked about what kind of campaign she was going to run in 1994 when she sought Wyoming's at-large congressional seat. They asked her about going door to door and she replied, "I would rather eat roadkill than go door to door."

That didn't play well.

—*Scott Cottington*

'Vote for the Crook'

Factoid: Edwin Edwards won a fourth term as governor of Louisiana in 1991 when he defeated David Duke, 61-39.

T he bumper stickers and signs that erupted in the 1991 Louisiana governor's campaign were just great. The famous one that people remember was a bumper sticker that said, "Vote for the Crook. It's important."

A friend of mine, who was the cinematographer for the Edwards campaign, made a 4 x 8 sign and put it in his yard. It had a beautiful fleur-de-lis painted on it. The sign said, "Vote Edwin, he's no saint, but he's no Nazi."

—*Bill Fletcher*

'Little Lady, How Are You Different?'

Factoid: Jo Ann Emerson, widow of Congressman Bill Emerson, won election in the 8th district of Missouri as an independent in 1996. In the regular general election, Emerson got 50.5%, Democrat Emily Firebaugh got 37% and Republican Richard Kline got 10%. In the special election held on the same day, Emerson, running as the Republican, beat Firebaugh 63-34.

Jo Ann Emerson was running in a special election after her husband, Congressman Bill Emerson, died of lung cancer. Bill Emerson had been the congressman for eight terms for the 8th district in Missouri.

Jo Ann is one of the few people who were born in Washington, D.C. Her dad, A. B. Herman, was special counsel to General Dwight Eisenhower. I first met him at the Republican National Committee where he was the counselor to RNC Chairman Mary Louise Smith. So Jo Ann had not spent a lot of time in the boot heel of Missouri, which is a fairly rural and agricultural area in the southeastern part of the state.

One of her first challenges when she was getting ready to give her announcement speech was what to wear. She invented the black pants suit long before Hillary Clinton started wearing them. She was quite sophisticated. She kind of scowled at me and said, "I brought my little sundress, my sweater and my flats and I'll be just fine." She understood that she had to adapt to the culture of the Missouri congressional district.

During one of her first big appearances, at a barbecue, she stood up and talked about the key issues of the district, such as agriculture and taxes, and how she agreed with Bill Emerson on these issues. She wrapped it up and asked for questions.

A crusty old guy in the back raises his hand and says, "Well, little lady, you told us about all the ways that you are like Bill Emerson. How are you different from him?"

This is just a couple of months after Bill died, so Jo Ann looks around for a moment, then she turns back and says, "Bill Emerson wasn't a National Rifle Association shooting champion when he was 14."
                                                                    —*Ladonna Lee*

Gore, That 'Snake,' Spreads Rumors About Me

I had become a strong Clinton supporter in the early 1980s. He was governor of Arkansas and then lost and came back in 1982, so during that period I became pretty close to him while working at the Democratic National Committee.

In May of 1987, when the presidential race was heating up, Clinton was looking at running. He hadn't jumped in yet, and the Gary Hart/Donna Rice episode exploded onto the scene.

It was midnight, early in May, when I got a phone call from Clinton and he just started to talk about the news of Hart's escapade. His first question to me was, "Is this going to be a problem for all of the candidates?" I told him that, yes, the *New York Times* had already sent out a questionnaire to every Democratic candidate running in the primaries, like Paul Simon, who said you can come and look in his bedroom window, so this was becoming a major issue.

His next line was, "Al Gore, that snake, he spreads these rumors about me."

Clinton wanted to be the only Southern candidate in 1988 in a crowded field, and Gore had gotten in and screwed up that plan. Clinton had always regarded Gore as a rival. At the time it didn't surprise me at all that Clinton thought Gore was a snake.

However, four years later he picked Gore for his vice president. It was a shock, because I knew what the true feelings were. It became another episode of what Clinton will do and how he will set aside his own situation for what will work politically for him, despite his own feelings.　　　　　　　　　　　*—Brian Lunde*

The Flicker of an Old Flame

Governor Ronald Reagan was running for president in 1979. One night we are campaigning in Texas. We're coming back to the airplane. It's nine o'clock at night. They have the Secret Service and the press and people screaming and yelling, and some little old lady gets my attention so I walk over there to the rope line. She says she was one of Ronnie Reagan's girlfriends. I ask her name and she writes it down. I figure this is good for a laugh if nothing else.

On the plane, we're flying to Chicago in the middle of the night. Nancy is asleep and I go over and sit down and say, Governor, at the last stop there was this little lady who said she was a former girlfriend of yours. Her name was such and such. Reagan is on the window side and he turns his head to look out the window. It seemed like an eternity to me, but he finally turns back and with this big grin says "No, Stu, not a girlfriend."

He was so bad with names, but I realized that he remembered her name.

—Stu Spencer

The Wit of Hubert Humphrey

Factoid: Hubert Humphrey's first attempt at elective office came in 1943, when he ran for mayor of Minneapolis and lost. He ran again in 1945 and was elected handily.

There were many times between 1968 and 1972 when I would be driving former Vice President Hubert Humphrey around Los Angeles. I was taking him to the airport on the I-10 freeway, and I was driving quite fast because I didn't want to miss his plane. He turned to me and said, "You know, Harvey, I'd rather be Hubert Humphrey late than the late Hubert Humphrey."

Another time during the 1972 California primary, on the campaign plane, there was bad turbulence and Humphrey said, "You know, you don't want this plane to crash." Everybody was agreeing. He said, "No, you don't understand. If this plane crashes, the headline will read 'Hubert Humphrey Dies in Plane Crash.' Your name won't even make the jump."

In Los Angeles, we used to do what was known as the "Fairfax Walk." On the Sunday before Election Day, there was a big rally in the Fairfax district for Democratic candidates to get out the Jewish votes. You finished it at Canter's, a great old deli on Fairfax.

In this booth at Canter's are Hubert Humphrey, Sam Donaldson, Joe Cerrell and even Walter Cronkite. News cameras were rolling everywhere, capturing these guys sitting down to have lunch. They bring this huge sandwich out for Humphrey. It's a triple-decker with pastrami and everything in the world on it. Humphrey takes a fork and knife and starts cutting it.

Later I said, "Senator, I don't understand. That was a great sandwich." I'm a Jewish kid, and this guy is from Minnesota, so what does he know?

"Harvey," he said, "if I had opened my mouth and picked up that sandwich, that would be the headline and the photograph in tomorrow's paper." —*Harvey Englander*

I Could Have Been Mayor

Factoid: Richard Nolan won a third term in Congress in 1978 when he defeated Republican Russ Bjorhus in the 6th district in Minnesota, 53-45.

Russ Bjorhus was running for Congress in southwest Minnesota in 1978 against a Democratic incumbent, Richard Nolan, who had betrayed the pro-life forces in a little town called Freeport, in west Stearns County, which is about 99.2 percent German Catholic.

On Election Day Bjorhus gets 90 percent of the vote in Freeport. On election night, when it was clear we were going to lose the general election, Bjorhus says, "Wow! We got 90 percent in Freeport. I should have run for mayor of Freeport."

—*Scott Cottington*

Jim Baker Lookalike

Factoid: James Baker, who was manager of President Gerald Ford's campaign in 1976 and later managed two other nationwide campaigns, ran for Texas attorney general in 1978 and lost to Mark White.

James Baker told this on himself. After directing a presidential campaign, he decided to run himself, so he announced as a candidate for Texas attorney general in 1978. He was out campaigning in a dusty little Texas town and some old geezer saw him and walked up to him on the street and said, "Did anybody ever tell you you look like Jim Baker?"

Baker said, "Yes, sir."

The old geezer said, "Well, doesn't that piss you off?"

—*Gary Hymel*

Still Going Strong at 98

One night after I'd been in a meeting with Senator Conrad Burns, my daughter Jessie, who was then about 13 years old, was at my office with me. Burns invited us over to his fundraiser, so we walked over to the Republican Senatorial Campaign Committee office on Capitol Hill.

When we get there, I tell Jessie she can either come into the reception with us on the first floor, or she can sit out in the chairs in the lobby, because it would only be 10 or 15 minutes. As a normal 13-year-old, she wasn't very interested in going to a cocktail party, so I tease her and say, "Oh, come on, be the second generation of Lee women to get pinched on the ass by Senator Thurmond." Thinking nothing of it, off we go. She elects to sit out in the lobby and wait for me.

A couple of weeks later, I have a dinner party and as children always do, in terms of getting even by embarrassing you, she looks at me and smiles as she says, "Mom, which senator is it that always pinches you on the ass?"

Several years later, in 2000, we are at a dinner party where Mildred Giacametto, wife of Leo Giacametto, then Burns's chief of staff, is also a dinner guest.

They get to talking about Strom Thurmond, and someone mentions that he still has an eye for the ladies at 98 and still likes to have an occasional hug. Mildred explains how he is known to hug you all the way around and cup your breast as he gives you a big hug. One of the other women at the dinner party was appalled that any woman would allow anyone to do that to them, much less a United States senator.

Mildred, who is a delightful and charming woman, smiled and said, "Oh, he's 98."

—*Ladonna Lee*

The Real Barbara Bush Speaks Out

We were in Detroit one day in 1986. We started out at five o'clock in the morning with the vice president and Mrs. Bush. It was a very stressful day. That day their son Marvin had gone into the hospital. The doctors couldn't figure out what the problem was, but he ended up having to have a colonoscopy as a young man. It was very serious.

I was afraid the Bushes might have to go back to Washington.

We were campaigning all day long working on the delegate selection process. It was about 11:30 at night and we had just finished a fundraiser in a Detroit suburb. We had a 45-minute motorcade, which at that time of day is not much fun. We finally get to the hotel and get on the elevator with the vice president and Mrs. Bush.

Everyone's image of Barbara Bush is of the ultimate grandmother, someone who is always nice. She usually is, but on this night, after 19 hours, her goodwill was wearing thin. She's standing there and looks over at the vice president and in a less than sweet tone says, "I wonder what that nice young lady who schedules you is doing at this moment? Maybe we should call her to see if she is well rested?"

All I could think was, when are we going to get to the 20th floor?

—*Bill Phillips*

Doing Business in New York

Factoid: Nelson Rockefeller won four consecutive terms as governor of New York, starting in 1958. He resigned as governor in 1973 and was nominated to be vice president of the United States in 1974.

When Nelson Rockefeller was governor of New York, some guy had acquired some property in a really upscale neighborhood on which he wanted to build a health club and spa, but the neighbors didn't like the idea. The local community couldn't dissuade him from building this health club/spa, so finally they got the governor to call him.

The governor said, "You know, it really would be better if you didn't do this. It's just a bad idea."

The guy responded, "Well, no, I've got the financing lined up and all my permits ready, and I'm going ahead."

"Have you checked all your permits to make sure they're okay?" Rockefeller asked.

"Yeah, they're all okay," the guy replied.

Rockefeller said, "No. Have you checked them tomorrow?"

—*Scott Cottington*

'When You're Right, I'll Be With You'

Factoid: Earl K. Long was governor of Louisiana three separate times. As lieutenant governor in 1939, he succeeded governor Richard Leche, who had resigned. He was elected governor for one term in 1948 and another term in 1956.

One of Governor Earl Long's leaders had gone against him on a vote in the Louisiana State Senate. Long then went down on the Senate floor and was chewing this person out. The senator said, "Look, Governor, I've told you before, when you're right, I'll be with you, but when you're wrong, I'll be against you."

Earl said, "Hell, when I'm right, I don't need you!"

—*Gary Hymel*

'Mama, Meet Phil Donahue'

Newt Gingrich is at the Coweta County Fair in 1978, seeing folks and shaking hands. This young woman comes running up and looks at Newt in adoration and tells him, "Oh, I have always wanted to meet you. And my mama really wants to meet you. Won't you come over and meet Mama?"

So Newt and the daughter go to meet this little old lady who was sitting down. "Mama," she says, "this is the man you have always wanted to meet. I would like you to meet Phil Donahue."

And Newt, without batting an eye, says, "So nice to meet you. How do you like the show?"

I mean, what could he do? He had that great silver hair and at a distance he did kind of look like Phil Donahue. —*Carlyle Gregory*

Talking Like Lyndon Johnson

Hubert Humphrey and I were in a car driving around Minnesota, and it was raining so hard the driver had to pull over to the side of the road. I observed to Humphrey, "It's raining like a cow pissing on a flat rock."

Humphrey starts laughing and turns around and says, "You're the only person in my life that talks like Lyndon Johnson." He later told that to Johnson.   —*D.J. Leary*

Bumper Sticker Advice

Factoid: In 1973, President Nixon fired Attorney General Elliot Richardson and then Deputy Attorney General Bill Ruckelshaus when they refused to fire Special Prosecutor Archibald Cox.

Right after the so-called Saturday Night Massacre on October 20, 1973, when President Richard Nixon caused the firing of the special prosecutor, an interesting bumper sticker showed up around the nation's capital. The special prosecutor who was fired was former Harvard law professor Archibald Cox.

The bumper sticker said, "Impeach the Cox Sacker."

—*Terry Cooper*

Gore and the Secret Service

Mike Pigott was a journalist working for the *Nashville Banner* covering Al Gore's first presidential race in 1988. Gore was 39 years old at the time. You have to know Pigott to really understand this, but he has an incredibly dry sense of humor.

He's standing in a group of reporters, and they travel together so they're all kind of road weary. He looks over at one of the reporters on their eighth stop of the day and says, "You know how to tell the difference between Gore and the Secret Service agents?" The other guy says, "No, how?"

Mike says, "Gore's the stiff one."

Everyone got a hoot out of it, but the funny thing was it ended up in one of the lead stories of either *Newsweek* or *Time*.

—*Dave Cooley*

Conte's Favorite Appropriation

Factoid: Silvio Conte was elected to Congress for 32 years from the 1st district of Massachusetts. Often, he was the only Republican in the Massachusetts delegation.

Louisiana Congressman Bob Livingston was chairman of the House Appropriations Committee when he told a story about Congressman Silvio Conte, who had been the ranking Republican on House Appropriations for many years.

Conte was famous for his opposition to pork-barrel appropriations, which meant the appropriation was not for his district in Massachusetts. He would put a fake pig nose on and go on the House floor to talk about pork when there was an appropriations bill up.

After Conte passed away in 1991, a dinner was held every year called the Joy of Politics Award, and Livingston was the recipient one year. He put on a fake pig nose to make this speech. He told about Conte's favorite project, which was providing money for the Atlantic salmon fish ladder.

Livingston said, "Every year Conte would insist they appropriate money to this project. One year we decided to add up all the money we had appropriated for the Atlantic salmon fish ladder, and we found out it would have been cheaper to send them by cab."

—*Gary Hymel*

She Bore an Amazing Resemblance to Her Brother

Paul Rexburg Thatcher, who was Vice President Hubert Humphrey's treasurer in the 1968 national campaign, would often tell of Humphrey's sister, Mrs. Francis Humphrey-Howard, who lived in Washington for many years. She was with one of the

273

national endowment groups. Mrs. Humphrey-Howard is evidently feared by all, including the D.C. cops, who don't dare ticket her, so she parks wherever she wants. She bore a rather amazing resemblance to her brother.

Thatcher was at a reception when Humphrey was vice president. Mrs. Humphrey-Howard, in very blue eye shadow up to her forehead, sailed into a room where Thatcher was sitting with French diplomats. They inquired, "Who's that?"

He said, "Please don't say anything; that's the vice president. He likes to dress up that way sometimes."　　　　*—Dee Long*

'You Don't Need Me Then'

Factoid: Dan Quayle won a second term in the U.S. Senate in 1986, when he defeated Jill Long, 61-39, in Indiana.

I worked for the National Republican Senatorial Senate Committee in 1986. We were over in Senator Dan Quayle's Senate office in the conference room, meeting with the media people, the pollster, the strategists and the chief of staffs.

While we were talking, Dan Quayle stuck his head in and said, "Hey, guys. What are you doing?"

His chief of staff, Tom Duesterberg, said, "We're just planning your re-election."

Quayle replied, "Oh, okay. You don't need me then." And off he went.　　　　*—Scott Cottington*

Iowa Hog Farm Reminds Agnew of Democrats

Factoid: Spiro Agnew was elected county executive of Baltimore County in 1962. He was elected governor of Maryland in 1966. Republican presidential nominee Richard Nixon chose Agnew as his running mate in 1968.

Spiro Agnew was the new vice presidential nominee in 1968. The Nixon campaign sent him on his obligatory first trip to small markets where he couldn't make big mistakes. The trip out of the box was to Cedar Rapids, Iowa.

I was the point person with the Iowa State Republican Committee who had to try to do something with the visit. One of the things we had to do was find a farm to take Agnew to because every candidate that comes to Iowa has to go to a farm. We found this farm north of Cedar Rapids, and when the governor got to the state, we were going to take him out there in the morning. He had a daylong schedule of activities, but the first thing on the itinerary was the farm. I'm sure Spiro Agnew had never been on a farm in his life, and he certainly had never been on an Iowa hog farm before.

Remember, in 1968 there were all these riots at the Democratic National Convention in Chicago.

The first thing Agnew saw on the pig farm was hogs farrowing (giving birth). The farmer started explaining to him about the hogs, and Agnew, in kind of the first indication he was going to be outspoken, said, "It looks to me like delegates at the Democratic National Convention."

Needless to say, it was the sound bite that led the evening news, and it was the first of many quotable remarks Spiro Agnew uttered.

—*Joe Gaylord*

Bibliography

☆ ☆ ☆

A ll told, more than 60 storytellers contributed to this book, plus one person identified as "anonymous." While the author spent eight months going around with his trusty tape recorder, visiting most of the storytellers face to face, these stories are really their stories, told in their own words. They were there, in the midst of the campaigns they tell about, when the events took place.

John Ashford is chairman and chief executive officer of the Hawthorn Group in Alexandria, Virginia. Originally from Missouri, Ashford started in campaigns in 1968 working in Tom Eagleton's first Senate race.

Dean Barkley is director of the Minnesota State Planning Agency in St. Paul. He was Governor Jesse Ventura's campaign chairman. Barkley got started in politics working for Congressman Don Fraser in Minneapolis in 1968.

Allyson Bell, of Salt Lake City, Utah, is involved in grassroots campaigns and fundraising events. In her first campaign job, she was finance director for Linda Chavez's unsuccessful campaign for U.S. Senate in Maryland in 1986.

Buddy Bishop lives in Panama City, Florida, where he consults on campaigns in Alabama, Georgia and Florida. He started in the business in 1966 working on the Bo Callaway campaign for governor of Georgia.

Bob Bissen is vice president of public relations at APCO Worldwide in Washington, D.C. He was the volunteer campus coordinator at St. Cloud State University in 1978 for Minnesota Senate candidate Rudy Boschwitz.

Charlie Black is the principal in the government relations firm of BKSH & Associates in Washington, D.C. He started in politics professionally as the political organization director in Jesse Helms' first Senate race in North Carolina in 1972.

Jay Bryant, of Upper Marlboro, Maryland, has produced television and radio commercials for Republican candidates nationwide. He started in politics in 1972 scheduling the Illinois state Republican ticket, led by gubernatorial candidate Richard B. Ogilvie.

Richard Bryers works for The Garth Group in New York City. His first campaign was in 1977, when he campaigned for a fraternity brother, Mathew Wolfe, running in the GOP primary in West Philadelphia for Ward Leader. "Let's make Wolfie a political boss" was successful.

George Burger is a principal in the public relations firm of Lunde and Burger in Washington, D.C. His first campaign experience came in 1978, working for Congressman Stan Lundine's first re-election effort in the New York 39th.

Martha Chayet works for a "headhunter" firm in Boston called The Oxbridge Group. She was Massachusetts co-chairman for finance in 2000 for George W. Bush. She started in politics by hosting a small-dollar fundraiser in 1982 for Republican lieutenant governor candidate Leon Lombardi.

Dave Cooley is a Democratic political consultant and partner in the firm of McNeely Piggott & Fox Public Relations in Nashville, Tennessee. He was chief of staff to Nashville Mayor Phil Bredesen and is managing his campaign for governor.

Terry Cooper, of Arlington, Virginia, does opposition research for Republican candidates. His first political experience came in 1978, while working for Motorola, doing battle on Capitol Hill in Washington, D.C.

Scott Cottington, of Minneapolis, Minnesota, is a consultant for Republican candidates. His first political experience was managing Russ Bjorhus' campaign for Congress in 1978 in Minnesota's 5th district.

Fred Davis is president of Strategic Perception, a TV firm in Hollywood. His first campaign experience came in 1974, working for his uncle, Jim

Inhofe, in his unsuccessful campaign for governor in Oklahoma.

John Deardourff, of McLean, Virginia, started in campaigns managing the first re-election campaign of Congresswoman Jessica M. Weis, in the 38th district of New York in 1960. He was a principal in the Republican consulting firm of Bailey-Deardourff.

Bob DeViney, a longtime political figure in Jefferson Parish, Louisiana, started in politics in 1970 knocking on doors in Boutte for Public Service Commissioner Frank E. Stire, handing out fans in 100-degree weather.

Harvey Englander is senior vice president and general manager of The MWW Group in Los Angeles. He volunteered in Bobby Kennedy's 1968 presidential campaign in California, as part of a college class project.

Bill Fletcher is president of Fletcher & Rowley Consulting in Nashville, Tennessee. He was press secretary and occasional TV spot producer for Bart Gordon's successful congressional campaign in 1984 in the 6th district of Tennessee.

David Garth is the founder of The Garth Group in New York City. His first campaign experience came in 1960 when he helped organize the New York State Draft Stevenson Committee.

Joe Gaylord is the principal in Chesapeake Associates in Arlington, Virginia. He started in politics right out of college in 1967 working as a field man in eastern Iowa for the Iowa Republican Party.

Leo Giacometto is in public relations in Washington, D.C. At the age of 23, he ran successfully for a seat in the Montana House of Representatives in 1986.

Tom Gildemeister is a minister at Christ United Methodist Church in Franklin, Tennessee. His first campaign experience was working for John Nance Garner, the Republican congressional candidate in the 2nd district of Washington in 1976.

Daryl Glenney, of West Palm Beach, Florida, is a Democratic strategic planner and communications consultant who heads The Glenney Group. Her first campaign was as a volunteer for Richard Nixon's 1962 campaign for governor of California.

Greg Graves is a Republican consultant working out of Las Cruces, New Mexico. He started in politics as a field man for Senator Pete Domenici's re-election campaign in New Mexico in 1978.

Carlyle Gregory is president of The Carlyle Gregory Company, a political consulting firm in Falls Church, Virginia. In his first campaign in 1974, he was the campaign coordinator and field man for Congressman Caldwell Butler in the 6th district of Virginia.

Josh Griffin is vice president of the McMullen Strategic Group, a public and government relations firm in Las Vegas, Nevada. He was the University of Nevada Reno chairman for Bush-Quayle in 1992.

Shane Hedges, of Helena, Montana, was the campaign manager for Judy Martz's successful campaign for governor. His first look at politics was as a page in the U.S. Senate in 1990.

Dave Hunter, of Helena, Montana, is a consultant for Democratic candidates. He was the volunteer director of the door-to-door campaign for Pat Williams' run for Congress in Montana's 1st district in 1978.

Tim Hyde is a principal in the DCI Group in Washington, D.C. He started in the late 1970s as a state legislative staffer working on Iowa legislative campaigns.

Gary Hymel co-authored *All Politics Is Local* with Speaker Thomas "Tip" O'Neill. He is vice chairman at Hill and Knowlton in Washington, D.C. He started in campaigns working for Congressman Hale Boggs in 1966, in the 2nd district of Louisiana.

Ron Kaufman is a principal in the Washington, D.C., firm of Dutko Associates. His first political experience came as a volunteer for Senator Ed Brooke's 1972 campaign in Massachusetts.

Tom King is a principal in the Democratic media consulting firm of Fenn and King in Washington, D.C. He started in politics in 1971 gathering signatures to put Boston Mayor Kevin White on the ballot again.

Steve Kinney is the West Coast representative for Public Opinion Strategies, a Republican survey research firm. Steve's office is in

Hermosa Beach, California — a block from the beach. He started in 1972 managing the successful state senate campaign of Cale Hudson in Chanute, Kansas.

Paul Kirk is a Boston lawyer in the firm of Sullivan and Worcester. He started in politics working for Kenneth O'Donnell, who had been a special assistant to President John Kennedy, when he ran unsuccessfully in the 1966 Massachusetts gubernatorial primary.

Hans Kaiser is the East Coast representative of Moore Information, a Portland, Oregon, polling firm. His first campaign experience was as a volunteer handing out literature in Annapolis, Maryland, for the Nixon presidential campaign in 1972.

Kenny Klinge, long active in Virginia politics, was the Southern field man for the Reagan campaigns in 1976, 1980 and 1984. He started in politics as a precinct captain in Arlington, Virginia, for Barry Goldwater's presidential campaign in 1964.

Celinda Lake, of Washington, D.C., is a Democratic pollster. Originally from Montana, she started in politics in 1972 as head of Students for Nixon in Massachusetts.

Gary Lawrence is the principal in Lawrence Research in Santa Ana, California, where he does public opinion research for corporations and Republican candidates. While on an LDS mission in 1961, Lawrence became interested in politics watching the Berlin Wall being constructed in East Germany.

D.J. Leary, of Minneapolis, Minnesota, was a Duluth radio manager when he joined Vice President Hubert Humphrey's campaign for president in 1968. He is co-editor of "Politics in Minnesota," a statewide political newsletter.

Bill Lee, of Warrenton, Virginia, is president of Telopinion Research, a public opinion firm. He is chairman of the National Association of Republican Campaign Professionals. While in high school, he handed out brochures for Barry Goldwater in Amarillo, Texas, in 1964.

Ladonna Lee is a strategic communications consultant in the Washington, D.C., office of Foley & Lardner. She started campaigning for her dad, Walt Younglund, who won the first of nine terms in the Colorado House of Representatives in 1968.

Emmy Lewis heads Lewis and Company Marketing Communications Inc., in Washington, D.C., specializing in direct-mail fundraising. She started in politics in Michigan, where she was Young Americans for Freedom state chairman in 1964.

Dee Long, of Minneapolis, Minnesota, was elected to the Minnesota House of Representatives for 10 terms, from 1978 to 1998. She volunteered for Eugene McCarthy's presidential campaign in 1968 and then managed the state senate campaign of Bob Tennessen in 1974, who won handily.

Brian Lunde is a principal in the Washington, D.C., public relations firm of Lunde and Burger. He started in Florida as a field man working on Jimmy Carter's 1976 presidential campaign.

Eddie Mahe is a strategic communications consultant in the Washington, D.C., office of Foley & Lardner. He started in politics in 1965 as the executive director of the Bernalillo County, New Mexico, Republican Committee.

Tony Marsh is a principal in the firm of Russo, Marsh and Copsey Inc. in Washington, D.C. He started in politics putting up yard signs in Upland, California, for Ronald Reagan when he ran for governor in 1966.

Tom Mason is the managing partner at Mason Smiley Larson Ltd., a marketing communications firm in Minneapolis, Minnesota. His first campaign experience was in 1982 as the press secretary for Minnesota gubernatorial candidate Wheelock Whitney.

Larry McCarthy, president of McCarthy, Marcus and Hennings Ltd. in Washington, D.C., produces political television spots for Republican candidates. He started in 1974 as a "press grunt" delivering press releases around New York City for Senator Jacob Javits in his re-election campaign against Ramsey Clark.

Kiki McLean, of the Dewey Square Group in Washington, D.C., has done advance work for several Democratic presidential campaigns.

Steve McMahon is a partner in Trippi, McMahon & Squire, of Alexandria, Virginia, where they produce TV commercials for Democratic candidates. He got involved in politics at the University of Nebraska in 1980 in the "Kennedy for President" campaign.

Dick Minard is deputy general manager at the Washington, D.C., office of Hill and Knowlton. He was an unsuccessful candidate for the Washington House of Representatives in 1974, running in the 5th district in Spokane County.

Bob Moore is a Portland, Oregon, pollster for Republican candidates. His company is Moore Information. He was a field representative in 1972 for the Oregon Committee to Re-elect the President (Nixon).

Vance Opperman, of Minneapolis, Minnesota, is the principal at Key Investments Inc.

Eileen Padberg is the principal in Eileen Padberg Consulting in Irvine, California. She started in politics in 1967, when she was in charge of the volunteer operation for assembly candidate Bruce Nestande in Anaheim.

Sandy Patano is the state director for Senator Larry Craig. She lives in Coeur d' Alene, Idaho.

Tony Payton, the author, was a Republican political consultant working out of Arlington, Virginia. His first campaign experience was as deputy press secretary and Cow County organizer for the "Ed Fike for Governor" campaign in Nevada in 1970.

Bill Phillips is the deputy mayor of Nashville, Tennessee. His first political campaign job was as press secretary for Nevada Attorney General Bob List's campaign for governor in 1978.

Phil Reberger, raised in Caldwell, Idaho, is the chief of staff to Idaho Governor Dirk Kempthorne. In 1973, he was campaign director for Mills Godwin's successful campaign for governor of Virginia.

Rick Reed is a principal in the media production firm of Stevens Reed Curcio & Company in Alexandria, Virginia. He was a national youth field man in Florida for Ronald Reagan's 1976 presidential campaign.

Don Ringe, of Burnsville, North Carolina, produces television spots for Republican candidates. His first campaign experience was working on Proposition 1, known as "Healthy One," in California in 1970.

Steve Sandler is a principal in the firm of Sandler-Innocenzi in Alexandria, Virginia. They produce political television spots for Republican candidates.

Selma Sierra, originally from Anthony, New Mexico, is the press secretary to Republican Congressman Joe Skeen, of the 3rd district of New Mexico. In her first campaign job, she hired on as press secretary for John Irick in his unsuccessful campaign for governor in 1982.

Phil Smith is the president of Captel, a Washington, D.C., firm. While attending college in 1975, he worked part-time at the Republican National Committee finance division opening the donor mail and depositing the contributions.

Stu Spencer started in campaigns in 1950 working in Earl Warren's third campaign for governor, turning out Democrats in the east Los Angeles barrios in a time when candidates could file in both party primaries. After hundreds of campaigns, he retired to Palm Desert, California.

Jay Stone, a Louisiana native, is vice president of Van Scoyoc Associates, a Washington, D.C., government relations firm. His first political experience was in 1971 as director for David Treen's first campaign for governor of Louisiana.

Ray Strother is the principal in the Democratic consulting firm of Strother Duffy Strother in Washington, D.C. He started in politics in Louisiana, running a successful campaign for state treasurer candidate Mary Evelyn Parker in 1968.

Cathy Thomas is a fundraising consultant in Nashville, Tennessee. She started in politics riding in a Jeep in the 1976 Mule Day Parade in Columbia, Tennessee, with Senate candidate Jim Sasser, who offered her a job as campaign field person that day.

David Towell won election to the U.S. House of Representatives from Nevada's at-large congressional seat in 1972.

Joe Trippi is a partner in the firm of Trippi, McMahon & Squire in Alexandria, Virginia. His first campaign experience was as a volunteer for Iola Williams when she ran for city council in San Jose, California, in 1976, and again in 1978 when she became the first black elected to the city council.

Jack Walsh is a Boston political consultant. He started in politics by handing out literature for relatives in 1959 in their campaigns for the Boston City Council and the Boston School Board.

George Young is president of George Young and Associates in Marina del Rey, California. His first campaign experience came in 1963, working for Del Clawson, who won a special congressional election in the 23rd district in southeast Los Angeles County.

About the Author

☆ ☆ ☆

Tony Payton's keen understanding of political numbers and messages was forged in small-town journalism and real grass-roots politics.

Payton was raised by journalist parents in Clayton, New Mexico, and saw firsthand how local politics directly affected everyday lives. He continued the family tradition as an award-winning reporter and editor for several newspapers in Arizona, California and Nevada.

Long before e-mail, Payton's ability to communicate was honed in an era "when you had to put together a story in your head and succinctly phone it in to the city desk."

Going beyond a chronicler of public events and politics, Payton became a grassroots crusader in the historic 1964 Goldwater presidential campaign, where it never occurred to him — or anyone else in Orange County, California — that Goldwater would not win.

Having tasted the thrill of political participation, Payton went on to work for successful congressional candidates and later became a Western states field man for the Republican National Committee during the early 1970s. Wrapping all this personal and professional experience together, Payton hung out his own political consulting shingle in 1977 and since then has successfully influenced the outcome of campaigns from Alaska to Alabama.

Payton pulled several shifts on Capitol Hill in Washington, D.C., serving as chief of staff to a congressman from Nevada and for U.S. Senators from New Mexico and Montana. Before going straight and getting into the campaign business, he spent a decade in the newspaper business. He was a beat reporter for the *Arizona Daily Star* in Tucson and the *Orange Coast Daily Pilot* in Orange County, California, before becoming editor and co-publisher of two weekly newspapers in Nevada. He won more than a dozen newspaper writing awards in Nevada, California and Texas. He attended four colleges in four states but never finished at any of them.

When legendary Democrat consultant Matt Reese died, Payton was inspired to start this book, claiming, "Matt's stories shouldn't have died with him." Unfortunately, he was called to the Great Campaign in the Sky on December 2, 2002, before he saw the publication of *War Stories From the Campaign Trail*.

Payton was proud of his five out of five winning record in 2002 and left his mark on a host of colleagues and friends who learned from his gentle guidance. He reveled in his family and friends, and many a weekend found him flying his Cessna 180 up and down the East Coast looking for the proverbial $100 hamburger. He enjoyed finding the best place in town for dinner, had a great wine collection long on California Zins and Cabernets, and had the good fortune to find a profession where he could work hard for 12 to 15 months out of each election cycle and then spend the balance of the "off-year" learning something new. He is missed.

Index

☆ ☆ ☆

A

Abrams, Hugh, 48
Abscam, 177
Actors in politics, 21
Adams, Brock, 73
Adams, John, 130
Adams, John Quincy, 130–131
Adams, Sherman, 133
Advertising, 56–57
 counter-punching in, 114–115
 television commercials, 56–57, 80–81, 91–92, 132, 193–194
Agnew, Spiro
 Despite Bad Luck, Bauman Beats Malkus in Maryland Special (Buddy
  Bishop), 190
 Iowa Hog Farm Reminds Agnew of Democrats (Joe Gaylord), 274–275
Ailes, Roger, 81–82
Alexander, Shana, 128–129
Allain, Bill, 199
Allard, Wayne, 107–108
Amato, Jimmy, 124
Anderson, John
 Bush Edges Reagan in 1980 Iowa Caucus (Tim Hyde), 135
 The Great Nashua Debate Strategy (Charlie Black), 151, 152, 154
 On the Run From the Press in New Hampshire (Charlie Black), 136
Anderson, Wendell, 219–220
Atwater, Lee
 'Onward Christian Soldiers' in Iowa (Bill Phillips), 142–143
 Vice President Pulls Boulter Over the Line in Texas (Ron Kaufman),
  215

B

Bad luck, 187–188

Bailey, Doug, 32
Baker, Howard
      Bush Edges Reagan in 1980 Iowa Caucus (Tim Hyde), 134, 135
      The Great Nashua Debate Strategy (Charlie Black), 150–154
      On the Run From the Press in New Hampshire (Charlie Black), 136
Baker, James
      Jim Baker Lookalike (Gary Hymel), 268–269
      Winning and Losing With Buddy Roemer (Ray Strother), 246
Baker, Tom, 33
Barkley, Dean, 16
Barrett, Laurence I., 176
Barthelemy, Sidney, 233
Batt, Phil, 256
Baucus, Max, 191
Bauman, Bob, 190–191
Beam, Abe, 39
Beatty, Warren, 21
Beilensen, Anthony, 225
Benson, Duane, 254
Bentsen, Lloyd
      Bentsen Social Security Spot Widely Used (Ray Strother), 85–86
      debate with Dan Quayle, 249
      When the Spirit Is With Matt, There's No One as Good (John Ashford),
        34
Berens, Bill, 170
Berg, Charlie, 219, 220
Bernardin, Bishop, 226
Bethune, Ed, 187
Bingaman, Jeff, 193
Bjorhus, Russ, 268
Black, Charlie, 215
Blackburn, Dan, 252
Bloomberg, Michael, 68
Boggs, Hale, 254–255
Bongignore, Lou, 134, 135
Bono, Sonny, 28–29
Boschwitz, Rudy
      Boschwitz's Biggest Mistake (Tom Mason), 182–183
      We Want Jesse, We Want Jesse (Dean Barkley), 16
Boulter, Beau, 213–216
Boyce, Jimmy, 235
Bradley, Bill, 172
Bradley, Tom, 34, 35
Breen, Jon, 154
Brinkley, David, 260

Brokaw, Tom, 249
Brothers, Jay, 90
Brown, Bob, 44
Brown, Edgar, 7
Brown, George, 100
Brown, John, 208–211
Brownell, Herbert, 31
Bryan, Richard
 Richard Bryan's Worst Day (Josh Griffin), 220–222
 When the Spirit Is With Matt, There's No One as Good (John Ashford), 32, 33
Bryan, William Jennings, 31, 145, 158
Buckley, William F., 39
Bunning, Jim, 22
Burdick, Quentin, 99
Burger, George, 33
Burns, Conrad
 contributions to 1988 campaign, 205
 'Get Serious Day' in Montana (Gary Lawrence), 62–63
 Kalispell press conference, 188
 Showdown in Virginia City, Montana (Leo Giacometto), 217–219
 Still Going Strong at 98 (Ladonna Lee), 269
Burns, Phyllis, 218, 219
Burr, Aaron, 130
Burris, John, 191
Burson, Holm, 250
Bush, Barbara
 'Onward Christian Soldiers' in Iowa (Bill Phillips), 143
 The Real Barbara Bush Speaks Out (Bill Phillips), 270
Bush, George H. W.
 Bush Edges Reagan in 1980 Iowa Caucus (Tim Hyde), 134–135
 Bush Goes One for One for Denver Bears (Ron Kaufman), 10–11
 Clinton's defeat of, 131
 'Get Serious Day' in Montana (Gary Lawrence), 62
 Getting Even With Pierre the Fourth in New Hampshire (Ron Kaufman), 173–174
 Giving Dukakis a Hard Time in Massachusetts (Ron Kaufman), 115–117
 The Great Nashua Debate Strategy (Charlie Black), 150–154
 The Low-water Mark for the Republicans (Eddie Mahe), 146
 'Onward Christian Soldiers' in Iowa (Bill Phillips), 142, 143
 Raising the Money at the Non-fundraiser (Ladonna Lee), 73–74
 The Real Barbara Bush Speaks Out (Bill Phillips), 270
 Richard's humor against, 263
 The Rolls Royce With the du Pont Bumper Stickers (Tim Hyde), 173

On the Run From the Press in New Hampshire (Charlie Black), 136
Vice President Pulls Boulter Over the Line in Texas (Ron Kaufman),
213–216
'You Ought to Be in Charge' in Dallas (Tony Marsh), 161–162
Bush, George W.
Bush Speaks Spanish Like They Speak in the Bars (Celinda Lake),
163–164
election of, 159
Giving Dukakis a Hard Time in Massachusetts (Ron Kaufman), 115
The Great Nashua Debate Strategy (Charlie Black), 150
and leaking of campaign information, 176
presidential campaign of, 2, 64
in presidential debates, 98
Strom Thurmond's Longevity (Bob Bissen), 7
Butz, Earl, 190–191

C
Cabral, Mike, 188–189
Caddell, Pat, 209–210
Cade, John, 247
Campaign professionals
legendary, 31–32
road warriors, 50–51
strategies of, 101–105
Carmen, Gerald, 151
Carper, Tom, 174
Carrick, Bill, 155
Carruthers, Garry, 126–127
Carson, Brad, 200, 202
Carter, Jimmy
Carter Has Bunny Story for 6-year-old (Jack Walsh), 250–251
and election laws, 132
'I Love Ronald Reagan...but' (Gary Lawrence), 164, 165
and Iran hostage crisis, 110–111
Jordan as campaign manager for, 32
and leaking of campaign information, 176–177
in presidential debates, 98
Raising the Money at the Non-fundraiser (Ladonna Lee), 73
Reagan Opens Campaign at the Neshoba County Fair (Kenny Klinge),
159, 161
road warriors of, 50–51
self-defeating behavior of, 180–181
The Wit of Gene McCarthy, 9
Casey, Bill, 137–138
Celeste, Richard, 14

Chappie, Gene, 51–52
Cheney, Dick, 13
Church, Frank
    The Superglue Trick (Phil Reberger), 171
    The Wit of Gene McCarthy, 9, 10
Churches, politics and, 2
Ciresi, Michael, 169–170
Clark, Herman, 13
Clausen, John, 257
Clay, Henry, 131, 144
Clements, Bill
    Clements Starts Cleaning Up Supreme Court (John Deardourff), 178
    'I'm Not Even Listening,' Clements Said (John Deardourff), 222–224
Clinton, Bill
    and 1996 election, 4
    Action America Supports Huckabee Travel (Greg Graves), 227
    and election laws, 132
    election of, 131
    fundraising stops for, 21
    Gore, That 'Snake,' Spreads Rumors About Me (Brian Lunde), 266
    Inhofe Wins Senate Special With Dancing Convicts (Fred Davis),
        87–88
    road warriors of, 50–51
    White Beats Clinton on Car Tags and Cubans (Bill Lee), 113
Clinton, Hillary Rodham, 113
Clute, Steve, 28, 29
Coburn, Tom, 200
Coleman, Norm, 106
Coles, Michael, 117–118
Collins, Jim, 85
Comedy in politics, 263–264
Commercials, 56–57, 80–81, 91–92, 132, 193–194
Condit, Gary, 114–115
Connally, John
    Bush Edges Reagan in 1980 Iowa Caucus (Tim Hyde), 134, 135
    The Great Nashua Debate Strategy (Charlie Black), 150–152
Conte, Silvio, 273
Conventions, 144–145
Coolidge, Calvin, 133, 145
Cooper, Bill, 224
Cooper, Larry, 170
Cory, Ken, 75–76
Corzine, Jon, 68, 103
Coulter, Nate, 227
Counter-punching, 114–115

Coverdell, Nancy, 119
Coverdell, Paul, 117–119
Cox, Archibald, 272
Cox, Jack, 5
Craig, Larry, 114
Crane, Phil
> Bush Edges Reagan in 1980 Iowa Caucus (Tim Hyde), 135
> The Great Nashua Debate Strategy (Charlie Black), 151, 152, 154
> On the Run From the Press in New Hampshire (Charlie Black), 136
Cranston, Alan
> Mondale Tops Cranston in Maine, Iowa Straw Polls (Joe Trippi),
> 140–142
> Taken to the Woodshed on Social Security (Paul Kirk), 252
Crawford, William, 131
Cubin, Barbara, 264
Cummings, Howard, 31
Cunningham, Jack, 73

D
Daley, Richard J., 4
Daniel, Robert, 253
Daub, Hal, 189–190
Daugherty, Harry, 31
Davis, Jimmy, 243–244
Davis, John W., 145
Dayton, Mark, 170
Deardourff, John
> Clements Starts Cleaning Up Supreme Court (John Deardourff), 178
> 'I'm Not Even Listening,' Clements Said (John Deardourff), 222–224
> Making a TV Spot About a Bull's Operation (John Deardourff), 96
> Raising the Money in 10 Minutes (John Deardourff), 72
> as Republican statewide campaign manager, 32
Deaver, Mike, 136
Debates, 98–99
> consequences of, 149–150
> illegal activities related to, 176–177
Democracy, xi
Democratic National Convention, 144–145
Denton, Jeremiah, 255
Deukmejian, George, 34–35
Dewey, Thomas, 149, 159, 166
Diamond, Harris, 246
Dinkins, David, 122, 123
Diprete, Edward, 170
Dirty tricks, 169–170

Disney, Walt, 56, 159
Dole, Bob
    and 1996 election, 4
    Bush Edges Reagan in 1980 Iowa Caucus (Tim Hyde), 135
    Getting Even With Pierre the Fourth in New Hampshire (Ron
        Kaufman), 173
    The Great Nashua Debate Strategy (Charlie Black), 151, 152, 154
    'Onward Christian Soldiers' in Iowa (Bill Phillips), 142–143
    The Rolls Royce With the du Pont Bumper Stickers (Tim Hyde), 173
Domenici, Pete, 250
Donaldson, Sam, 26
Doucet, Pat
    Traveling With the Band Across Louisiana (Ray Strother), 243
    Women Wore White Gloves to Fundraisers (Ray Strother), 238
Douglas, Helen Gahagan, 172
Douglas, Stephen, 145
Duesterberg, Tom, 274
Dukakis, Mike
    'Get Serious Day' in Montana (Gary Lawrence), 62–63
    Giving Dukakis a Hard Time in Massachusetts (Ron Kaufman),
        115–117
Duke, David
    The Master Turns a Phrase (Bill Fletcher), 40
    'Vote for the Crook' (Bill Fletcher), 264
    Winning and Losing With Buddy Roemer (Ray Strother), 245–247
    The World Watched Louisiana (Bill Fletcher), 242
    Writing a 30-minute TV Show for Edwards (Bill Fletcher), 231, 232
Du Pont, Elise R. W., 174
Du Pont, Pierre
    Getting Even With Pierre the Fourth in New Hampshire (Ron
Kaufman), 174–175
    'Onward Christian Soldiers' in Iowa (Bill Phillips), 142
    The Rolls Royce With the du Pont Bumper Stickers (Tim Hyde), 173
Durning, Marvin, 73

E
Eastwood, Clint
    Eastwood Kept His Promise (Eileen Padberg), 41–42
    Eastwood Wins Mayor's Race in Carmel (Eileen Padberg), 22–25
Edwards, Edwin
    Johnston Loses Gubernatorial Race, Wins Senate Race (Rob Couhig),
        239
    The Master Turns a Phrase (Bill Fletcher), 40–41
    Moore Wins Congressional Re-run in Louisiana (Jay Stone), 236
    'Vote for the Crook' (Bill Fletcher), 264

Winning and Losing With Buddy Roemer (Ray Strother), 245–247
The World Watched Louisiana (Bill Fletcher), 242–243
Writing a 30-minute TV Show for Edwards (Bill Fletcher), 231–232
Eggers, Paul, 183–184
Eisenhower, Dwight
 and 1952 campaign, 167
 campaign manager of, 31
 in New Hampshire primary, 133
 political ads by, 56, 132, 159
Electoral College, 130–131
Ellender, Allan J., 239, 240
Ellison, Pam, 42
Emerson, Bill, 265
Emerson, Jo Ann, 265
Erlichman, John, 190
Ewing, Andy, 200–202

F
Fadem, Barry, 41
Fahrenkopf, Frank, 69
Fame, 4–5
Faricy, Ray, 257
Fears, Bill, 65
Fenger, George, 46–47
Fike, Ed, 120
Firebaugh, Emily, 265
Fitzgerald, Jerome, 96
Fitzmorris, Jimmy, 247
Flood, Daniel, 177–178
Flynn, Ray, 116
Folson, James, Jr., 255
Ford, Gerald
 Bishops Suggest Stevens for Supreme Court (Stu Spencer), 225, 226
 campaign manager for, 32
 and election laws, 132
 The Low-water Mark for the Republicans (Eddie Mahe), 146
 in presidential debates, 98
 at Republican National Convention, 145
 self-defeating behavior of, 180
Ford, Whitey, 10
Franks, Bob, 68, 103
Fremont, John C., 144
Friedler, Frank, 239
Friedline, Doug
 We Want Jesse, We Want Jesse (Dean Barkley), 17

The Winning Strategy on a Bar Napkin (Dean Barkley), 106
Fuller, Craig, 143
Fullerton, Byron, 184
Fulton, Richard, 216–217
Fund raising, 67–68

G
Galifianakis, Nick, 18
Gallup, George, 59
Ganhus, Christine, 169–170
Garth, David
    Filming Mr. Yankee in Brooklyn (Richard Bryers), 83–84
    The Garth Theory of Running Campaigns (David Garth), 35–37
    Keeping Giuliani Cool With the Press (Richard Bryers), 123
Gephardt, Dick, 154–156
Gerry, Elbridge, 55
Gerrymandering, 55–56
Giacometto, Leo
    Running for the Legislature in Big Sky Country (Leo Giacometto),
      47–49
    Showdown in Virginia City, Montana (Leo Giacometto), 217–219
    You're in North Dakota Right Now (Leo Giacometto), 253–254
Giacometto, Mildred, 269
Gibbons, Jim, 222
Gill, Steve, 92–93
Gingrich, Newt
    Mama, Meet Phil Donahue' (Carlyle Gregory), 271
    No Revolution in the Back of a Limo (Joe Gaylord), 12–14
    Old Gingrich Film Proves Useful (Bill Fletcher), 92–93
    You Say a Thousand From Whom? (Carlyle Gregory), 74
Giuliani, Rudy
    Filming Mr. Yankee in Brooklyn (Richard Bryers), 83–84
    Keeping Giuliani Cool With the Press, 122–124
    legend status of, 4
Glenn, John
    multiple campaigns of, 21–22
    Reagan Letter Pays for Entire 1984 Campaign (Phil Smith), 70
Goldwater, Barry, 4–5, 57, 167
Goodman, Bob, 80
Gordon, Bart, 92
Gordon, Steve, 75
Gore, Al
    and 1999-2000 presidential campaign, 2, 159
    and Bush's drunk driving conviction, 64

Bush Speaks Spanish Like They Speak in the Bars (Celinda Lake), 163, 164

and election laws, 132

Giving Dukakis a Hard Time in Massachusetts (Ron Kaufman), 115

Gore, That 'Snake,' Spreads Rumors About Me (Brian Lunde), 266

Gore and the Secret Service (Dave Cooley), 272–273

and leaking of Bush's campaign information, 176

No Debate Without the Frontrunner (Kiki McLean), 154–157

in presidential debates, 98

Graham, Billy, 147–148

Gramm, Phil, 215

Grams, Rod, 170

Graves, Greg, 213–214

Graves, Joe, 124–125

Greenspun, Hank, 120

Gregg, Hugh, 151

H

Halderman, Bob, 190

Hance, Kent, 222

Hanna, Mark, 31

Hannaford, Pete, 139

Hansen, Clifford, 37–38

Harding, Warren, 31

Harrison, William Henry, 264

Hart, Gary

Chop It Off in Troublesome Gulch (Joe Trippi), 259–260

Gore, That 'Snake,' Spreads Rumors About Me (Brian Lunde), 266

Mondale Puts Down Boxing Gloves in Pennsylvania (Joe Trippi), 19

Mondale's humor against, 263

No Debate Without the Frontrunner (Kiki McLean), 155

Reagan Letter Pays for Entire 1984 Campaign (Phil Smith), 70

Hart, Lee, 260

Hayes, Rutherford B., 131

Hayes, Wayne, 254–255

Hearst, William Randolph, 120

Hecht, Chic

Richard Bryan's Worst Day (Josh Griffin), 220, 221

When the Spirit Is With Matt, There's No One as Good (John Ashford), 32

Heineman, Dave, 46

Helms, Jesse, 18

Herman, A. B., 265

Heston, Charlton, 21

Hicks, Loise Day, 78

Hightower, Jack, 213
Hill, John
Clements Starts Cleaning Up Supreme Court (John Deardourff), 178
'I'm Not Even Listening,' Clements Said (John Deardourff), 222
Hillings, Pat, 37–38
Hillsman, Bill, 94
Hoffman, Philip, 72
Hopkins, Larry, 196
Huckabee, Mike, 227–229
Huckaby, Jerry, 241–242
Huddleston, Dee, 81–83
Humor in politics, 263–264
Humphrey, Gordon, 153
Humphrey, Hubert
Ground Zero in the Anti-war Movement (Vance Opperman), 212, 213
'Maggie, They're Trying to Screw One of Your Old Friends' (D. J. Leary), 206–207
presidential campaign of, 159
She Bore and Amazing Resemblance to Her Brother (Dee Long), 273–274
Talking Like Lyndon Johnson (D.J. Leary), 272
'Textual Deviant' Make the Plain Dealer (D.J. Leary), 121–122
The Wit of Hubert Humphrey (Harvey Englander), 267–268
Humphrey, Hubert, III, 106
Humphrey-Howard, Francis, 273–274
Hutchison, Sue, 41

I
Illegal activities, 176–177
Inhofe, Jim, 87–90
Iowa caucus, 133–134

J
Jackson, Andrew, 55, 131, 144
Jamail, Joseph, 178–179
Jamison, Cy, 188
Javits, Jacob, 207–208
Jefferson, Thomas, 130
Jenrette, John, 177
Johnson, Chuck, 186
Johnson, John, 219
Johnson, Lyndon
"daisy girl" commercial by, 57, 167
Goldwater campaign against, 5
Talking Like Lyndon Johnson (D.J. Leary), 272

Johnston, Bennett, 239–240
Jones, Brereton, 196
Jordan, Hamilton
      as Carter's manager, 32
      'You Ought to Be in Charge' in Dallas (Tony Marsh), 162
Jorgensen, Earl, 15–16
Judge, Tom, 198

K
Karnes, David, 189
Kefauver, Estes, 133, 150
Kelly, Richard, 177
Kemp, Jack
      campaign of, 21
      Getting Even With Pierre the Fourth in New Hampshire (Ron
          Kaufman), 173
      'Onward Christian Soldiers' in Iowa (Bill Phillips), 142
      The Rolls Royce With the du Pont Bumper Stickers (Tim Hyde), 173
      Vice President Pulls Boulter Over the Line in Texas (Ron Kaufman),
          215
Kempthorne, Dirk, 53–54
Kennedy, John F.
      campaign manager rewarded by, 31
      debates by, 132
      as legend, 5
      in presidential debates, 98, 149
      in West Virginia primary, 32
      When the Spirit Is With Matt, There's No One as Good (John Ashford),
          32
Kennedy, Robert, 31
Kennedy, Ted, 145–146
Kerry, John, 74–75
Ketchum, Bill, 211–212
King, Martin Luther, 112
Kirk, Paul
      Kirk Elected DNC Chair, DLC Formed (Brian Lunde), 145–146
      Taken to the Woodshed on Social Security (Paul Kirk), 252
      They Won't Say He Couldn't Raise His Hat (Paul Kirk), 68–69
Klein, Walt, 107
Kline, Richard, 265
Klinge, Kenny, 199
Knags, John, 184
Kohl, Herb, 22
Kroc, Joan, 68–69

L
LaBlanc, Sam, 239
LaCaze, Jeff, 233–236
Lake, Celinda, 186
Lake, Jim
  The Great Nashua Debate Strategy (Charlie Black), 150, 151, 153, 154
  On the Run From the Press in New Hampshire (Charlie Black),
      136–139
Lambert, Louis, 236–237
Landon, Alf, 59
Latimer, George, 60
Lauder, Ron, 122
Laxalt, Paul
  The Great Nashua Debate Strategy (Charlie Black), 152, 153
  Reagan Letter Pays for Entire 1984 Campaign (Phil Smith), 69
Leavitt, Mike, 128
Leche, Richard, 271
Lee, Keith, 32, 33
Lee, Ladonna, 205
Legendary campaign professionals, 31–32
Legendary political figures, 4–5
Levy, Chandra, 114
Lewis, Emmy, 70
Lewis, Frank, 46
Lewis, John, 244
Lightfoot, Jim Ross, 194–195
Lightfoot, Nancy, 194, 195
Limbaugh, Rush, 90
Lincoln, Abraham, 144, 145
Lindsay, John
  Buckley's challenge of, 39
  The Garth Theory of Running Campaigns (David Garth), 35
  Lindsay Goes to Harlem When King Is Slain (David Garth), 111–112
List, Bob, 125–126
List, Michelle, 125, 126
Livingston, Bob, 273
Loeb, William, 180
Loeffler, Tom, 222
Long, Earl, 271
Long, Gillis, 239, 244–245
Long, Jill, 274
Long, Russell, 245
Losing campaigns, 166–168
Lott, Trent, 160, 161
Loyd, Gary, 171

Lozano, Juanita Yvette, 176
Lunde, Brian, 209

M
Magnuson, Warren, 207
Malkus, Fred, 190
Manatt, Chuck, 208, 209
Manning, Timothy, 226
Marciano, Rocky, 37
Marichal, Juan, 10
Martin, Fred, 156
Martz, Judy, 184, 185
Matalin, Mary, 246
Matheson, Scott, 146
Maxwell, John, 194
Mazeroski, Bill, 2
McCain, John
        and election laws, 132
        Not Following the Schedule (Ladonna Lee), 181
McCarthy, Eugene
        Ground Zero in the Anti-war Movement (Vance Opperman), 212, 213
        The Wit of Gene McCarthy (Vance Opperman), 9–10
McConnell, Mitch, 81–83
McCormick, Mike, 110
McCotter, Lane, 127
McCurdy, Dave, 87–89
McDaniel, Karen, 126, 127
McDaniel, Red, 181–182
McDougall, Mel, 71–72
McGee, Lloyd, 134
McGovern, George, 134
McGrath, Howard, 31
McIntyre, Francis, 225–226
McKiethen, John, 239
McKinley, William, 31, 56, 158
McLister, Mike, 253
McWherter, Ned, 255–256
Meese, Ed, 136
Meir, Golda, 207, 208
Melcher, John
        'Get Serious Day' in Montana (Gary Lawrence), 62, 63
        Showdown in Virginia City, Montana (Leo Giacometto), 217, 218
Mellman, Mark, 231
Milford, H.C., 95
Miller, March, 51

Mills, Bill, 190
Mills, Wilbur, 206–207
Minn, Steve, 225
Minner, Ruth Ann, 191
Mintz, Donald, 233
Mitchell, John, 31
Mochary, Mary, 172
Modern political campaigns, 55–58
Mondale, Walter
    humor used by, 263
    'Maggie, They're Trying to Screw One of Your Old Friends' (D. J.
        Leary), 206–207
    Mondale Puts Down Boxing Gloves in Pennsylvania (Joe Trippi),
        18–20
    Mondale Tops Cranston in Maine, Iowa Straw Polls (Joe Trippi),
        140–142
    Reagan Letter Pays for Entire 1984 Campaign (Phil Smith), 70
    Running Cigars From Canada (Joe Trippi), 52–53
    The Wit of Gene McCarthy, 9, 10
Montgomery, Terry, 61–62
Moore, Henson
    campaign of, 230–231
    Election Night in Louisiana (James Farwell), 247
    Moore Wins Congressional Re-run in Louisiana (Jay Stone), 233–236
Morgan, Bill
    The Master Turns a Phrase (Bill Fletcher), 40
    Writing a 30-minute TV Show for Edwards (Bill Fletcher), 231
Morial, Marc, 233
Morris, Dick, 113
Morris, Robert, 172
Morrison, Sid, 110
Mowad, George, 242
Murphine, Ralph, 34
Murphy, George, 29–30
Murphy, John, 177
Murphy, Michael, 177
Murphy, Tom, 12
Murphy's Law, 187–188
Muskie, Edmund, 133–134, 169, 180

N
Nace, Paul, 79
Nemerov, Irv, 212–213
New Hampshire primary, 133
Newspapers, 120–121

Nixon, Richard, 31
    Bishops Suggest Stevens for Supreme Court (Stu Spencer), 225
    Bumper Sticker Advice (Terry Cooper), 272
    Caught With His Pants Down (Hans Kaiser), 260–261
    debates by, 132
    and dirty tricks, 169
    and Iowa caucus, 134
    The Legendary Trickster Dick Tuck (Don Ringe), 172–173
    The Low-water Mark for the Republicans (Eddie Mahe), 146
    Nixon Gives Spencer Credentials (Stu Spencer), 38
    presidential campaign of, 159
    in presidential debates, 98, 149
    'Textual Deviant' Make the Plain Dealer (D.J. Leary), 121
    Watergate Wasn't Nixon's Only Problem (David Towell), 210–212
Nofziger, Lyn
    Reagan Opens Campaign at the Neshoba County Fair (Kenny Klinge),
        160
    On the Run From the Press in New Hampshire (Charlie Black), 136
Nolan, Richard, 268
Norment, Tommy, 65
North, Ollie, 120–121
Nunn, Louis, 208

O
Obenshain, Dick, 25
O'Callaghan, Mike, 120
O'Donnell, Harry, 112
O'Keefe, Mark, 184–186
O'Malley, Walter, 29
O'Neill, Tip
    Carter Has Bunny Story for 6-year-old (Jack Walsh), 251
    Taken to the Woodshed on Social Security (Paul Kirk), 252
Orton, Bill, 128
Osborne, Bill, 39–40

P
Packwood, Bob, 65–66
Parker, Mary Evelyn
    Making B/W Television for Mary Evelyn Parker (Ray Strother),
        240–241
    Women Wore White Gloves to Fundraisers (Ray Strother), 237–238
Peachy, Judy, 27
Percell, Patrick, 117
Percy, Charles, 197–198
Perot, H. Ross

election outcome altered by, 131
    personal money spent by, 68
    'You Ought to Be in Charge' in Dallas (Tony Marsh), 161–163
Perpich, Rudy, 60–62
Philips, Wayne, 48, 49
Phillips, Tom, 178
Pickens, T. Boone, 214
Pickering, Charles, 199
Pigott, Mike, 272–273
Plesser, Tully, 148
Political campaigns, 55–58
Political conventions, 144–145
Politics, 1–3
Polling, 59
Positioning, 102
Presidential campaigns, 130–132, 158–159
Presidential debates. *See* Debates
Press, 120–121
Public office seekers, 39–40
Public opinion research, 57, 59–60
Pulitzer, Joseph, 120
Purcell, Bill, 216–217

Q
Quayle, Dan
    debate with Lloyd Bentsen, 249
    press attacks on, 121
    'You Don't Need Me Then' (Scott Cottington), 274

R
Racicot, Marc, 188
Radio
    advertising on, 56, 91–92
    debates on, 98, 149
Raising money, 67–68
Ramirez, Jack, 198–199
Rarick, John, 233–234
Raven, Eddie, 243–244
Ray, Bob, 96–97
Rayburn, Sam, 244–245
Reagan, Nancy
    Meeting Ronald Reagan the First Time (Emmy Lewis), 5
    Reagan Endorses Assembly Candidate (Tom Gildemeister), 259
    Reagan Opens Campaign at the Neshoba County Fair (Kenny Klinge),
        160, 161

at Republican National Convention, 145
On the Run From the Press in New Hampshire (Charlie Black), 138
Reagan, Ronald, 32
Bush Edges Reagan in 1980 Iowa Caucus (Tim Hyde), 134–135
The Flicker of an Old Flame (Stu Spencer), 266–267
The Great Nashua Debate Strategy (Charlie Black), 150–154
'I Love Ronald Reagan...but' (Gary Lawrence), 164–165
and Iran hostage crisis, 111
Just Handing Out Brochures, the Hard Way (George Young), 43
and leaking of Carter's campaign information, 176–177
Life magazine Gives Reagan a Jab (George Young), 128–129
Locking Up the Opponent in New Jersey (Rick Reed), 172
Meeting Ronald Reagan the First Time (Emmy Lewis), 5–6
Moore Wins Congressional Re-run in Louisiana (Jay Stone), 234
Not Following the Schedule (Ladonna Lee), 182
Politics Is Just Like Show Business (Stu Spencer), 261–262
Reagan Endorses Assembly Candidate (Tom Gildemeister), 258–259
Reagan Letter Pays for Entire 1984 Campaign (Phil Smith), 69–71
Reagan Opens Campaign at the Neshoba County Fair (Kenny Klinge),
159–161
On the Run From the Press in New Hampshire (Charlie Black),
136–140
The Speaker Is Out Fencing (Cathy Thomas), 255–256
Reberger, Phil, 53
Rebozo, Bebe, 210
Reese, Della, 73
Reese, George, 239
Reese, Matt, 32
The Loveable Matt Reese (Daryl Glenney), 34
Playing Atlantic City With John Y. Brown (George Burger), 209
When the Spirit Is With Matt, There's No One as Good (John Ashford),
32–34
Whorehouse Owner Gets Lucky, Gives 50 Gs to Lambert (Stu
Spencer), 237
Religion, politics and, 2
Republican Party convention, 144
Research
on campaign opponents, 64–65
public opinion, 57, 59–60
Rhodes, Jim, 14–15
Rice, Donna, 260
Richards, Ann, 263
Riley, Ed, 155
Road warriors, 50–51
Robb, Chuck, 120–121, 146

Roberts, Bill, 32, 35, 261
Roberts, Steve, 134
Robertson, Pat, 142
Rockefeller, Nelson, 270–271
Rodham, Hillary, 113
Roemer, Buddy
      The Master Turns a Phrase (Bill Fletcher), 40, 41
      Winning and Losing With Buddy Roemer (Ray Strother), 245–247
      Writing a 30-minute TV Show for Edwards (Bill Fletcher), 231, 232
Rollins, Ed, 161–163
Romney, George, 5
Roncalio, Teno, 37
Roncallo, Angelo, 211–212
Roosevelt, Franklin D., 31, 56, 59
Roosevelt, Theodore, 56, 131, 250
Rose, Bob, 125
Ross, Jack, 200–202
Rove, Karl, 223
Rowley, John, 92–93
Royko, Mike, 88
Ryall, Marty, 119

S
Salinger, Pierre, 29
Sandy, R.C. "Buzz," 93
Sanford, Terry, 146
Sardoni, Andy, 177–178
Sasser, Jim, 258
Schmitt, Jack, 193
Schreck, Frank, 33
Schunk, Bill, 42
Schunk, Mae, 42–43
Schuster, Bob, 264
Schwinden, Ted, 198–199
Sears, John
      The Great Nashua Debate Strategy (Charlie Black), 150–153
      On the Run From the Press in New Hampshire (Charlie Black),
         136–139
Segretti, Donald, 169
Self-defeating behaviors, 180
Sellers, Richard, 72–73
Shalala, Donna, 188–189
Shaw, Bernard, 62
Sheppard, Virginia, 74
Sherman, Norman, 121

Sherwood, Beverly, 93–94
Shorress, Melvin, 236
Shrum, Bob, 156, 157
Simon, Paul
      Attack Spot Backfires in Illinois (Larry McCarthy), 197, 198
      Gore, That 'Snake,' Spreads Rumors About Me (Brian Lunde), 266
      No Debate Without the Frontrunner (Kiki McLean), 155
Sisisky, Norman, 253
Smebakken, Ted, 219–220
Smith, Dan, 259
Smith, Earl, 48
Smith, Mary Louise, 146, 147
Smith, Preston, 183
Smith, Red, 37
Smith, Rod, 147
Smith brothers, 74
Snider, Howard, 100
Spahn, Warren, 10, 11
Speed of campaigns, 57
Spencer, Stu, 32, 37–38
Sports figures in politics, 21, 22
Squire, Bob, 32
Stallings, Richard, 53
Stangeland, Arlan, 108–109
Stars in politics, 21–22
Stassen, Harold, 4, 149, 166–167
Steinberg, Arnie, 41
Stevens, John Paul, 225, 226
Stevenson, Adlai
      at Democratic National Convention, 145
      in presidential debates, 149–150
      television commercial by, 56–57, 132
Stone, Roger
      Locking Up the Opponent in New Jersey (Rick Reed), 172
      The Rolls Royce With the du Pont Bumper Stickers (Tim Hyde), 173
Strategies, campaign, 101–105
Street organizations, 77–78, 103
Strickland, Ted, 107–108
Strinden, Earl, 99
Sturgulewski, Arliss, 80
Sullivan, Michael, 108
Sundlun, Bruce
      Sundlun in Diprete's Future (George Burger), 170–171
      That Wasn't Shalala on the Phone (George Burger), 188–189
Symms, Steve

Aiming at Table Rock (Tony Payton), 53
The Superglue Trick (Phil Reberger), 171
Synhorst, Tom, 194

T
Taft, Robert, 133, 166, 167
Taft, William Howard, 131, 250
Tarrance, Lance
      Looking for Dee Huddleston (Larry McCarthy), 81
      White Beats Clinton on Car Tags and Cubans (Bill Lee), 113
Taylor, Elizabeth
      Elizabeth Taylor Revealed in Williamsburg (Kenny Klinge), 27
      Elizabeth Taylor's Lucky Dress (Don Ringe), 25–27
Teeter, Bob, 146, 147
Television
      commercials on, 56–57, 80–81, 91–92, 132, 193–194
      impact of, 31–32
      presidential debates on, 98, 132
Thatcher, Paul Rexburg, 273–274
Thaxton, Dick, 147
Thompson, Frank, 177
Thurmond, Strom
      as oldest man in Senate in 2001, 4
      recognition of, 4
      Senator Thurmond Lives On (Tom Mason), 8
      Still Going Strong at 98 (Ladonna Lee), 269
      Strom Thurmond's Longevity (Bob Bissen), 7
Tilden, Samuel, 131
Timiley, Joseph, 78
Timmons, Bill, 160
Todd, Eleanor, 71
Todd, Webster B., 71–73
Toledano, Ben, 239
Torres, Anastasio, 250
Tower, John, 184
Townsend, Charlotte, 22, 24
Townsend, Larry, 208–209
Treen, David
      Election Night in Louisiana (James Farwell), 247–247
      losing campaign of, 167
      Whorehouse Owner Gets Lucky, Gives 50 Gs to Lambert (Stu
            Spencer), 236–237
      Working to Get the Alien Center in Oakdale (Bob DeViney), 241–242
Treen, Doty, 247
Truman, Harry, 31, 133, 158–159

Tuck, Dick
     dirty tricks by, 169
     The Legendary Trickster Dick Tuck (Don Ringe), 172–173
Tucker, Jim Guy, 227
Tully, Paul, 260
Tunney, John, 29
Twilegar, Ron, 114
Tyler, John, 264

U
Unruh, Jesse, 15–16
U.S. House of Representatives, 55
U.S. Senate, 56
Utley, Garrick, 139

V
Vale, Thomas, 122
Veccio, Pat, 112
Ventura, Jesse, 21
     'Do You Have Any Idea Who Jesse Ventura Is?' (Dean Barkley), 42–43
     Ventura Almost Blows Bank Loan With Drugs, Prostitution Position
          (Dean Barkley), 224–225
     Ventura's TV Puts Him Over the Top (Dean Barkley), 94–95
     We Want Jesse, We Want Jesse (Dean Barkley), 16–17
     The Winning Strategy on a Bar Napkin (Dean Barkley), 106–107
Ventura, Teri, 17
Vickery, Bill, 228, 229
Vilsack, Tom, 194–195
Voters
     lists of, 57–58
     reasons for choosing candidates, 102–103

W
Walker, David, 44–45
Walker, Olene, 128
Wallace, George, 121, 159
Wallace, Mike, 179
Wallop, Malcolm, 80
Warner, John, 25–27
War stories, 203–206
Washington, George, ix, 130
Weaver, Jim, 65
Weill, Al, 37
Weld, Bill, 74–75
Wellstone, Paul

Boschwitz's Biggest Mistake (Tom Mason), 182
Ventura's TV Puts Him Over the Top (Dean Barkley), 94
We Want Jesse, We Want Jesse (Dean Barkley), 16
Westfall, George, 95
White, Bryon, 22
White, Frank, 113
White, Kevin
Carter Has Bunny Story for 6-year-old (Jack Walsh), 251
Taking a Soaking for the Mayor (Tom King), 78–79
White, Mark
'I'm Not Even Listening,' Clements Said (John Deardourff), 222, 223
Jim Baker Lookalike (Gary Hymel), 268
Whitley, Charles, 181
Whitman, Christy Todd, 71
Wilkinson, Martha, 196–197
Wilkinson, Wallace, 196
Williams, Harrison, 177
Wilson, Woodrow, 131, 250
Wirthlin, Dick
On the Run From the Press in New Hampshire (Charlie Black), 136
Winning and Losing With Buddy Roemer (Ray Strother), 247
Wood, Bob, 43–44
Wood, Leonard, 133
Woods, Rosemary, 37
Worley, David, 12
Wynn, Steve, 209

Y
Yacich, Paul, 240
Yaekel, Steve, 48, 49